Stockpiling Strategic Materials

Chandler Publications in
POLITICAL SCIENCE
Victor Jones, *Editor*

Stockpiling Strategic Materials

↑ 933401

Politics and National Defense

Glenn H. Snyder
State University of New York at Buffalo

CHANDLER PUBLISHING COMPANY
124 Spear Street, San Francisco, California 94105

Contents

Institute of War and Peace Studies

Stockpiling Strategic Materials: Politics and National Defense is one of a series of publications sponsored by the Institute of War and Peace Studies of Columbia University. Other books from the Institute are: Alfred Vagts, *Defense and Diplomacy: The Soldier and the Conduct of Foreign Relations* (1956); Seymour Melman, editor, *Inspection for Disarmament* (1958); William T. R. Fox, editor, *Theoretical Aspects of International Relations* (1959); Kenneth N. Waltz, *Man, the State, and War* (1959); Samuel P. Huntington, *The Common Defense: Strategic Programs in National Politics* (1961); Samuel P. Huntington, editor, *Changing Patterns of Military Politics* (1962); Warner R. Schilling, Paul Y. Hammond, and Glenn H. Synder, *Strategy, Politics, and Defense Budgets* (1962); Zbigniew Brzezinski and Samuel P. Huntington, *Political Power: USA/USSR* (1964) (sponsored jointly with the Russian Institute, Columbia University); Amitai Etzioni, *Political Unification* (1965).

Preface

This book is a substantial revision of my doctoral dissertation, which was completed in 1956. I had not intended to publish it until a subcommittee of the Senate Armed Services Committee under Senator Stuart Symington held extensive hearings on stockpiling during 1962 and 1963, in the course of which a considerable amount of previously classified information was made public. The release of this material, supplemented by interviews, made it possible for me to bring my manuscript up to date, and also to document in detail the history of the stockpile program during the Eisenhower Administration, which the original dissertation had treated in rather general terms.

Since the Symington subcommittee did not go into the history of stockpiling prior to 1953, the documentary foundation of the earlier chapters remains as it was in the dissertation, although these chapters have been rewritten and condensed. This earlier part of the narrative is based, in about equal proportion, on public documents and on interviews with governmental participants in the stockpile program, interviews which were carried out during the summers of 1954 and 1955. An exception to this is Chapter I on the legislative history of the Stockpiling Act, which is based almost entirely on unclassified materials from the National Archives and the files of the Office of the Army Adjutant General. At no time during the research process did I have access to classified documents. My request for such access or for the declassification of documents was denied. I have been assured, however, by persons who have had such access, that my story is factually accurate and that it adequately covers all essential aspects.

The book as it stands is slightly over half the size of the original manuscript, despite the inclusion of the additional material from the Symington hearings. The reader who is interested in more detail should consult my dissertation in the Columbia University library.

My interest in the stockpiling program dates back to my service as a Washington reporter for *The Wall Street Journal* during 1950 and early 1951, which brought me into occasional contact with the program and other governmental activities related to it. This previous contact interlocked with an interest in the general field of civilian-military relations which I acquired later during my graduate study at Columbia, chiefly under Professor William T. R. Fox. The original manuscript was one of several case-study "inputs" for a broad investigation into contrasting civilian and military perspectives or attitudes toward national security policy, a project which was undertaken by the Institute of War and Peace Studies at Columbia. The over-all findings of this project will be incorporated in a forthcoming book by Professor Fox, Director of the Institute. I am deeply grateful to Professor Fox for his advice, stimulation, and encouragement, and for the financial assistance rendered to me by the Institute.

I must also acknowledge my indebtedness to Professor Samuel P. Huntington of Harvard University, who read the original version, made valuable suggestions regarding its revision, and encouraged me to proceed toward publication. The governmental officials who gave me their time for interviews are too numerous to list, and many of them wished to remain anonymous; I can only say that without their gracious cooperation this book would not have been possible. Nor would it have seen the light of day without the encouragement and interest of Professor Victor Jones of the University of California, the editor of the series of which this book is a part. Of course, I must add the usual caveat that I alone am responsible for any errors or deficiencies in the book.

GLENN H. SNYDER

Buffalo, N.Y.
January 1965

Stockpiling
Strategic
Materials

Introduction

In this age of hydrogen bombs and intercontinental ballistic missiles, when the overwhelming concern of most students of national security policy has become the avoidance of nuclear annihilation and the rational integration of these horrendous weapons into foreign and defense policies, a book about stockpiles of copper, lead, zinc, goose feathers, castor oil, shellac, and other raw materials, as elements in national security policy, may seem anachronistic if not absurd. Yet the fact is that the United States government now owns more than $8 billion worth of such "strategic and critical" materials—about $3 billion more, incidentally, than its "stockpile" of surplus agricultural commodities. The "strategic" stockpile has been built up gradually since World War II as insurance against deficiencies in supplies of essential raw materials in the event of another major war. Although a portion of this stockpile has been declared surplus because of changes in military technology, most of it is still considered essential for national defense, and plans are under way to establish stockpile requirements for survival and industrial recovery after a nuclear exchange. In the official view of the United States government, the stockpile program is still an integral, if minor, part of our over-all defense posture.

However, it is not the primary purpose of this book to appraise

1

the relevance of raw-materials stockpiling to contemporary national defense problems. The aim is twofold: It is, first, simply to
tell the history of a program which has been almost totally ne-
glected in other studies of postwar national defense policy, a
program which few Americans even knew existed until Senator
Stuart Symington's dramatic exposé during 1962 and 1963. Second, it is to analyze that history in terms of the political forces,
both within and outside the government, which impinged upon it
and shaped its progress, and thus to contribute something to our
extremely meager empirical knowledge of "the politics of national defense." It is, therefore, primarily a study in political science,
rather than in history or economics. The political scientist will
find it most relevant to those sectors of the discipline usually labeled "administrative behavior," "decision making," or "civilian-
military relations," although no attempt is made to arrange the
data according to any particular theoretical framework which
may be suggested by these labels. In brief, it is a study in how
governmental decisions are made: the allocation of roles, the origin and development of attitudes and interests, the exercise of
influence and pressure, and so on.

Stockpiling is a good subject for the study of administrative
politics because of its inherently hybrid nature. Although its sole
official function and purpose, ostensibly at least, is that of national defense, it also impinges on other governmental policies and
programs, such as foreign economic policy, natural resource policy, and policies toward business generally. Because of this
mixed character, its administration has always been marked by a
wide dispersal of functions and responsibilities and a high degree
of interdepartmental collaboration. The Department of Defense
participates because of its concern with the ultimate purpose of
the program; the Department of State because of its responsibility for international economic policy (specifically its concern for
the effects of stockpile buying on foreign producers and consumers of materials); the Department of the Interior because of its
responsibility for domestic resources policy, its technical exper-

tise regarding the objects to be stockpiled, and its concern for the welfare of the domestic mining industry; the Department of Commerce because of its responsibility for domestic business interests, particularly materials-consuming industries; the Department of Agriculture because some of the stockpiled materials are agricultural in origin and because of the close relation which has developed between stockpiling and the agricultural price-support program; and, finally, the agency responsible for industrial mobilization (now the Office of Emergency Planning) because stockpiling is essentially an aspect of industrial mobilization. Standing behind several of these agencies are their "constituencies"—the private-interest groups which have occasionally brought pressures to bear on the program independently, either directly upon the program's administrators or indirectly via their friends in Congress. Incidentally, the dispersal of functions and representation in the Executive Branch has been mirrored in a similar dispersal of interests and responsibilities toward the program among several committees of Congress.

Naturally enough, this fractionalization of responsibility and the diversity of the interests concerned have produced friction and conflict from the very outset. The national defense interest has been paramount, but the sponsors of other interests have attempted, with considerable success, to push stockpiling policies off the straight and narrow track of national security into the service of other values, such as the support of domestic minerals prices or the alleviation of materials shortages. A pervasive theme which runs through the story of stockpiling is the tension between management of the stockpile according to the ground rules of national security and its manipulation as a "buffer stock" to stabilize or otherwise affect the prices and production of materials. Each of these purposes generates its own logic, which conflicts sharply with the logic of the other, and, in the abstract, a pure, single-value stockpiling policy could have followed one or the other. In reality, the program has been multi-valued, despite its labeling as a national security measure, and its administration has pursued both security and "economic" functions. The word "economic" is placed within quotation marks because no participant ever openly urged that stockpiling policy should support the aim of economic stabilization in its pure, objective sense, except very briefly in the bargaining which produced the basic legislation in 1946. To the extent that stockpiling has promoted economic-stabilization ends, this was the result, not of open, straightforward *economic* arguments, but of *political* pressures, and arguments which were almost always couched in the language of national security. In other words, the limited degree to which the economic function was realized was the haphazard, almost unconscious, result of politics and bargaining among the interested and participating groups, each arguing, not always hypocritically, that its own particular interest in certain price and economic effects was really consistent with—in fact, required by— the objective of national security. An interesting related theme is the stiff and fairly successful resistance to these "extraneous" pressures which the Department of Defense waged when the program was under essentially military control, compared with the marked weakening of resistance when it was transferred to a civilian industrial-mobilization agency in 1953.

The "outputs" of stockpiling policy decisions have, in a sense, followed from "inputs" consisting of both technical, logical calculations and subjective interests and pressures. Like a good deal of national defense policy generally, policy was the product of a continuous interaction between logic and politics. More accurately, perhaps, those who were responsible for running the program as a national security measure generated a complex assortment of technical procedures and formulae, not only as aids to administration, but also as defenses for the national security interest (or their conception of it) against the assaults of those who spoke for subnational or other-national interests. The "special interest" attackers were therefore forced to attack the logical formulae and the assumptions behind them in order to justify their own demands; and when they were successful in forcing a deviation in their favor, it was usually legitimized by manipulating the technical calculus, thus protecting both the administrators and the pressure groups from the suspicion or charge of boondoggling, and preserving a public façade of strict rationality in the service of the over-all national interest. This preservation of the appearance of objectivity by technical, disinterested calculation was one reason why Senator Symington's disclosures of political chicanery in 1962 and 1963 came as a considerable surprise to all but the insiders.

The national security rationale for having a stockpile of raw materials rests fundamentally on the simple fact that the United States is not self-sufficient in most of the materials which its industrial process consumes. Although nature has indeed endowed us richly with natural resources, and although our *degree* of self-sufficiency is high in comparison with most other industrialized nations, about a third of the more than 100 minerals we use come almost entirely from other lands, and we are a net importer of all metals but vanadium and molybdenum. The Stockpiling Act of 1946 was dedicated to the proposition that we must accumulate government stocks of the most essential of these minerals and other imported materials, in case enemy military or naval action in some future war should block our access to them, and thus prevent or hinder the wartime production of munitions and other essentials. The validity of this proposition seemed confirmed by the experience in World War II, when Japanese conquests in Asia deprived us of most of our natural rubber, tin, and other materials, and enemy submarines not only sent tons of vital materials to the bottom, but also forced the diversion of scarce naval power to convoy duty. On the other hand, the war also proved the considerable capacity of the American industry and people to "rise to the occasion" by the ingenious development of synthetics, the use of substitutes, and the conservation of scarce materials by consumer belt-tightening. The astounding achievements of Germany in these respects were also significant. However, the prevailing opinion among those in the United States

government who were responsible for industrial-mobilization
planning was that such measures might not be sufficient in another war, and, in any case, that a stockpile was worth having to
avoid their cost and inconvenience.

The reader who is familiar with the history of the United States
national defense policy since World War II may be puzzled by
the seeming detachment of the stockpile program from the con-
stantly changing developments in military technology and strategic doctrine which took place at higher levels of the defense decision-making structure. Logically, a program of industrial mobilization should be in constant contact with military hardware programs and strategic planning. It is true that stockpiling, once
under way, tended to perpetuate itself along lines originally conceived in 1946 and earlier, more or less in blissful isolation from
changing defense concepts and capabilities, most notably the advent of nuclear plenty and the related concepts of deterrence
and limited war. At certain critical points, high-level national
policy broke through and made contact with stockpiling, sometimes with rather drastic consequences. On the whole, however,
the sense of at least semidetachment from the mainstream of
national defense policy accurately reflects the reality.

This autonomous character of the stockpiling program is
another characteristic which, along with its multi-value and
multi-interest nature, makes it a good laboratory for observing
the politics of national defense decision-making. Stockpiling
might be described as a "middle-level" program, the kind of program which was not important enough to appear very often on
the desk of the President or even on the desks of the highest
officials of the agencies concerned, but nevertheless important
enough to engage the attention and energies of lower-level
officials responsible for relevant aspects of their agencies' interests. Thus, decisions tended to be made largely by a process of
pure "horizontal bargaining" (to borrow Samuel P. Huntington's phrase) between divisions or bureaus of the interested
agencies, relatively uninhibited by interference from the vertical

hierarchy of authority. In other words, the stockpiling story is interesting and important for what it reveals about administrative politics "in the raw," as a study in how decisions are made in a context of maximally free play of power and parochial interest, relatively unstructured or "uncorrupted" either by a strong common sense of a well-defined national interest or by authoritative direction from the top. A much more important program presumably would have been more subject to hierarchical direction and to integration with an evolving national policy, and conflicts would have been more promptly settled by authoritative decision; a lesser one might not have impinged sharply enough upon agency interests to produce much conflict. Falling between these two poles, stockpile policy-making tended to be both conflictful and undirected. Once it was "wound up," so to speak, in 1946, the program simply kept going, more or less autonomously and under its own momentum, along lines determined primarily by the vector sum of the political power of the interested agencies and groups. It was not until twelve years later, in 1958, that the contradiction between stockpiling policy and over-all defense policy was finally perceived to be so blatant as to require decisive intervention by the highest authorities. At that time a Presidential decision resulted in the administrative "creation" of huge surpluses; that is, amounts of materials in the stockpile which were recognized as being unneeded when measured against prevailing strategic plans and strategic assumptions concerning the nature of future war. Further modest attempts have been made since then to introduce more consistency between stockpiling and other aspects of national security policy; at this writing (early 1965) the nature and eventual consequences of such integration are still being worked out.

I

The Stockpiling Act of 1946

Our story appropriately begins with the background and legislative history of the Stockpiling Act of 1946. This Act not only established rough guidelines for postwar stockpiling policy, but also determined the agency participants in policy making and allocated authoritative power among the participants. The background of discussion in both the Executive Branch and Congress, prior to passage of the legislation, provides a preview of the often conflicting perspectives, interests, and pressures which continued to generate controversy throughout the subsequent history of the program.

The Act of 1946 was the outcome of a power struggle among the Departments of War, the Navy, the Interior, and State; the Bureau of the Budget; the Office of War Mobilization and Reconversion; the Senate and House Military Affairs Committees; and the mining bloc in Congress, consisting of congressmen from minerals-producing states. The struggle centered on two broad subjects: the *purposes* which stockpile policy was to serve; and the *roles* and *procedures* for making policy, which, in effect, would determine the degree of influence for each of the interested agencies, and the allocation of power between the Executive Branch and Congress.

The struggle was importantly influenced by the fact that a stockpiling law was already on the books, the Strategic Materials

Act of 1939. This Act authorized the Secretaries of War and the Navy "acting jointly" with the Secretary of the Interior "through the Army-Navy Munitions Board," to build a stockpile of "strategic" raw materials, in view of the threat of loss of vital imports as the result of Japanese conquests in Asia and the possibility of war in Europe. This Act had become virtually inoperative by the summer of 1940, when it was superseded by broader and more urgent mobilization programs, and very little material was accumulated during its year of operation. Nevertheless, the precedents of military control and of military collaboration with the Department of the Interior were to have important consequences in the bargaining which took place prior to the enactment of the 1946 Act.

Policy Differences

While the agency differences on policy content were closely related to the issue of control, it is convenient to treat them separately.

The policy perspectives of the War and Navy Departments centered on the proposition that the stockpile should be accumulated solely for the purpose of national security. The materials to be acquired, and their amounts, should be determined entirely by an objective calculation of wartime mobilization requirements and possible supply shortages. The program must not be tainted by economic or political aims, such as supporting the domestic mining industry, stabilizing world raw-materials prices, or political bargaining with producing nations. Nor should it be used for other purposes of foreign policy, such as supporting foreign-aid programs. Purchases should be made at the lowest possible price, regardless of source, and the source of most acquisitions would naturally be foreign since the major purpose of stockpiling was to hedge against an interruption of wartime imports of those materials for which the United States was substantially dependent on foreign supplies.

The Army and Navy wished to eliminate, or at least to modify, the "Buy-American" clause which had been written into the pre-war law, requiring preference for domestically produced materials. But above all, the military participants, especially those from the Army, wanted to keep the stockpile program free of all political or economic objectives and influences. Such objectives would make the program controversial; they would pervert and distort the program from its proper security function and generally convert it into a "political football." They even opposed the idea of stockpiling for civilian requirements during war; the stockpile should comprise only materials required for producing military equipment. If other agencies wished to make provision for nonmilitary production and civilian wartime requirements, this was all right, but they should ask for separate legislation and a separate stockpile for this purpose, and not try to introduce this objective into the military stockpile. Thus the military participants, particularly on the Army side, tended not only to stigmatize all possibly nonsecurity functions of stockpiling as irrelevant, frivolous, even vaguely immoral, but also to define the national security function in the narrowest military terms. No doubt this attitude reflected in part a desire to keep the stockpile small so as to minimize its competition for the military budget dollar; but it also showed a failure to recognize what World War II had amply demonstrated—the dependence of the cutting edge of a military effort on the efficiency of the economy as a whole, and the consequent requirement for minimum satisfaction of some nonmilitary needs.

The military departments wanted all surplus strategic materials which were held by the government at the end of the war to be turned over to the national defense stockpile. They wanted fairly flexible authority to sell or dispose of stockpiled materials, flexible enough to permit disposal of deteriorated and obsolete materials, but for no other reason except for use in war or national emergency as declared by the President.

The State Department's policy views coincided with those of the War and Navy Departments on some points and conflicted on others. The Department was opposed to any preference for domestic suppliers, partly because this contradicted the Department's cherished free-trade policy as codified in the Reciprocal Trade Agreements Act, partly because of a belief that domestic purchasing would deplete domestic reserves and thus reduce (or at least not contribute to) national security in raw materials. Mindful of the interests of foreign producers, the Department wanted all World War II surplus stocks to be frozen in a permanent stockpile to avoid the price depression which might result from their sale. In addition, the State Department wished to avoid an abrupt decline in United States purchasing of raw materials at the end of the war, with consequent disruption of the economies of the producing countries; therefore it was anxious to get new stockpile legislation enacted before the end of hostilities so that stockpile purchases could be used to smooth the transition from wartime to peacetime demand.

Like the military, the Department of State was inclined to favor a small stockpile, but for somewhat different reasons. The reasons stemmed largely from a rather pacifistic orientation manifested chiefly in a high degree of faith in the efficacy of the international organization which was to be set up to keep the peace. There was some feeling that unilateral military preparedness, including stockpiling, at too high a level would demonstrate lack of faith in the organization and thus undermine it. One State Department memorandum said, for example: "The United States cannot logically at once devote its energies to the maintenance of international peace and prepare for global war."

State Department views ran counter to the military's on the over-all purposes of the stockpile program and the related issue of disposal authority. While they conceded that the primary purpose of stockpiling should be national defense, State Department participants also spoke of using the stockpile as an "instrument of international political and economic policy" and of placing it "within the framework" of whatever international raw-materials controls and price-stabilization agreements might be nego-

tiated after the war. Stockpile purchases from foreign sources
should be carried out so as to minimize economic dislocation and
"maximize long-term economic and political benefits" to the
supplying nations. To carry out such policies, the stockpile administrators would need "wide discretion to sell as well as to
buy" in order to be able to "take advantage of changes in prices
and market conditions."

Although the State Department favored a small stockpile, it
wanted the stockpile to provide for civilian as well as military
requirements in war; in any case, the Department believed, it
was difficult if not impossible to draw a clear line between the
two sets of needs in a modern wartime economy.

The Office of War Mobilization and Reconversion also wanted
the stockpile to provide for the total strategic-materials deficit
of the economy in case of war, not just for military requirements.
It differed with the military departments, the State Department,
and the Department of the Interior, in desiring to sell most of the
wartime surplus materials to consuming industries after the war
to facilitate reconversion. It also wanted a relatively high degree
of disposal flexibility, so that stockpiled materials might be released to combat shortages and inflationary price trends in the
postwar period.

The Department of the Interior favored a large stockpile,
heavy emphasis on domestic purchasing, tight restrictions on disposal, and transfer of all war-surplus materials to the stockpile. If
disposal authority were not strictly limited, government stocks
might be thrown on the market, thus depressing prices to the detriment of domestic suppliers. Obviously, these policy positions
reflected Interior's commitment to its domestic mining constituency.

The Question of Control

There were three contenders for control of the postwar stockpile program: the Army-Navy Munitions Board, the Department

of the Interior, and the Office of War Mobilization and Reconversion. The Department of State was a highly interested party but did not want control; it tended to favor vesting policy control in the OWMR or its postwar successor.

The military arguments for sole or dominant control by the ANMB were closely related to the military policy views. Since the purpose of stockpiling was, or should be, national security and nothing else, control should logically be vested in a military agency, although the civilian agencies might play limited advisory roles. The program under military control would not be diverted to nonsecurity ends, which the Army and Navy considered illegitimate. The military departments and the ANMB were relatively immune to political pressures which might corrupt and distort the program, whereas the civilian agencies were vulnerable to such pressures, either domestic or foreign. The civilian agencies were incapable of assessing the effect of changes in weapons technology on requirements for strategic materials. The ANMB was best qualified by experience since it had been in charge of the short-lived prewar program. Control or significant participation by the civilian agencies would prejudice the passage of legislation in Congress. The military participants asserted that the civilians were unwilling to accept a mere advisory status because they hoped to introduce economic and political aims into the program. The civilians, the military charged, were trying to do this covertly, "under the guise of national defense." Such policies would not only discredit the program; they would also absorb funds needed elsewhere for national security.

While the military departments wanted exclusive control, through the ANMB, they at least considered certain compromises at various stages of bargaining. One such was the idea of having separate military and civilian stockpiles. As one War Department memorandum put it:

The civilian agencies, although denying that this is the purpose, are, in effect, trying to obtain a larger stockpile than necessary for defense but needed for economic or diplomatic reasons. If this is desirable, they should frankly and honestly go to Congress and seek a separate stockpile for such purposes, rather than try to ride on our backs.[1]

Thus the civilian agencies might present a bill which would give them control of a stockpile for *their* purposes; at the same time, the prewar law would be extended and revised to provide for a purely military stockpile.

Another variant was to put the stockpile formally and administratively in the hands of a civilian agency, which would, however, be required to stockpile minimum requirements declared by the military before spending funds for other materials. The military departments would not participate in the program's administration at all, not even in an advisory capacity, except to send over their requirements. It is noteworthy that neither of these alternatives allowed for any significant collaboration with civilian agencies. The military tended to want either complete control or no real participation at all but with their interests protected by law—but preferably complete control.

The Interior Department's case for vesting control in its hands was based on the nature of the objects to be stockpiled rather than on the purposes of stockpiling. It was the department in which expertise on metals and minerals was concentrated, and the technical prowess of the Department's Bureau of Mines, it was said, was essential to efficient administration. A corollary argument was that the military departments were not equipped to make the necessary technical judgments.

The claim of the OWMR was based on the assertion that planning and action in the field of industrial mobilization was properly a civilian function, since many values and interests other than military were involved. Stockpiling must necessarily make provision for the materials needs of the whole economy and population in war, and the military services were poorly suited for this job in terms of interest, inclination, and expertise. Furthermore,

[1] Memo, Julius Amberg, Special Assistant to Secretary of War, to Robert P. Patterson, Under Secretary of War, March 2, 1944. Office of the Army Adjutant General [hereafter cited as AGO] File No. 400.13.

the civilian agency in charge of stockpiling should not be beholden to any particular domestic interest group, as Interior was.

The State Department, as noted above, tended to favor the OWMR, but was willing to support control by other agencies or a new special agency provided that State was granted an advisory role carrying sufficient influence to protect the country's foreign-policy interests.

The Distribution of Power

In the bargaining process, the military departments enjoyed a clear superiority of power over the civilian agencies. The essential problem, of course, was to get a piece of stockpiling legislation through Congress. By tradition, stockpiling was the concern of the Military Affairs Committees in both houses, committees which would be expected to favor the military viewpoint and particularly the Army view. The advantage of precedent was on the military's side, the prewar law having placed the Army-Navy Munitions Board in substantial control. At the time the legislation was being considered, the war was still on, and the military were riding on a high crest of prestige. Many congressmen had not really absorbed one of the major lessons of World War II: that industrial mobilization must be a civilian function, since it involves making broad choices between security and nonsecurity values and requires a sound grasp of theoretical economics as well as a rich empirical knowledge of the nation's economic system.

In addition to the advantage of administrative logic, the OWMR could count on the support of the civilian agencies without interested domestic constituencies (notably the State Department and the Bureau of the Budget), as well as the Department of Commerce, which tended to represent the interests of materials-consuming industries. It was also closer to the President administratively than the older "line" agencies, and it generally enjoyed the President's confidence and support in matters of industrial mobilization.

The Department of the Interior wielded considerable influence in Congress, largely because of the interests it shared with representatives from mining states. Precedent favored it, too, for it had been one of the policy-making agencies, along with the War and Navy Departments, in the prewar stockpile program. These two factors were to give Interior a pivotal role in the bargaining, even though all the other Executive Branch participants recognized and deplored Interior's special-interest bias.

The Department of State was weakest in bargaining power. Unpopular in Congress, distrusted by many in the military services, more or less ignored by the President in the making of major wartime policy, State had to substitute intellect and personal energy for political power in defending its interests.

The First Round

The struggle in the Executive Branch was precipitated in Congress by the introduction of a mining-bloc bill[2] in the summer of 1943 by Senator James Scrugham of Nevada, Chairman of the Mining and Minerals Subcommittee of the Senate Special Committee on Small Business. The bill was pointed essentially toward keeping in business the small, high-cost domestic mines which were operating during the war under the stimulus of premium prices and subsidies. Stockpile purchases were to be made at prices high enough to provide such companies with a reasonable profit, and no foreign materials were to be bought which were available domestically at any price. The stockpile would be accumulated and administered by an interagency committee chaired by "an outstanding member of the mining industry."

This bill, with its flagrant domestic-subsidy feature, was unacceptable to all the executive agencies except Interior. It was necessary to come up with an Administration bill to head off its pas-

[2] S.1160, 78th Congress, 1st session.

sage, and the Department of State took the lead, in the person of
Herbert Feis, Economic Adviser to the Secretary of State. Besides preempting the Scrugham bill, State's initiative was promp-
ted also by its general interest in postwar economic planning, its
own special interest in locking up the wartime surpluses of some
materials whose indiscriminate sale might injure foreign producing countries, and by its desire to head off military control of the
program and install it instead in a permanent civilian industrial-
mobilization agency. Feis organized an interagency committee to
draft the bill. Besides State, the committee included representatives from the War Production Board, the Foreign Economic Administration, the Department of the Interior, and several other
civilian agencies. The military departments were not at first invi-
ted.

The committee soon found itself in disagreement, most seriously on the degree of restriction to be placed on the disposal of
materials once acquired. This issue reflected a broader disagreement about the proper purpose and function of a stockpile
program, which in turn reflected agency interests. In advocating tight disposal restrictions, Interior, represented by Elmer
Pehrson, emphasized the national security objective, but also
stressed the need to protect the domestic minerals producers
against indiscriminate or unpredictable sales from the stockpile.
The Department of Commerce felt that some flexibility was desirable to permit the release of materials to combat high prices or
shortages. The Foreign Economic Administration, represented by
Paul Nitze, favored uninhibited disposal authority, so that the
stockpile might be used as a buffer stock to stabilize world prices
of primary commodities. The Department of State was of two
minds: it was sympathetic to the FEA view in principle, but it
was also aware of the practical political fact that certain foreign
producing countries, notably in Southeast Asia, might object to
the price-breaking potential of a stockpile which was not tightly
frozen. The committee finally agreed provisionally that although

it was theoretically desirable to have wide discretion to sell as well as buy materials, it was necessary to limit this discretion for political reasons.[3]

Apparently the State Department had not initially intended to bring the military services into the discussions. However, invitations were extended to the War and Navy Departments after the second meeting of the committee—significantly perhaps, after strong urging by the Interior representative. Pehrson undoubtedly hoped to gain support from the military by exploiting their association with Interior in the prewar program and their common interest in resisting the use of the stockpile as an instrument of commodity price stabilization. It had become known that the military departments had begun work on a stockpiling bill of their own based on an extension of the prewar law, with control to be vested in the Army-Navy Munitions Board. Undoubtedly, the State Department realized that if Congress were confronted with both a civilian and a military bill, or even a civilian bill which was opposed by the military, the military, with its great wartime prestige, would emerge the winner. It was necessary, therefore, to get military support for a single Administration bill, even at the cost of significant concessions.

Military participation in the Feis committee's meetings was rather indifferent. Officers did not attend until three months after the invitations had been extended. Different officers represented the War and Navy Departments at different meetings, and they consistently took a rather dogmatic, uncooperative line. Stockpiling should serve no other purpose than national security, they insisted. They doubted whether it was proper to accumulate a single stockpile for both civilian and military needs. They seemed unimpressed by Feis' arguments about the indivisibility of industrial-mobilization planning; they tended to equate national security with military security and appeared to believe that any

[3] Feis committee, *Minutes*, second meeting, June 24, 1943.

accumulation for wartime civilian requirements would give the stockpile an unsavory political and economic coloring.[4]

In the end, however, the committee was able to agree on a bill which reflected some of the preferences of all participants, with significant concessions to the military. The bill stated that the only purpose of stockpiling was national security. The stockpile administrators were to give priority to "requirements of the minimum stockpiles deemed necessary by the armed forces," and the Army and Navy would be allowed to maintain separate "working stocks" of strategic materials for their exclusive use. In return for these concessions, the military representatives agreed that the main stockpile should take account of civilian as well as military requirements. Common interests of the military and the Department of the Interior were reflected in the proviso that the President could release materials from the stockpile only "for national defense" instead of "in the public interest" as earlier drafts had put it. Interior must have been disappointed, however, when at military insistence a provision making the stockpilers directly responsible for the "development of domestic resources" was deleted, though the bill did provide for "conservation and development" activities to be carried on independently by the Department of the Interior. The bill omitted any reference to commodity price stabilization, foreign economic development, and other nonmobilization functions; those in State and the FEA who had favored incorporating such functions had to be satisfied with a statement that acquisition goals should reflect "shifts in international political relations."[5]

Actually, the committee failed to reach complete agreement on the critical question of who was to control and administer the stockpile program. The bill called for the President to create "appropriate governmental machinery" to operate under the direc-

[4] *Ibid.*, sixth meeting, September 16, 1943.
[5] WPB Document No. 273. October 7, 1943. National Archives, WPB File No. 112.

tion of a Governing Board, consisting of representatives of State, War, and Navy, and "such other agencies as might be determined by the President."[6] Naturally, this designation was gall and wormwood to Interior, which had expected to have the leading role. The military departments reluctantly agreed to naming the State Department only after Feis persuasively pointed out the impact on foreign policy of stockpiling operations. Feis paid a high price for this military concession; in addition to the policy changes mentioned above, he handed over to the military departments the right to sponsor the bill and guide it through Congress. The armed services also reserved the right to suggest changes in the bill without consulting the other agencies during the legislative process.[7] In a sense, however, this price only recognized a political reality: the pronounced hostility of many congressmen toward the Department of State and hence the low likelihood that any State-sponsored stockpiling bill could pass muster in Congress.

The upshot was that the military had succeeded in revising the civilian bill to fit their own policy preferences and in obtaining dominant control—at the very small price of allowing minor State Department participation. Feis had assured them during the negotiations that State would consider its function to be purely advisory, that it was interested only in the source of purchases (foreign vs. domestic), and that it would leave all major policy decisions to the military.[8] In short, the results were the fruit of an alliance between the military and the Department of State, with the military very much the dominant partner, even though State had taken the initiative in writing the bill. Interior's move to bring the military into the discussions had backfired: instead of joining forces with Interior, the military had lined up with State, leaving Interior isolated.

[6] Ibid.
[7] Memo, Admiral Keleher, ANMB, to James V. Forrestal, Under Secretary of the Navy, September 30, 1945. National Archives, Special File No. 401.1.
[8] Ibid.

The Second Round

The military-State alliance proved to be unstable, however. One suspects that the military departments' commitment to the Feis bill and their capture of the sponsorship of the bill were simply holding tactics designed, in part at least, to delay the introduction of any stockpiling legislation until the military were ready with their own. At any rate, early in 1944 the Under Secretaries of War and the Navy, Judge Robert Patterson and James Forrestal, respectively, were persuaded by their subordinates that they should disengage their departments from the Feis bill, chiefly because it failed to provide for exclusive Army and Navy control and made reference to certain "extraneous considerations, such as relations with other nations, developing of domestic resources, etc."[9] The Army-Navy Munitions Board began drafting a set of amendments to the prewar stockpiling law which would leave the ANMB in control, with the civilian agencies playing only an advisory role.

Julius Amberg, Special Assistant to the Secretary of War, brought the bad news to Charles Taft, who had succeeded Herbert Feis as Chief of State's Office of Wartime Economic Affairs. Naturally, Taft expressed considerable dismay and said the Department would insist on having more than a weak advisory role. Taft persuaded Amberg to agree to a meeting of all the interested agencies, to reach some sort of civilian-military compromise.[10] The meeting took place on February 10, with Dean Acheson, Assistant Secretary of State for Economic Affairs, presiding. All the arguments for civilian versus military control were recited, with considerable vehemence on both sides. In the end, the military representatives refused to budge from their determination to prevent any significant civilian role in stockpiling,

[9] Memo, Julius Amberg, Special Assistant to the Secretary of War, to Robert P. Patterson, Under Secretary of War, January 5, 1944. National Archives, File No. 032.3.

[10] *Ibid.*, January 31, 1944. National Archives, Special File No. 401.1.

but they did agree to allow the civilian agencies to participate in the drafting of amendments to the prewar law. A committee under Julius Amberg was appointed for this purpose.[11]

Before the first meeting of the Amberg committee, a new coalition, between State and Interior, took shape. The State Department, now convinced that the Army and Navy really intended to renege on their earlier agreement, swallowed its distaste for Interior's domestic-mining bias in a desperate attempt to put the stockpile program in civilian hands and preserve a measure of influence for itself. Interior, while it might have been satisfied with a simple extension of the prewar law (which would have given it a role at least formally equal to that of the Army and Navy), now feared that the military departments intended to exclude it as well. The fruit of this alliance was a new civilian bill which would have established a Stockpile Board, consisting of the Secretary of the Interior as Chairman; the Secretaries of State, War, the Navy, and Commerce; and the heads of the OWMR, the War Production Board, and the FEA. The bill was supported by all the interested civilian agencies. The earlier lineup, which had pitted the "foreign interest–small stockpile" advocates against the "domestic interest–big stockpile" agency (Interior) and had resulted in a superficial victory for the former, had now been transformed, as a consequence of the defection of the armed services from the alliance with State, into a straight civilian-military division.

As a "carrot" for the armed services, the civilian bill provided that the Stockpile Board would stockpile at least the quantities determined necessary for military needs by the Secretaries of War and the Navy. However, it would purchase them "at such times as it may determine." In other words, the military amounts would not enjoy priority in procurement as they would have under the Feis bill. The new bill contained a "Buy-American" clause, reflecting the interests of Interior, and a requirement that the Board give "due consideration to the needs of the domestic economy," reflecting the consumer-oriented interests of the Commerce Department and the industrial-mobilization agencies.

The bill was discussed at the first meeting of the Amberg committee on February 24. Amberg, presenting the War Department's view, expressed firm opposition on the familiar grounds that any stockpiling beyond military requirements would make the program "a political issue" and that the military departments could not accept a minority position on the board. Perhaps as a lure to Interior, he suggested a simple extension of the prewar law, with a single amendment permitting the transfer of war-surplus stocks to the ANMB's stockpile. But the State Department, in the person of Charles Taft, refused to accept this proposal.

Then the united front of the armed services broke with a crash (at least temporarily) when Struve Hensel, Special Assistant to the Under Secretary of the Navy, announced that the Navy Department would accept the civilian bill if the Navy were simply left off the Governing Board. This would mean, if the War Department went along, that the armed services would simply present their estimated military requirements to the Governing Board but would not otherwise participate in stockpile policy making. Variations on this theme had appeared earlier in intramilitary discussions. The notion had the support of a relatively sophisticated group of temporary wartime officers and civilians, chiefly Navy, who felt that stockpiling was not properly a military activity and should be left to the civilians, preferably to a permanent industrial-mobilization agency in the Executive Office of the President. The meeting closed with a decision to refer the Hensel proposal back to the departments.[12]

As it turned out, this apparent breakthrough came to nothing because of strong opposition from the War Department and the

[12] Minutes of Interdepartmental Meeting on Stockpile Legislation, February 25, 1944. AGO File No. 400.13.

ANMB. The ANMB's Executive Committee, composed of military officers from both services, rejected the Hensel scheme because it would not assure protection of the military interest in stockpiling and because, with civilian agencies in control, the program would become "political" and "highly controversial"; even if the Army and Navy did not participate, they would be considered responsible for any maladministration because of the inherent military nature of stockpiling.[13]

With the situation again deadlocked, the only solution was to submit the dispute to higher authority. The appropriate referee was James Byrnes, head of the Office of War Mobilization, one of whose functions was to arbitrate interagency disputes on mobilization matters. Byrnes decided to defer his decision until after Congress had acted on a surplus-property bill then under consideration.

Congress passed the Surplus Property Act in October 1944.[14] The military departments had been working to get war surpluses of strategic materials held by other agencies transferred to the ANMB after the war, to be held as the nucleus of a postwar stockpile under authority of the prewar stockpiling law. Collaborating with mining-state congressmen, who feared the dumping of these materials on the market, the ANMB was successful in getting this transferral written into the Act. In addition, the Act directed the ANMB to submit to Congress within three months the maximum and minimum amounts of each strategic mineral or metal which it thought should be held in the postwar stockpile. This provision and the ANMB activity and subsequent report that it produced were instrumental in showing a congressional preference for, and strengthening the precedent of, military control of the postwar program, and considerably strengthened the military hand in the further bargaining within the Executive Branch.

[13] Report of meeting of Executive Committee on Stockpile Legislation, February 29, 1944. National Archives, Special File No. 032.3.
[14] Public Law 457, 78th Congress.

The Third Round

Meanwhile the Scrugham bill had failed because of congressional inaction. Another, less extreme mining-bloc bill appeared during the 1945 congressional session. Drafted by the American Mining Congress, it was introduced by Senator Elbert Thomas of Utah and Representative Andrew May of Kentucky, who, besides having mining interests in their states, were Chairmen of the Military Affairs Committees. The bill was significant, first because it placed administrative supervision of stockpiling in the ANMB, and second because it provided a high degree of congressional supervision. The ANMB was authorized to decide what materials to stockpile and to establish quantitative goals for each, but once established the goals could not be changed without specific congressional authorization. Sales from the stockpile were subject to tight legal restriction and close congressional supervision. Stockpile purchases were to be made in accordance with the "Buy-American" Act of 1933, which required the purchase of government supplies domestically whenever possible. The Stockpile Board which was to supervise the program in the Executive Branch would consist of the Secretary of War as Chairman and the Secretaries of the Navy, State, the Interior, and Commerce.

The Navy Department and some of the lower-ranking Army officers, mainly temporarily uniformed technicians, found the Thomas-May bill acceptable, except for the freezing of stockpile goals. The War Department opposed the bill because it left the military departments in a minority position on the Stockpile Board.[15]

This bill precipitated a new initiative in the Executive Branch. Fred Vinson, who had succeeded Byrnes as head of the Office of War Mobilization and Reconversion, appointed an interagency committee to draft an Administration bill, chaired by Kenneth C.

[15] Captain Regenstein to Executive Secretary, ANMB, April 9, 1945. AGO File No. 400.13. Also letter, Secretary of War Henry L. Stimson to Senator Elbert Thomas, undated, AGO File No. 400.13.

Royall, Special Assistant to the Secretary of War. The other members were Lewis Strauss, Special Assistant to the Secretary of the Navy, Michael W. Strauss, Assistant Secretary of the Interior, Harold Stein, Planning Advisor in the OWMR, and Richard H. Templeton, Jr., representing the Bureau of the Budget. The Department of State later asked to be represented and was allowed to send an observer. The most significant overt facts about this new decision-making unit were the seizure of initiative by the OWMR, the weak position of the Department of State, and the War Department's leading position in the drafting of legislation.[16]

The drafting committee immediately split into a "tripolar balance of power," with the military departments making up one unit, the OWMR, the Bureau of the Budget, and the State Department another, and the Interior Department the third. Each of these three coalitions presented separate bills.

In fact the division was at least tentatively bipolar because the military bill called for establishing a Stockpile Board in the Department of the Interior, with a chairman to be appointed by the Secretary of the Interior. Evidently, the military agencies were attempting to engineer a new reversal of alliances by making overtures to Interior. It was a very small carrot, however, because, although Interior would have the administrative responsibility and the housekeeping burdens which went along with it, the ANMB was to determine "which materials are strategic, the quality and quantity of each such material which shall be stockpiled, the maximum time within which each shall be acquired, and the priority with respect to acquisition as among the several materials and quantities thereof . . ." This allocation left little for the Stockpile Board and Interior to do except advise the ANMB and carry out the onerous details of purchasing, storage, and maintenance. The military bill may also have reflected a rising current of opinion in War and Navy—that these departments should divest themselves of nonmilitary- or semicivilian-type ac-

---

[16] Interview with Harold Stein, May 6, 1954.

tivities as the war drew to a close. Thus the bill provided for formal location of the program in a civilian agency—no doubt with an eye to reducing its competition with military programs for national security budget dollars (presumably scarce after the war) and to taking the military largely out of the line of political fire which the controversial program might provoke. The military departments chose Interior as their prospective "front" because of their earlier experience in working with Interior, because of the technical expertise of the Bureau of Mines, and because they believed Interior would be less likely to let loose of materials once acquired than would some other civilian agency.[17]

But Interior wanted to be more than general manager and purchasing agent. Its proposal also placed the chairmanship in the Department of the Interior, but with real powers: the chairman would determine the total amounts to be stockpiled and would generally control stockpiling policy. However, he would be bound to stockpile *at least* the amounts desired by the ANMB and to give priority to their acquisition. This last provision, representing Interior's overture to the military, went quite a distance toward the military departments' position. Nevertheless, as we shall see, the military-Interior alliance took a long time to jell, chiefly because Interior insisted on the freedom to stockpile any amount of materials *in addition* to those the ANMB would designate as military requirements.

The OWMR, the Bureau of the Budget, and the Department of State agreed on a draft bill which would allow the President to establish a Strategic Materials Stockpiling Board in whatever agency he might choose. The chairman would be appointed by the head of that agency and would be advised by the secretaries of the other interested agencies as members of the Board. The authors of the bill recommended that the Board be placed in the OWMR or in its successor as the postwar industrial-mobilization agency. With the advice of the Board, the President would determine what kinds of materials to stockpile, their quantities and

[17] Interview with Kenneth Royall, August 12, 1955.

qualities, and the dates by which they should be acquired. He could delegate this authority. Naturally, the authors of this bill recommended that he delegate it to the OWMR.[18]

The drafting committee held several meetings to discuss these proposals. The arguments were much the same as those advanced during the previous negotiations. Interior stressed its technical expertise; the other agencies objected to Interior's close identification with producing interests and its ignorance of the strategic and international aspects of stockpiling. The other civilian agencies emphasized the mixed civilian-military nature of stockpiling, which required placement in a civilian mobilization agency, able to take an over-all view of the national economy and to assess objectively both civilian and military requirements, and uncorrupted by any bias resulting from specialist attitudes and particular domestic interests. As for the military bill, these agencies asserted that the armed services were not qualified to plan for civilian wartime needs and probably would seriously underestimate such needs. The Army and Navy just as firmly held that since stockpiling was a national security program, they should have ultimate control over policy. They asserted that any civilian mobilization agency would have an uncertain future and would be vulnerable to domestic political pressures.[19]

Although there was some sentiment in the lower ranks of the ANMB for accepting the Interior plan as a compromise, Royall and Strauss held out for the military bill. Consequently, when the committee voted on the question of who should control stockpile objectives and procurement policy, the OWMR-Budget-State proposal received a plurality. The Army, the Navy, and the Department of the Interior each voted for its own plan. Royall could have created a stalemate by not counting the vote of the State Department's observer, but he elected to count it because some decision had to be made.

On the question of the location of the Stockpile Board, the De-

[18] Interview with Harold Stein, May 6, 1954.
[19] Letter, John Snyder to President Truman, September 7, 1945. Also interview with Harold Stein, May 6, 1954.

partment of State *was* demoted to observer status, thus avoiding a tie vote. Interior and the military departments joined to defeat the OWMR and the Bureau of the Budget.[20]

The resulting compromise bill was rather an oddity. The President was to determine general stockpile policy, but it was recommended that he delegate this function to the OWMR or its successor. At the same time, he was *instructed* to place the Stockpiling Board and its chairman administratively in the Department of the Interior. This contradictory outcome satisfied nobody, although it was perhaps most favorable to Interior. If the bill were to become law, the President might find it administratively necessary, however distasteful, to delegate policy control to the new unit which would be set up in the Interior Department.

When Royall reported to John Snyder (who had succeeded Fred Vinson as head of the OWMR), he left the distinct impression that the bill was an unsatisfactory patchwork of selections from the three bills and would require further discussion. Snyder decided that a Presidential decision was necessary. He sent copies of the three rival bills, with a memo setting out the views of the agencies, to President Truman. The President decided in favor of the OWMR-Budget plan, which would empower the President to place the Board and its chairman in the agency of his choice and which recommended the OWMR.

Of course, the military departments might have foreseen this outcome, considering the administrative location of the OWMR in the Executive Office of the President and especially in view of the close personal ties between John Snyder and President Truman. If so, why did they not strike up an alliance with Interior when they had a chance, by accepting the Interior plan in full? In addition to a fear that Interior would corrupt the program by indiscriminate domestic subsidies and price-support operations, the most likely explanation is that they expected to get what they wanted anyway from the congressional Military Affairs Committees, whatever bill the Administration proposed.

[20] Memo, Royall to Snyder, August 22, 1945. National Archives, Special File No. 401.1.

The approved Administration bill went first to the Senate Committee on Military Affairs. After a preliminary hearing, at which the military representatives supported the bill, the Committee's staff wrote a new bill, combining features from the Administration measure and the Thomas-May bill. From the latter were taken the Buy-American clause, other language intended to favor domestic suppliers, and tight congressional control over sales from the stockpile. Otherwise the Administration bill, with its provision for civilian control, was left intact. The Executive Branch agencies (the military quite reluctantly) agreed to the Committee's changes. This compromise bill passed the Senate on December 20 and went to the House Committee on Military Affairs the next day. The session was approaching its end, and nearly all interested parties, except the military departments, were anxious that the bill pass before adjournment. The prime consideration was that after January 2, government agencies would no longer be legally required to turn over their surplus strategic materials to the stockpile. To the mining industry and its governmental supporters, this deadline raised the specter of dumping; to the prospective new government stockpilers it might mean a loss of considerable amounts of free materials.

A representative of the American Mining Congress called all the interested agencies on December 21, urging that they request House Speaker Sam Rayburn to push the bill through by unanimous-consent procedure, without hearings. The Bureau of the Budget, the OWMR, and the Department of the Interior did call Rayburn to this effect. Rayburn told Snyder that he could get it through if the Administration could pry it out of the Committee.[21]

Royall was working to block this move. He wrote Rayburn, asking that no action be taken by the House without hearings because the War Department wished to be heard.[22] Royall also asked Representative Carl Durham, Acting Chairman of the

[21] Memo, Brig. Gen. Edgar P. Sorenson to Kenneth Royall, January 18, 1946. AGO File No. 400.13.
[22] *Ibid.*

House Committee on Military Affairs, to "put the bill in his pock-
et." The result was that when Snyder tried to contact him, Durham made himself unavailable.[23] So the session ended.

By the opening of the next session in January 1946, the War
Department had virtually decided to withdraw its support from
the pending bill and try to get instead a simple extension of the
prewar stockpiling law, which provided for formal military control with some collaboration with Interior. Royall's first move,
however, was to write to Snyder, suggesting a compromise which
would leave most aspects of policy under the control of the
OWMR, but give the ANMB the right to establish minimum
stockpile goals, which would be given priority in acquisition. In
a follow-up letter, he threatened to "prevent the passage" of the
pending legislation and to "rest on the present statutes relating
thereto"—that is, the prewar law—if his compromise proposition
were rejected.[24]

Snyder rejected Royall's demand, pointing out blandly that it
would be "entirely proper" for the War Department to use the
ANMB as its representative to advise the OWMR in the determination of stockpile goals.[25] Of course, this counterproposal did
not satisfy Royall or the War Department, which wanted more
than the right to give advice, something that was provided for
anyway in the pending bill.

Royall then proceeded to carry out his threat. He had the
Army side of the Munitions Board staff prepare *two* statements
as briefing for his appearance before the House Committee. One
was a formal statement in support of the Senate bill. The other
expressed the "fundamental objections" of the War Department
to that bill.[26]

After first hearing a representative from the OWMR, the

[23] Interview with Harold Stein, May 6, 1954.
[24] Letters, Royall to Snyder, January 26 and 28, 1946. AGO File No.
400.13.
[25] Letter, Snyder to Royall, February 1, 1946. AGO File No. 400.13.
[26] Memo, Major General S. P. Spalding to Royall, February 21, 1946.
AGO File No. 400.13.

House Committee on Military Affairs, chaired by Andrew May of
Kentucky, called Royall to testify on February 26. May was a
strong partisan of joint control of stockpiling by the military departments and the Department of the Interior. This preference
naturally followed from the combination of his Committee role
and the mining interests of his state. While there is no proof, the
conversation between May and other Committee members and
Royall at the hearing amply suggests that they had reached a
meeting of minds beforehand as to the desirable form of stockpile legislation and how Royall's views were to be brought out at
the hearing.

Royall began by reading the formal statement of War Department support for the Senate bill. Then, patiently probing and
leading their witness, May and others induced Royall to admit
that legal authority for stockpiling under military control already
existed and that therefore there was no need for new legislation
except for appropriations. Asked for his "personal view" on the
question of civilian versus military control, Royall revealed that
the War Department originally had disagreed with the Administration's bill and had sponsored a different bill providing for policy control by the War and Navy Departments, and now favored
a simple extension of the prewar statute.[27]

The Committee then proceeded to rewrite the bill along the
lines of the prewar law. The Secretaries of War, the Navy, and
the Interior, "acting jointly" through the ANMB, were authorized
to decide what materials were "strategic and critical" and the
total amounts and qualities of each to be stockpiled. This was
the function of establishing stockpile objectives. The Secretaries
of State, the Treasury, Agriculture, and Commerce were to
"cooperate" in this function.

The other major aspect of stockpiling policy—decisions on the
amount of each material actually to be bought each year, including, by inference, the preparation of the annual budget request for

[27] U.S. Congress, House, Committee on Military Affairs, "Stockpiling,"
Hearing, 79th Congress, 2nd session, 1946.

stockpiling—was to be controlled only by the Secretaries of War and the Navy. In other words, while Interior gained a greater role than the other civilian agencies in the determination of stockpile objectives, it was given no special influence on the vital function of procurement policy, which was more immediately significant than the somewhat formal function of setting ultimate goals.

Actual purchases were to be made by the Procurement Division of the Department of the Treasury under the direction of the Secretaries of War and the Navy. The Procurement Division was made responsible also for the storage and maintenance of the materials acquired, again, however, subject to policy guidance from the military departments.

Materials could be released from the stockpile in time of war or by Presidential order when "required for the purpose of the common defense." They could also be sold, short of a defense emergency, for reasons of technical obsolescence or deterioration, but such sales required a notice to the Military Affairs Committee of each house of Congress and a public announcement in the Federal Register at least six months in advance of the sale. Disposal of materials for any other reason required the express approval of Congress.

Domestic producers were protected in various other ways. The stated purpose of the Act—to "decrease and prevent wherever possible a dangerous and costly dependence of the United States upon foreign nations for supplies of these materials in times of national emergency"—was to be pursued not only by the "acquisition and retention" of stockpiles, but also by the "conservation and development of sources of these materials within the United States." Stockpile procurement was made subject to the Buy-American Act of 1933, and imports for the stockpile were to be subject to tariff duties. The Departments of the Interior and Agriculture were authorized to make scientific investigations "in order to determine and develop domestic sources of supply."

Domestic industrial *consumers* were likewise protected by a

proviso that the stockpile could buy only materials "in excess of
the current industrial demand." Government agencies were to
transfer to the stockpile, free of charge, all surpluses which fell
within the stockpile's quantitative goals and quality specifications.
But the Civilian Production Administration in the Department of Commerce could block the transfer and force the sale
of any such surpluses deemed necessary to United States industry.

The Committee's bill passed the House, was approved by a Sen-
ate-House conference committee without significant change, and
then quickly was approved again by both houses of Congress. It
was signed by President Truman on July 23, 1946.[28]

[28] See Appendix B for the full text of the Act.

II

Organization and Administration

An organizational chart of the administrative machinery of the stockpile program through most of its history would resemble nothing so much as a Rube Goldberg cartoon—of a contraption performing an essentially simple operation by an amazingly complicated process. Among critics of the program, a favorite game was to count up the large number of agencies or committees involved in one way or another. The Congressional Joint Committee on Foreign Economic Cooperation in 1949 counted 16 executive agencies and 11 congressional committees.[1] After the proliferation of new stockpiling apparatus during the Korean War, an official of the Defense Production Administration (who, incidentally, wanted his agency to take over the entire program) compiled a list of 54 agencies, 5 major interdepartmental committees, 9 congressional committees, and 5 international organizations.[2]

Such estimates should be taken as impressionistic rather than

[1] U.S. Congress, Joint Committee on Foreign Economic Cooperation, *Report, ECA and Strategic Materials*, Senate Report No. 140, 81st Congress, 1st session, 1949, p. 11.

[2] Senate Committee on Interior and Insular Affairs, *Stockpile Hearing*, 1953 and 1954, Part 2, pp. 462 ff.

accurate, for they usually were based on a rather loose definition of what constituted an agency and included some agencies and groups whose relationship to the central program was tenuous and administratively insignificant. Nevertheless, as impressions, they made a valid point—that the organization for stockpiling was highly decentralized and dispersed. The principal reason lay in the many-sided nature of the program itself: it could not be made to fit neatly into any one administrative slot. It involved the activities, responsibilities, and interests of so many agencies that it was necessarily a cooperative affair. Another reason is that the organization was built up piecemeal: as new functions and agencies with a stockpiling relationship were created, they were simply grafted onto the existing organization, with little or no attempt to revise or reintegrate the basic organization at the several stages of its growth. Third, Congress has been imaginative in legislating methods other than originally contemplated for accumulating materials and, in the process, making the stockpile program serve other ends, notably the disposal of agricultural surpluses and getting something "in return" for foreign aid. Finally, to protect the interests of groups affected by stockpiling operations, Congress gave some influence in stockpile policy making to agencies responsible for those interests.

This chapter briefly describes the organizational structure and decision-making process prior to the Korean War. The purpose is to lay a necessary background for the discussion of policy in subsequent chapters and to point up certain organizational and procedural problems.

Munitions Board

The principal stockpiling agency before mid-1950 was the Army-Navy Munitions Board, reorganized and renamed the Munitions Board in 1947. Although the Stockpiling Act had given the ultimate policy-making authority to the Secretaries of War, the Navy, and the Interior, the military Secretaries soon delegated their stockpile functions to the Board. Legally, of course, the functions concerned with the establishment of stockpile objectives still had to be shared with the Secretary of the Interior, who had a veto power.

The Board had other duties besides stockpiling. Since its creation by administrative action in 1922, it had been concerned generally with industrial-mobilization planning and the coordination of military procurement by the armed services.

The National Security Act of 1947, as amended in 1949, gave the Munitions Board statutory status and reorganized it. The Act prescribed the Board's membership as the under secretary or an assistant secretary from each of the three military departments, with a civilian chairman appointed by the President. The under and assistant secretaries, when sitting as members of the Board, did not officially represent their superiors but acted solely as members of the Board, which was responsible to the Secretary of Defense. The chairman was given the power of decision when the service representatives could not agree.

By administrative action, two deputy chairmen were added, one civilian and one military. The all-military Executive Committee, which had existed under the old ANMB, was expanded to include an Air Force member. The military deputy chairman held the rank of lieutenant general or vice-admiral; the members of the Executive Committee were usually two major generals and a rear admiral. The Executive Committee headed a secretariat comprising six administrative divisions, including a Materials Division, which was responsible for stockpile planning. The Materials Division was headed by a military officer from each service, at the colonel and (Navy) captain rank, with a small staff, primarily of civilian technicians.

The roster of the ANMB and its staff for February 1947 indicated a slight majority for military people over civilians in the professional positions—26 and 22, respectively. As time went on, the staff increased, and the proportion of military officers to civilians declined. By April 1952 the military proportion was just under one fourth—111 out of a total of 413.[3] Military men continued to fill the high policy-making positions just below the chairman. In stockpiling matters, however, the strongest influence undoubtedly was wielded by a civilian, Carl Rolle, who had been with the program since its inception before World War II. He bore the title of Minerals Adviser but was jocularly referred to as "Mr. Stockpile."

Advisory Committees

The Munitions Board was advised by a number of interagency committees, chief among which was the Strategic Materials Committee, later changed to the Interdepartmental Stockpile Committee. This committee was the vehicle by which the Departments of State, the Treasury, the Interior, Agriculture, and Commerce cooperated with the military departments in establishing stockpile goals, as specified in the Stockpiling Act, with Interior enjoying a rather privileged position. The rationale for membership of these agencies, of course, was that they had not only significant advice to contribute but also bureaucratic and constituency interests to protect. The actual representatives on the Strategic Materials Committee varied from meeting to meeting, but they were of intermediate rank, usually the head or assistant chief of the division in each agency most concerned with stockpile matters. In addition to the civilian agencies, the War and Navy Departments, and the Air Force after 1947, were also represented on the Committee by military officers.

In March 1949 the Interdepartmental Stockpile Committee replaced the Strategic Materials Committee. The membership changed in two respects: the military departments were demoted to observer status, and the individual members generally held positions of greater responsibility in their own departments. Rep-

[3] U.S. Congress, Senate, Preparedness Investigating Subcommittee of the Committee on Armed Services, *Investigation of the Preparedness Program, 38th Report, Munitions Board,* committee print, 82nd Congress, 2nd session, 1952, p. 13.

resentatives from other agencies, for example, the Atomic Energy Commission and the Bureau of the Budget, often sent observers to meetings. The Munitions Board provided the chairman, in the person of either the Chairman of the Board or the highest-ranking military officer on the Board's staff.

The Munitions Board appears to have relied rather heavily on the advice of the Strategic Materials Committee and its successor. The advice was followed fairly religiously on principally nonmilitary matters—for example, the general economic impact of stockpile purchases, estimates of availability of particular materials, reasonableness of prices, and projections of future production. By contrast, when strategic factors were foremost, such as the making of basic assumptions for estimating supplies from foreign sources in wartime and the scheduling of relative procurement urgencies, the Munitions Board made its own decisions and usually stuck to them, sometimes against the opposition of almost the entire committee.

By 1949, the Board and the Interdepartmental Stockpile Committee were being advised by 13 interdepartmental commodity committees, each dealing with groups of related materials. Each committee included representatives of the military services and civilian agencies interested in the commodity, usually Interior, Agriculture, and Commerce. Their basic function was to consolidate data received from the various agencies on past and probable future supplies and requirements of all essential materials likely to be scarce during war.

The Stockpiling Act directed the Munitions Board to appoint industry advisory committees "to the fullest extent practicable." In January 1949 there were 11 such committees divided into 35 subcommittees. They worked with the corresponding interagency commodity committees and also advised the Board directly. Their membership was supposed to be a cross section of both producing and consuming industries, and including small as well as large firms. They contributed advice on available supplies, market conditions, industrial quality standards, industrial quantitative requirements, buying techniques, changing technology, and storage and rotation of perishables.[4]

National Security Resources Board

The National Security Act complicated matters by also establishing a new civilian mobilization agency, the National Security Resources Board. Its function was to advise the President concerning "the coordination of military, industrial and civilian mobilization," including "policies for establishing adequate reserves of strategic and critical materials, and for the conservation of these reserves."[5]

The NSRB was an interagency committee chaired by a civilian appointed by the President, and with a small civilian staff. The Board consisted of the Secretaries of Defense, the Interior, the Treasury, Commerce, Labor, Agriculture, and State.

At first the authority of the Board rested with the Board as a group; that is, the Chairman had no independent authority except to direct the work of the staff. In May 1950 the powers of the Board were transferred to the Chairman, and the Board was made advisory to him.

The National Security Act made it clear that the NSRB was to take over some of the functions formerly performed by the Army-Navy Munitions Board in the field of mobilization planning. The Munitions Board's general area of concern was somewhat narrower than that of its predecessor: it was responsible only for the "military aspects" of industrial mobilization. The NSRB had over-all responsibility to weigh military against civilian needs. The NSRB had no power of direct command, but its position as adviser to the President put it in a good position to make its wishes prevail. The NSRB was clearly expected to take on the leading role in stockpile policy making.

[4] House Committee on Armed Services, *Stockpiling Hearing*, 1950, pp. 7512 ff.

[5] Public Law 216, 81st Congress, Section 103(a).

From the beginning, there was confusion about the respective jurisdictions of the two agencies. This confusion was partly because of the rather general language of the law, partly because of the inherent difficulty of separating military from other aspects of mobilization, and partly because of the Munitions Board's already having formulated plans and policies and put programs into operation, while the NSRB had to start from scratch. Some of the Munitions Board staff thought the NSRB was invading their bailiwick by trying to go too deeply into details; the NSRB staff members, for their part, were critical of what they called the Munitions Board's "cut-and-dried" approach and "rigid" formulae— they considered themselves more flexible and imaginative.

The Munitions Board made clear that it regarded the NSRB's communications merely as suggestions or recommendations, not as directives. When the NSRB proposed modifications in policy, the Munitions Board insisted that these were subject to negotiation and agreement before going into effect.[6] On the other hand, NSRB Chairman Arthur M. Hill told a congressional committee in March 1948 that it was the job of the Munitions Board to administer the stockpiling program, defend appropriations, and direct purchases, but that the NSRB established the policies.

Frictions were encountered in the establishment and feasibility testing of wartime requirements, a process directly related to the calculation of stockpile objectives. According to the National Security Act, the Munitions Board was supposed to evaluate, in the light of probably available resources, the feasibility of military wartime requirements estimates based on the strategic plans of the Joint Chiefs of Staff. The NSRB combined the military requirements with its estimate of civilian requirements and tested the feasibility of the whole, in view of *its* measure of the resources available. The question arose: which should be estimated first, military requirements or civilian requirements? The Munitions Board asked the NSRB for a statement of civilian require-

[6] Interview with Dewayne Kreager, former Executive Secretary of NSRB, August 26, 1955.

ments to be used as a floor for the establishment of military requirements. From its point of view it could not effectively evaluate the feasibility of military strategic and logistic plans without first knowing how much of the available resources would be held back for civilian use.

The NSRB tended to see the problem the other way around: the extent of the required civilian sacrifice would depend in part upon the size of the military requirements. The military services should base their requirements on needs, rather than availabilities. In other words, the NSRB preferred to have military requirements come from the Munitions Board uncolored by considerations of civilian needs; in order to assess the relative urgency of military and civilian requirements, it had to be sure that military requirements were "pure." In the process of weighing total requirements against total resources, perhaps both military and civilian requirements would be cut; but while neither could be finally determined without benefit of the other, each would have to be estimated initially on its own merits.

The solution finally evolved was that the staffs of the two agencies collaborate in assessing the feasibility of military requirements. Yet in May 1950 the Munitions Board again asked for a "definite determination" of civilian requirements, and asserted: "The ability of industry to meet both civilian and military requirements then could be ascertained with much greater accuracy, thus increasing the accuracy of tests of the feasibility of strategic and logistic plans."[7]

Relations between the two agencies were clarified, somewhat to the advantage of the NSRB, by NSRB Document No. 99, which was signed by the President early in 1949. The NSRB was to "assure the adequacy" of stockpiling policies, assure the coordination of stockpiling with other resource security measures, obtain consistency in the gathering and evaluating of supply and

---

[7] Harry B. Yoshpe, *A Case Study in Peacetime Mobilization Planning: The National Security Resources Board, 1947-1953*, Executive Office of the President, April 30, 1953, pp. 17 ff.

requirements data in all resource planning, and "obtain the initiative" of the Munitions Board and other agencies in the formulation and efficient execution of stockpile policies. The Munitions Board was given two separate and distinct roles. First, it was to represent the views and interests of the armed services in stockpiling. Second, it was to "serve as a central staff agency in bringing together the agencies of the Executive Branch in the continuing formulation and follow-up on execution of stockpiling policies and programs." In the latter role, the document emphasized that the Munitions Board was to "objectively facilitate the coordination of Executive Branch interests and operations." In addition, the Board was directed to bring to the NSRB all the problems which could not be resolved by consultation with other agencies. The NSRB thus became the stockpiling referee or "review agency."[8]

By spelling out in detail various things that the NSRB could do short of action by the President, the order conferred substantial independent authority on the NSRB. The Munitions Board could hold out for Presidential determination if it wanted to, but in doing so, it would be in the face of a clear indication by the President that he expected the NSRB to make the decision whenever possible.

While increasing the powers of the NSRB, the order also whittled away some of the powers of the Munitions Board by making the Board an advocate of military views and at the same time a coordinator of the views of all the agencies. Not only was this position anomalous, it was also a clear step down from the Board's earlier role: that of *the* central policy maker, obliged to take advice from other agencies but ultimately responsible for decisions. By becoming a "staff agency" and being required to "bring together" all agencies "in the formulation of policy"—not to formulate policy itself—the Munitions Board was further

[8] A summary of, and excerpts from, the document are printed in the Munitions Board's *Report to Congress* for July 23, 1949, p. 11015, and January 23, 1950, pp. 9-10.

downgraded. Finally, by directing the Board to bring disputes to the NSRB, the document took away the Munitions Board's own power to resolve disputes.

Nevertheless, the existence of the NSRB was convenient for the Munitions Board and the Department of Defense, not only because the NSRB put its full support behind the stockpiling program, but also because it was a handy referee for controversial questions and policy issues. To put it another way, the Munitions Board was not unhappy to have the NSRB available as a maker of policy choices involving values other than national security, and security programs other than military. This left the Board more freedom to play the role it really preferred: that of a more or less technical agency, engaged in the rational pursuit of a single, unambiguous policy objective, namely, the accumulation of the planned stockpile in the shortest possible time at the least possible cost. The Department of Defense tended to refer to the NSRB policy decisions involving nonmilitary matters whose resolution was important for military planning.

It is no contradiction to point out that having the stockpile planning function lodged in a military agency was also politically valuable to the NSRB. When a representative of a military agency said the national security required that the program be run in a particular way, his opinion carried weight. Thus, having the Munitions Board available as a front-line guard against domestic political forces tended to make the NSRB's own job easier.

Some of the NSRB's power accrued from conflicts between the Munitions Board and other agencies. The NSRB was available as an umpire to whom the weaker antagonist could appeal its case. In a dispute with the Department of Commerce on the extent of permissible stockpile competition with industrial buyers, the Munitions Board had the politically weaker position, or thought it had; an appeal to the NSRB brought results in its favor. When the Department of the Interior was the weaker party in a dispute over stockpile objectives (discussed in Chapter IV), it appealed to the NSRB over the objection of the Munitions Board.

Through the membership of its chairman on the National Security Council, the NSRB was in a position to assess the consistency of the stockpile program with over-all foreign and military policies. Stockpiling was never a very prominent item in the business of the Security Council, but certain basic shifts in policy did come up for consideration, mostly during and after the Korean War.

General Services Administration

The Procurement Division of the Treasury Department was the first general manager and purchasing agent for the stockpile. In a 1947 reorganization, it became the Bureau of Federal Supply, still housed in the Treasury Department. The Federal Property and Administrative Services Act of 1949 transferred this function to the Federal Supply Service, a part of the newly formed General Services Administration. In 1950 the Emergency Procurement Service was established within the GSA as a specialized unit dealing with the purchase of materials for the stockpile. The core personnel remained rather constant through all these reorganizations, although the staff expanded steadily. In May 1950 the GSA employed 697 people who were concerned with stockpiling in one way or another.

The principal rationale for giving the purchase and management duties to the Treasury Department and later to the GSA was that these agencies were responsible for buying general supplies for the government. Thus they had a long background of purchasing experience and were knowledgeable in commercial practices and customs. The Munitions Board was not considered qualified for this function, and did not want it, first because it was a planning not an operating agency, and second because the purchasing of raw materials was not prominent among military skills and was not considered a military function.

The purchasing agency was guided by directives provided annually by the Munitions Board. These "shopping lists" were detailed and subject to frequent amendment. In addition, during the early years of the program, the purchasing agents were required to clear each transaction with the Board and the Strategic Materials Committee. The stringency of this control was a constant source of friction between the purchasers and the Munitions Board until it was relaxed by Presidential action in NSRB Document No. 99. This document further expanded the role of the purchasing agency by authorizing it to coordinate the stockpile "operations" of all agencies, as a corollary to the Munitions Board's coordination of "programs" and the NSRB's coordination of "policy."

Besides purchasing, the Department of the Treasury and later the GSA were responsible also for the storage and care of materials. This function included the selection of storage sites and types of warehousing, arrangements for transportation from mine or port to storage, inspection of materials for deterioration, sale of deteriorated materials and purchase of replacements, refining and processing of below-grade materials, inventory accounting, research to improve storage practices, and a host of other related details. The Munitions Board provided general guidance on storage standards. Both the Board and the GSA were assisted by an Interdepartmental Stockpile Storage Committee, consisting of members from the Munitions Board, each of the three armed services, the GSA, and the Departments of the Interior and Agriculture. In addition, the industry advisory committees provided advice on problems relating to particular materials.

Storage policy attempted to combine economic and security considerations. The Joint Chiefs of Staff advised on the security aspects. Materials were to be stockpiled close to the point of their ultimate use, but not if this practice would mean undue concentration at one or two locations. Storage near the industrial consumers meant that transportation and time were being stockpiled as well as materials. Port areas were to be avoided whenever possible because of the probability that transportation and warehouse facilities in these areas would become congested during an emergency.[9] Not more than 5 per cent of the total stockpile of combustible materials, like rubber, was stored at one site.

Primarily for reasons of economy, materials were stored at military depots and other government-owned warehouses to the extent that such space was available, of suitable type, and at locations which fitted the approved distribution pattern. In January 1948, 70 military depots, 10 commercial warehouses, and 3 stand-by defense plants were being used as storage sites. As the stockpile grew, available military space did not increase proportionately, so that more and more commercial facilities had to be used. By August 1953 the stockpile was stored at 318 locations, consisting of 71 military depots, 9 GSA depots, 4 government-owned vaults, 6 commercial vaults, 165 commercial warehouses, 34 commercial tank-farms, 7 open-air commercial sites, 4 open-air government sites, and 18 industrial plants. The vaults were used for small but valuable items such as narcotics, diamonds, and jewel bearings. Tanks were used for liquid materials such as coconut oil and palm oil. Ores and metals not subject to deterioration by exposure, such as zinc, lead, and bauxite, were stocked at the open-air sites.[10]

The rotation of perishable materials became an important administrative function. The GSA's technicians periodically inspected the stocks of rubber, cordage fibers, oil, and other perishables. Before deterioration reached certain minimum standards, the material was sold and replaced.

Another administrative duty was to provide for "beneficiation" of low-grade materials taken into the stockpile as surplus transfers from other agencies. This was done only when the cost was less than buying an equivalent quantity of high-grade material.

By December 31, 1953, $210 million had been spent for maintenance and administration of the stockpile. This figure represented about 6 per cent of total expenditures up to that date.

[9] Munitions Board, *Stockpile Report to the Congress*, January 23, 1950, pp. 29-30.
[10] *Ibid.*, July 23, 1950, p. 16.

Economic Cooperation Administration

Passage of the Economic Cooperation Act (Marshall Plan) in
April 1948 was preceded by a lively debate between Congress
and various administrative agencies on whether the foreign-aid
program should be used to increase the supply of materials for
stockpiling. Many congressmen enthusiastically supported two
ideas: that the recipients of aid should repay the United States
with strategic materials, and that a maximum of the aid should
be invested in expanding production of strategic materials overseas. This seemed to be a good way to get something in return
for the aid and to make up part of the depletion of the United
States' own resources which inevitably would result from the aid
program.

During the preparation of the bill in the Executive Branch, the
Department of Defense and the NSRB took a position similar to
the one prevalent in Congress, against the vigorous opposition of
the Department of State. The Administration bill was a compromise: there was no specific provision for any *quid pro quo* for aid
grants in the form of strategic materials, but loans might be repaid in such materials "under certain circumstances." The bill
also provided for some use of aid funds to explore and develop
minerals deposits abroad.

At the hearings on the bill, the Administration split became
clearly visible under close probing by the congressmen. The Department of Defense and the Treasury Department witnesses
supported the Administration bill and hinted for stronger language to promote stockpile acquisitions. The Department of
State spokesmen stuck to the position they had held in the interagency bargaining. Their logic was compelling: strategic materials were readily salable for dollars; therefore any materials which
the aided countries had to turn over to the United States in return for grants would reduce their dollar income and increase
their dollar deficit, thus increasing the required grants-in-aid. On

balance, the United States would not gain. Moreover, the recovery program would be hampered by taking materials for the stockpile which were needed by the European countries themselves for their recovery; and to force the countries to take their own currency in payment for the materials (in the form of "counterpart funds" to be generated by aid grants), instead of dollars, would reduce incentives for new exploration and development.[11]

In the end, purchase of strategic materials with counterpart funds was not mentioned in the Economic Cooperation Act, but it did appear in the act authorizing appropriations for the program. Not less than 5 per cent of these funds was to be set aside for purchases of materials and for administrative expenses of the United States in the participating countries.[12] The Act itself, passed in April 1948, stipulated that the recipient countries agree to "facilitate" the transfer of materials in which the United States was deficient and to negotiate schedules of "minimum availability" and future delivery of such materials. The Administrator was directed to use aid funds and local currency deposits "to the greatest extent practicable" to stimulate expansion of production of these materials in the ECA countries and their possessions. He was to assist the other stockpiling agencies in their efforts to purchase materials and expand production abroad. Finally, the Economic Cooperation Administration was authorized to guarantee private investments in strategic-materials projects as well as others. The Act required that participating countries provide "suitable protection for the right of access" for American interests in the development of materials deposits in their territories on terms equivalent to those enjoyed by the country's nationals.[13]

---

[11] Dean Acheson, former Under Secretary of State, at the time a private citizen, made the following blunt comment: "If Congress will make its decision on the basis of getting recovery in Europe, it will not waste its time with things like this. This is a collateral issue. It has nothing to do with the point . . . Everybody is deceiving themselves by trying to believe we can make a cheap solution." House Committee on Foreign Affairs, *Postwar Recovery Hearings*, 1947 and 1948, p. 710.

[12] Public Law 793, 80th Congress, June 28, 1948.

[13] Public Law 472, 80th Congress, April 3, 1948.

Department of State

The stockpiling role of the Department of State comprised five general aspects:

1. It advised concerning the effect of stockpile operations on United States foreign relations and attempted to assure consistency of stockpile policy with foreign-policy objectives.
2. It took diplomatic action in support of stockpile acquisitions.
3. It provided information on foreign supplies and requirements.
4. It participated in international economic organizations and groups.
5. It appraised the probable wartime political orientation of source countries in connection with the establishment of stockpile goals.

While the Munitions Board controlled the program, prior to 1953, the State Department took a rather passive interpretation of its role as adviser on the foreign-policy effects of stockpiling. Its representatives on the Interdepartmental Stockpile Committee were always ready to speak to foreign-policy questions in a general way, but only two or three times did they suggest revisions to make stockpile plans conform more closely to foreign-policy objectives, and the suggested revisions were minor in character. According to one former Department of State representative on the Committee, the Department almost made a fetish out of refraining from injecting political considerations into stockpile discussions. The Department believed that the military viewpoint should be controlling, and in interagency discussions, the Department's representatives were usually on the side of the Munitions Board.[14]

Apparently the Department began to play a more active role

[14] Interview with G. W. Nichols, former Department of State representative on the Strategic Materials Committee, July 17, 1955.

after 1950 and to inject political factors into the decisions more often, especially after policy control was transferred to the Office of Defense Mobilization in 1953.

International organizations which had a bearing on stockpile accumulation and policy, and in which the State Department participated, included the International Rubber Study Group, the International Tin Study Group, the Combined Tin Committee, the Wool Study Group, the Economic and Social Council of the United Nations, and various commodity committees associated with the North Atlantic Treaty Organization. The Department also took the lead in establishing the International Materials Conference, which recommended international allocations of several materials during the Korean War.

After 1950 the State Department carried the responsibility for evaluating the political reliability of source countries in the event of war, in the determination of stockpile objectives. This aspect of its stockpiling role is described in Chapter IV.

Department of Commerce

The role of the Department of Commerce in the stockpile program was, first of all, to serve as a guardian of the public interest in a prosperous and stable economy and as a spokesman for the more specific interest of industrial consumers in a plentiful supply of raw materials. In this role, it acted as a brake on stockpile accumulation.

However, the Department carried on a number of other activities, the over-all effect of which was to support stockpile accumulation. It had authority to control the usage of tin in the interest of conservation, and until August 1949 it restricted the use of this metal in certain products in order to increase its availability for stockpile purchase. The Department of Commerce also contributed to progress in stockpiling natural rubber by prescribing a minimum content of synthetic rubber in certain rubber products, as authorized by the Rubber Act of 1948. Not only did this prescription diminish commercial demand for natural rubber, thus facilitating stockpile purchases; it also served to maintain operation of the synthetic rubber plants at the minimum levels deemed necessary for national security.

Department of the Interior

The Secretary of the Interior shared with the Secretaries of the Army, Navy, and Air Force (who delegated their functions to the Munitions Board) the responsibility for determining stockpile objectives. The Department's Bureau of Mines made available information concerning domestic and foreign production and supplies. Such information was useful both for establishing stockpile objectives and for estimating current availability. Through its Minerals Advisory Council and other contacts, Interior was in a position to know and to present in stockpiling discussions the viewpoint of minerals-producing industries.

The Stockpiling Act authorized the Department of the Interior to undertake research and field exploration directed toward the broad objective of increasing United States self-sufficiency in strategic and critical materials.

Department of Agriculture

The role of the Department of Agriculture was similar to that of the Interior Department in many ways. It provided supply information on commodities of agricultural origin and carried on research into the expansion of domestic or Western Hemisphere production of these items or development of substitutes. For example, the Department worked on techniques for producing natural rubber from the guayule bush, undertook the development of domestic substitutes for quebracho, cordage fibers, and pyrethrum, and investigated the feasibility of growing opium and castor beans domestically. Since most of the perishable materials were agricultural in origin, the Department conducted research to determine optimum storage conditions for these items, especially coconut oil, palm oil, and castor oil. It also contributed advice to the GSA on storage, inspection, and rotation of perishable materials.

Commodity Credit Corporation

By an amendment to the charter of the Commodity Credit Corporation in June 1949, Congress authorized that agency to accept strategic and critical materials in exchange for surplus agricultural commodities. The materials acquired were to be transferred to the stockpile, and the Corporation reimbursed out of stockpile funds at market value. The chief political impetus behind this program came from farm-state congressmen, who were interested in getting rid of a portion of the CCC's surplus stocks without seriously depressing market prices.

In the first year of the barter program, results were meager. Only two transactions were completed, exchanges of cotton and corn for chromite. The main difficulty seemed to be that foreign traders either wanted to get the agricultural commodities at far below market value or offered materials in exchange which the Munitions Board was not anxious to buy. Naturally, the CCC did not wish to trade its commodities at prices below its regular export price. Not only would this mean a loss for the CCC; it would also tend to depress the market prices and ultimately would require more purchases by the CCC to support domestic prices.

Foreign traders were unwilling to offer strategic materials which the stockpile needed urgently, according to CCC people, because they could always sell such materials for dollars. The CCC was unwilling to acquire and hold materials on its own account which it could not sell to the stockpile.[15]

[15] House Committee on Armed Services, *Stockpiling Hearing*, 1950, p. 7648.

During the Korean War, the CCC began to have more success in its bartering. To what extent this was a result of a greater sense of urgency or simply the accumulation of experience and commercial contacts, cannot be assessed. By June 30, 1953, the stockpile had acquired $56,727,000 worth of materials via CCC barter deals.[16]

[16] Munitions Board, *Stockpile Report to the Congress*, August 15, 1953, p. 5.

[III]

Stockpile Acquisition, 1946-1950

The transition to a postwar stockpile program was fairly smooth, for much of the groundwork already had been laid by the technicians while the interagency battle for control had been going on at the higher levels. The Army-Navy Munitions Board, working with the Strategic Materials Committee, had laid down the basic philosophy and purposes of postwar policy, defined the criteria for the selection of materials for stockpiling, drawn up a list of 52 materials to be stockpiled, established purchase goals, and prescribed quality specifications. All this was done by authority of the Strategic Materials Act of 1939 and the Surplus Property Act of 1944, and was adopted with only slight changes as the initial framework for postwar policy.

The Munitions Board estimated that reaching the targets would cost $2.1 billion and would take approximately five years. The five-year procurement period was based on practical rather than strategic considerations, it was stated; that is, the Munitions Board felt that availability of materials in the market would allow completion in about that period of time.[1]

---

[1] Interview with Department of Defense official, formerly Munitions Board staff member, June 30, 1955.

It was expected that some $300 million worth of materials would be transferred from the wartime stocks of other agencies, principally the Reconstruction Finance Corporation. This left $1.8 billion to be purchased. Initially, it was planned that the buying would be done in equal installments of $360 million a year for five years.[2] However, the first request for appropriations was for only $270 million. Officials of the Board explained that the request was limited to this amount in deference to the Civilian Production Administration, which felt that no more could be spared from industrial needs, and because the Board itself was doubtful whether it could spend the full $360 million in "unsettled world markets."[3] The Bureau of the Budget reduced the request to $250 million. Congress slashed it to $100 million.[4]

With this rather modest beginning, the business of building a stockpile got under way. From the start, the stockpilers had to grapple with a fundamental dilemma: should acquisitions policy be based on economic considerations or national security considerations or both, and if both, what kind of balance should be struck? The entire story of postwar stockpile procurement, including the differences between agency attitudes, can be told largely in terms of this choice.

The national security criterion, as interpreted and emphasized by the Munitions Board, suggested that all materials be purchased at a rate roughly corresponding to the five-year procurement schedule. Second, available funds should be allocated among the several materials so as to maximize their yield in national security. This meant, essentially, that the stockpile should be kept in balance, that it should be built up evenly across the

[2] U.S. Congress, Senate, Subcommittee of the Committee on Appropriations, *Hearing, Military Establishment Appropriation Bill for 1948*, 80th Congress, 1st session, 1947, p. 257.

[3] *Ibid., Hearing, First Supplemental Appropriation Bill for 1947*, 79th Congress, 2nd session, 1946, p. 7.

[4] U.S. Congress, House, Subcommittee of the Committee on Public Lands, *Hearing, Stockpiling of Strategic and Critical Metals and Minerals*, 80th Congress, 1st session, 1947, p. 21. [Cited hereafter as House Committee on Public Lands, *Stockpiling Hearing, 1947.*]

board—not letting procurement of some materials move far ahead of schedule while others lagged far behind. Third (and this point illustrates the close interrelation of the economic and security factors), national security maximization called for buying all materials at the lowest possible prices.

An emphasis on economic considerations would dictate holding off on stockpile purchases if there were a danger that such purchases would contribute to inflation or absorb materials urgently needed by manufacturers. Conversely, such an emphasis might call for heavy purchasing if prices were low or if producing industries were depressed. It would not require an even distribution of funds between the various materials, but rather, allocation of funds to materials which were most available in the marketplace, regardless of the size of the inventory of each already on hand.

Proponents of either emphasis could offer evidence from the Stockpiling Act to justify their position. The major purpose of stockpiling, the Act said, was to decrease and prevent a "dangerous and costly dependence" on foreign nations for raw materials in case of war. But the Act also stated that purchases were to be made "so far as is practicable, from supplies of materials in excess of the current industrial demand . . ." and were to encourage the development of supply sources within the United States.

Priority of Reconversion, 1946-1947

As a guide for planning, the Munitions Board drew up an ideal procurement schedule (to be described later) which was based almost entirely on security considerations. This schedule was largely academic in the first year of operations because economics, not security, was in the saddle. The Munitions Board agreed that during a limited period of reconversion from wartime to peacetime production, the needs of industry would have priority over stockpile requirements. It was not felt that security was being sidetracked in favor of economic considerations but that

these considerations—industrial reconversion and averting inflation—were themselves in the military interest and in the interest of national security. As late as June 1948 the Munitions
Board was saying that its policy was to "reconcile the national
security interest in reserves of essential materials with the national security interest in a prosperous and active economy."[5]

"Getting back to normal" was perhaps the dominant theme
both in public opinion and in government in mid-1946. The idea
was to shake off the burdens of war as quickly as possible and
return to the full enjoyment of peacetime comforts. This feeling
also dominated the congressional attitude toward stockpiling.
Some congressmen were skeptical about "preparing for war"
when supposedly the main business of the moment was consoli-
dating the peace. Fear of inflation further reduced their enthusiasm for stockpiling.

The Munitions Board pursued an extremely cautious price-
and-purchase policy in the early postwar period. The Treasury
procurement agents were forbidden to bid over the market price.
Even payment of the market price was allowed only for urgently
needed materials and materials whose price compared favorably
with prewar prices. Purchase for less than the market price was
often possible for materials of which the stockpile took a large
portion of the current supply and which were not particularly
scarce. As a rule of thumb, any price higher than one and one-
half times the prewar price was considered too high. The Munitions Board preferred to wait for the softening of prices which it
confidently expected would soon occur.

Even when the price was favorable, the Munitions Board did
not buy if the material was needed for industrial consumers. The
law required that industrial consumers were to get first call on
materials only "so far as is practicable," but the stockpilers disre-
garded this qualifying phrase.[6]

[5] *Ibid., Hearing, Strategic and Critical Minerals and Metals,* 80th Congress, 2nd session, 1949, p. 1010. [Cited hereafter as House Committee on
Public Lands, *Hearing, Strategic and Critical Minerals and Metals,* 1948.]
[6] *Ibid.*

In consequence of these policies, plus the fact that business activity and demand for materials was generally high immediately after the war and price trends were upward for a good many items on the stockpile list, procurement progress in the first year of the program was far below earlier expectations. Of the $100 million appropriated, $33 million was unobligated at the end of the fiscal year.[7]

Because of either high prices or strong industrial demand, some of the most urgently needed materials (such as copper, Manila fiber, chromium, and quartz crystals) were not purchased at all during the first year. On the other hand, greater amounts of some materials were available at reasonable prices than had been anticipated. The Board publicly took credit for preventing, by its purchase of these materials, cutbacks of production and losses of employment.[8]

In the first year, the purchasing agents in the Department of the Treasury were required to submit every offer to the Munitions Board for approval by the Board and the Strategic Materials Committee. One purpose of this requirement was to make sure the purchasing agents did not buy anything needed by industrial consumers.

On the Strategic Materials Committee, the dominant voice in determining whether a particular purchase was allowable was that of the member from the Civilian Production Administration in the Department of Commerce, Miss Marion Worthing. The CPA, as the successor to the War Production Board, was responsible chiefly for facilitating reconversion to a peacetime economy. The Stockpiling Act had designated the CPA as the agency to determine whether war-surplus materials were to go into the postwar stockpile or were to be sold to make up a deficiency in current industrial requirements. This authority did not extend explicitly to the determination of whether current purchases would infringe on industrial requirements, but in fact the CPA appears

[7] *Ibid.*, p. 932.
[8] *Ibid., Stockpiling Hearing,* 1947, p. 28.

to have enjoyed a veto power over all proposed cash acquisitions as well as surplus transfers.

In order to make certain that an amount offered was in excess of industrial needs, the CPA often required the purchasing agents to offer the material to a large industrial consumer before accepting it for the government. For certain materials, the Treasury procurement people were required to show three letters of refusal from potential industrial buyers.

Military and civilian members of the Committee split on the question of what weight to give to price considerations in purchase decisions. Civilians, led by the Commerce and State members, generally counseled delay when prices were deemed abnormally high. Representatives of the Army, Navy, and Air Force usually objected to delaying procurement for price reasons, although the Navy member, a civilian, sometimes went along with the civilian agencies. The Army and Air Force members, who were military officers, contended that the purpose of stockpiling was to accumulate the required amounts of materials in the time allotted, not price speculation. They declared further that any criticism of the program would be directed at the failure to complete this basic mission rather than at the high prices paid. The Munitions Board representative, a civilian himself, was willing to give some weight to price considerations, along with the other civilians.[9]

Disposal of the Wartime Stockpile

Much of the influence of the Civilian Production Administration stemmed from its control over the disposition of war-surplus materials, mainly the sizable inventory in the hands of the Reconstruction Finance Corporation. The Stockpiling Act provided that such materials were to be transferred to the new stockpile

[9] The material on the Strategic Materials Committee was obtained from interviews, during the summer of 1955, with sources who wished to remain anonymous.

except for amounts necessary to make up deficiencies in industrial supplies. The CPA was given authority to determine the deficiencies.

Materials transferred to the stockpile were without cost to stockpile funds except that stockpile money could be used to defray the expenses of transfer. The Army-Navy Munitions Board was permitted to reject offers of inferior-grade materials, but also was authorized to use stockpile funds to process such materials up to the desired quality.

Congressmen from mining states had opposed the deficiency provision before and during passage of the Act; they naturally preferred to have all the materials in government hands locked up in a permanent stockpile. Congressmen who spoke for producing interests charged that consuming interests had been chiefly responsible for this "loophole."

The CPA tended to favor consuming industries over the stockpile in its surplus-disposal policies. The Act was silent as to how an industrial deficiency was to be determined, and what period of time the estimate of a deficiency was to cover. The CPA made its estimates on the high side: often the amount of the deficiency was larger than the entire surplus stock, leaving nothing for the stockpile.

The net results of the policies of the CPA and its successor, the Office of Materials Distribution in the Commerce Department, was that during the first three postwar years, stockpiling, on balance, was *negative*. By June 1948 between $400 million and $500 million of materials which would have qualified for the stockpile had been sold to industry from stocks held principally by the RFC.[10] It was not until the close of fiscal 1949 that an equivalent amount of new material had been delivered.

The stockpile had received $457 million worth of government surplus materials by July 1949. By this time the bulk of the wartime surpluses had been disposed of in one way or the other.

[10] House Committee on Public Lands, *Hearing, Strategic and Critical Minerals and Metals,* 1948, p. 933.

Stockpile acquisitions were highly unbalanced: large quantities of some materials were received; little or none of others. This imbalance followed from the policies governing disposition of the surplus: the stockpile got only those materials which industry did not need. By way of example, considerable quantities of zinc, mercury, and vanadium were received, but practically no copper, chromite, and bauxite. For a few materials, surplus transfers completely filled the objective.

Much of the material transferred did not come up to stockpile quality specifications. The Stockpiling Act provided authority for "refining and processing," but little or no processing was done during the first two years. The reason, according to the Munitions Board, was that processing would have meant competition with industry. The Board interpreted the law's injunction against purchasing materials needed by industry to mean also a prohibition against competition with industry for the use of processing facilities.[11]

Reorientation, 1947-1948

The Munitions Board confidently assumed that industrial shortages would be temporary, that industry would finish reconverting in about a year, and that lower industrial demand and lower prices would then allow more progress in stockpiling, including the achievement of a better balance in the inventory. It believed that $360 million could be spent to good advantage during fiscal 1948, 80 per cent of which would be spent for materials lagging behind schedule in relation to the other materials.[12]

The Bureau of the Budget darkened this bright vista by allowing only $200 million of the Munitions Board's request. According to the Bureau, the Board was overoptimistic: there would not be $360 million worth of materials available for stockpile purchase in the next fiscal year.

[11] *Ibid.*, p. 116.
[12] *Ibid., Stockpiling Hearing,* 1947, pp. 29-30.

Congress once again appropriated only $100 million, but made up for the cash reduction by authorizing $75 million in contract authority, that is, permission to make contracts in this amount for delivery beyond the current fiscal year, to be covered out of later appropriations.

As high industrial demand and shortages of materials continued into the fall of 1947, with no sign of letup, the Munitions Board slowly began to shift its priorities. It began to feel that industry had had time enough to reconvert and that it was now time for the stockpile to start buying more aggressively and stop deferring to industry. International developments—the Greek and Turkish crises, the launching of the Marshall Plan, the Czechoslovakian *coup d'état*, the Berlin blockade, the general heightening of East-West tension—stimulated a feeling of urgency, including a nagging fear that the nation was again going to be caught short in raw materials.

This change in attitude was instrumental in bringing about several new measures and changes in policy, all directed toward speeding up stockpile procurement and making the stockpile something more than a mere "residual claimant" for materials.

In the Strategic Materials Committee, sentiment in favor of a more vigorous purchase policy increased in the fall of 1947 and early 1948, with the members from the armed services, especially the Army and Air Force, in the vanguard. Major S. M. Matelski, representing the Army, and Colonel C. C. Segrist, the Air Force, pressed for allowing the purchasing agents to buy whatever was needed for the stockpile, regardless of the needs of industry. They also wanted to remove the restrictions on price policy, that is, to permit the Treasury procurement officers to pay at least market prices.

The Interior member, Elmer Pehrson, and the Treasury representative, Harry Maull, agreed substantially with the military officers. Miss Marion Worthing, representing the Office of Materials Distribution, continued to insist that the stockpile should not buy in competition with industrial consumers. In this position she was usually supported by the State and Agriculture Departments and by the OMD's parent agency, the Commerce Department.

In December 1947 the Committee, by a vote divided along the above lines, recommended that the Munitions Board enter into full competition with industrial buyers, regardless of the scarcity of a material or the wishes of the OMD. But the Board, although it was "commencing to be alarmed," did not want to go quite this far. It did not want to make a general change in policy, arbitrarily overruling the OMD because then the question would have to be resolved at higher levels. However, the Board began to overrule the OMD occasionally on individual offers and began to pursue a generally more active purchase policy.[13]

The Munitions Board tried to persuade Commerce to halt disposals of war-surplus materials, as well as to relax its opposition to aggressive stockpile buying. Not much success was gained on either count until the National Security Resources Board entered the discussion. The NSRB strongly favored a more vigorous stockpiling effort. Dr. John Steelman, Acting Director, recommended to the President in June 1948 the following measures: acceleration of stockpile procurement regardless of industrial deprivation, voluntary allocation agreements with producers and importers, conservation of supplies by industry, stimulation of both domestic and foreign production and delivery, and arrangements with foreign governments to encourage the importation of strategic and critical materials.[14] President Truman approved the recommendation on July 16, 1948, and directed all agencies to "take steps to make substantial progress toward achieving stockpile objectives."

Although the stockpilers now had a green light to engage in vigorous competition with industrial buyers, they did not com-

---

[13] Interviews with former Munitions Board staff members in the Department of Defense, summer of 1955.

[14] Harry B. Yoshpe, *A Case Study in Peacetime Mobilization Planning: The National Security Resources Board, 1947-1953*, Executive Office of the President, April 30, 1953, p. 107.

pletely disregard market considerations. Procurement was stepped up, especially for the materials which were behind schedule, but not anywhere near the danger point to a "sound, healthy economy." In its January 1959 report to the Congress, the Munitions Board stated that "although it is no longer considered practical to purchase only materials found to be in excess of current industrial requirements, purchases in direct competition with industrial consumers are avoided where possible."[15] The policy of not bidding above the market price continued to prevail.

Given these attitudes, procurement of materials in short supply continued to be difficult. Although they were authorized to compete somewhat more aggressively against industrial buyers, the purchase officers in the Treasury still had the problem of finding suppliers who were willing to sell to the stockpile in preference to private industrial customers. Most suppliers preferred these private customers who represented their long-term "bread and butter" business; stockpile sales were erratic and were bound to end some day. Nor were most producers willing to expand their production capacities for what they believed was a temporary demand. A sudden stoppage of stockpile buying would leave them with a "white elephant" in the form of surplus capacity.

Despite such resistance, some progress was made in accelerating procurement. From July 1947 to April 1948, when the funds ran out, the stockpilers obligated $244 million as against $67 million in fiscal 1947. Expenditures were $78 million, against $9 million in fiscal 1947.[16] There was still vast imbalance in the inventory. Of 10 materials, there was none on hand, and one third of the materials being stockpiled were at less than 10 per cent of their scheduled second-year goals.[17] Yet final objectives for 7 ma-

[15] Munitions Board, *Stockpile Report to the Congress,* January 23, 1949, p. 24.

[16] *Ibid.,* p. 36.

[17] U.S. Congress, House Subcommittee of the Committee on Appropriations, *Hearing, Military Establishment Appropriation Bill for 1950,* 81st Congress, 1st session, 1949, pp. 12-13.

terials were completed or nearly completed. Some of the lagging materials, like kyanite, palm oil, pepper, quinidine, talc, and tin, were among the most strategic, that is, produced in distant sources. About 16 per cent of the aggregate objective was on hand; another 5 per cent was on order.[18] But originally 40 per cent had been programed for procurement by June 30, 1948.

Balance vs. Availability

At every stage of the procurement process, the stockpilers had to face the question whether to press toward the attainment of balance in the stockpile, that is, whether to place procurement emphasis on materials lagging behind schedule, or to allocate funds according to the relative availability of materials. This dilemma was another form of the perennial question of security versus economic values.

The stockpile has always been out of balance especially during the early postwar years. The fundamental reason was that the requirements for a balanced stockpile, which were largely conditioned by noneconomic factors, did not necessarily coincide with supply-demand conditions—that is, with the degree of availability of the individual materials. The imbalance was particularly acute during the early postwar period because stockpile acquisitions were determined almost entirely by market conditions. War-surplus stocks in the hands of the RFC and other agencies were unbalanced in the first place, and those which were transferred to the permanent stockpile were even more so because of the rule that the stockpile was to get only what industry didn't need. Purchase operations, since they followed the same rule, aggravated rather than corrected the imbalance.

As this rule was relaxed, the Munitions Board continuously pressed for the attainment of a better balance in the inventory. In general terms this meant two things: (1) putting vigorous effort into buying materials whose acquisition was lagging, de-

[18] *Ibid., Hearing, Second Deficiency Appropriation Bill for 1948*, 80th Congress, 2nd session, 1948, p. 25.

spite their scarcity in the market; and (2) not buying materials which the stockpile already had in relatively large amounts simply because they were plentiful. The agency line-up on the first point has been treated to some extent already. On the second aspect, the Munitions Board was supported only by the State Department. All the other participating agencies, including the three armed services, as a rule wanted to buy whatever materials were available on the market, regardless of the composition of the inventory on hand.

The Munitions Board determined the degree of balance and the relative urgency of acquiring the various materials by a rather complicated formula. Generally speaking, the ideal at which the formula aimed was to achieve and maintain, as between all the materials, equality of the following ratio:

$$\frac{\text{assumed nonstockpile wartime supplies plus stockpile currently on hand}}{\text{expected wartime requirements}}$$

This meant that emphasis in the early years of the five-year procurement period was to be placed on materials not expected to be transferred in large amounts from war surplus and normally supplied in considerable amounts by sources not expected to be militarily accessible to the United States in wartime, such as cobalt, manganese, and chrome. Procurement emphasis would gradually shift to materials produced to some extent in the United States and accessible sources, such as copper, lead, and zinc.

Thus "balance" did not mean maintaining the same percentage of the stockpile objective on hand for each material, but rather an amount which more or less equalized across the board the ratio of expected wartime supplies to wartime requirements. The stockpile objective represented different proportions of the expected wartime supply of the various materials; for example (in August 1950), 75 per cent for tin and 65 per cent for manganese, but only 20 per cent for zinc and 5 per cent for copper and lead.[19] Procurement of lead was not as urgent as purchase of tin, because considerable supplies of lead were certain to be avail-

[19] *The New York Times*, August 30, 1950, p. 38.

able even without a stockpile. In other words, balance required that the degree of completion of the tin objective be at all times higher than the degree of completion of the goal for lead.

There were other subsidiary considerations which entered into the formula. Some materials, such as industrial diamonds and quartz crystals, had to be bought at a fairly steady rate since their availability was not subject to ready increase or decrease, because of cartel policies and technological conditions. Purchase of others, such as copper, lead, and zinc, had to be spread over the entire five-year procurement period because of the large amounts needed. Although strict balancing of supply-requirement ratios might have entailed deferring all copper purchases, say, until the third or fourth year of the program, the Munitions Board felt that the sudden commencement of large stockpile purchases at that time would badly disrupt the copper market.

Finally, the Board decided to acquire as soon as possible at least a small amount of all materials on the list—even those of lowest priority according to the basic rule—in order to have something immediately available for highly essential uses should an emergency occur suddenly.[20]

The urgency formula did not include political considerations; for example, the possibility of procurement being slowed down or halted because of a source country's attitude before completion of the objective, in advance of full-scale war. The possibility of loss of certain sources through Communist conquest in a limited war did not enter into the calculations either, at least until 1950, when the Korean aggression dramatized this possibility.

The issue of balance vs. availability, or scheduled vs. opportunistic buying, arose, in the first instance, during the preparation of the annual budget requests. The practice was for the Munitions Board to draw up a tentative purchase program based

[20] The material on procurement scheduling was obtained from interviews with former members of the Munitions Board staff, summer of 1955, and from the testimony of Captain T. D. Jacobs (USN) in U.S. Congress, House, Subcommittee of the Committee on Appropriations, *Hearing, Military Establishment Appropriation Bill for 1950,* 81st Congress, 1st session, 1949, pp. 6-7.

on the relative urgency of acquiring the various materials, according to the formula described above. Then the Strategic Materials Committee prepared a schedule of estimated availabilities for the coming fiscal year. The opinion of the CPA (OMD) member was usually controlling on the question of availability, although the word of the Treasury representative carried weight where price, rather than quantitative industrial demand, was the issue. The Munitions Board then compared the two schedules and combined them into a single schedule which supposedly represented a compromise between the two orienting principles. Actually, this initial program emphasized balance, since it was composed more than six months before the beginning of the fiscal year, with the recognition that availabilities might change in the interim.[21]

The Bureau of the Budget evaluated the proposed program in terms of both urgency and availability, and of course in the context of other governmental programs relating to total government revenues and expenditures. However, the Bureau tended to place the greatest weight upon its own estimate of market conditions in the upcoming fiscal year. The Bureau's estimate that a projected purchase would constitute too large a deprivation for industrial consumers or would unduly contribute to inflationary pressures became the basis for a cut. This stress on availability was thought justified by the fact that by the time the Bureau considered the program, the beginning of the fiscal year would have moved several months closer than when the program was formulated, so that market conditions were more predictable.[22]

It would seem that by stressing balance or relative urgency in its request for funds, the Munitions Board may have set the stage for larger cuts than if it had given more weight to probable market conditions. That is, the emphasis on urgency tended to increase the number and size of scheduled purchases of materials

[21] Interview with Department of Defense official, former Munitions Board staff member, July 10, 1955.

[22] Interview with Joe Mayer, Budget Examiner, Bureau of the Budget, July 12, 1954.

in tight supply, thus making the whole program more vulnerable to cuts on the grounds of availability. It is true, at any rate, that during the first four years, the total of reductions made by the Bureau of the Budget was larger than that made by Congress.

The civilian agencies, especially Interior and the NSRB, tended to think that the Munitions Board was rather backward about asking for appropriations. In their view, the request should reflect not a neatly balanced procurement program for the year, but total availability of all materials, estimated liberally. The Munitions Board's usual answer to the charge of timidity was that budget estimates should be kept "practical," or "realistic," meaning, apparently, within the limit of what the Bureau and Congress might conceivably grant.[23] Also, the Board may have held down the budget requests because it was reluctant to make more progress in raw-materials security than was being made in other security programs. The January 1949 report to Congress stated, for example, that stockpiling "must be conducted in perspective with the entire national security program" and that "it is essential that this nation should seek to balance all the different programs for national security. . . . To advance one part of the national pattern of national security measures to the exclusion of the other component parts invites disastrous unbalance of the entire program."[24]

The purchase directive was prepared in a manner similar to that used in formulation of the budget request. Here again it was a case of comparing and combining the Munitions Board's schedule of urgencies with a schedule of availabilities worked out primarily by the Strategic Materials Committee. The Board was reluctant to allocate funds for materials which were already up to or over their scheduled objectives for the current fiscal year. On the other hand, funds were always allocated to materials which

[23] Interview with Department of Defense official, former Munitions Board staff member, July 10, 1955.
[24] Munitions Board, *Stockpile Report to the Congress*, January 23, 1949, pp. 9, 23.

were far behind schedule, even though their scarcity left doubt that all the funds allocated could be spent.

As noted earlier, the Munitions Board at first required the stockpile purchasing agents in the Treasury and in the GSA to clear each transaction with the Board and the Strategic Materials Committee. The principal purpose was to make sure the purchasers did not deprive industry of needed materials, but at the same time were properly aggressive in efforts to secure urgently needed materials. In the Committee's discussions of the individual offers (and of the purchase directive), all members except the Munitions Board and the Department of State usually favored accepting offers up to the *total objective* for a material, if the price was reasonable, rather than just up to the current annual procurement goal. For example, a vanadium offer was received in 1947 which would have brought the inventory of this material up to 90 per cent of the total objective. A majority of the Committee favored accepting the offer, but the Munitions Board, supported by the Department of State, voted "no" and the offer was rejected.[25]

The principal theme in the Munitions Board's reasoning was that a chain is only as strong as its weakest link. As the Board put it:

Balanced acquisition of all strategic and critical materials is at the very heart of the stockpile program. All materials being stockpiled are essential. . . . A plentiful supply of one item might be useless for want of another.

· · ·

Any alteration in these principles would have a serious adverse effect on the value of the stockpile to the national security. Stockpile procurement has been scheduled to provide the maximum of national security for every dollar spent. To shift our schedules would mean less security for the money.[26]

[25] Interview with Department of Defense official, former Munitions Board staff member, July 7, 1955.
[26] Munitions Board, *Stockpile Report of the Congress*, July 23, 1949, pp. 20, 23.

Underlying these arguments was the feeling, on the part of some in the Munitions Board, that the purchase of materials to the limit of their availability, ignoring the ideal of balance, would come dangerously close to using stockpile funds for economic stabilization—thus perverting the purpose of stockpiling, which was supposed to be national security and national security only.

Another major factor underlying the balance-vs.-availability debate was a difference in perspective concerning the timing of the security threat. Advocates of the availability criterion tended to ignore the question of when the war might start. They tended to approach stockpile procurement as a simple administrative problem: simply buying all the materials required to meet the total stockpile objectives in the shortest time at minimum cost. Not being responsible for broader aspects of national security planning, as were the Munitions Board and the State Department, they were not concerned with "external" factors in such planning, such as the possible intentions of the enemy. Hence, they did not worry much about the possibility that war might start before the stockpile was completed when it might be in a state of imbalance. The Munitions Board, on the other hand, *was* concerned. Its representatives would say that if anyone could guarantee no outbreak of war for at least ten or fifteen years, they would be glad to follow the availability criterion. But since no one could predict the date of "M-day," they adopted the conservative assumption that a war might occur at any time. This basic postulate was at the root of the Board's insistence on balance in the inventory. If a war could occur any time, it followed that stockpile funds should be spent so as to maximize the *current* security value of the stockpile. To put it somewhat differently, if a war should break out before the stockpile was completed, a balanced stockpile would have more wartime utility than an unbalanced one, for any given amount of prewar expenditure.

The running conflict between urgency and availability as

guidelines for procurement was complicated by differences of opinion as to what factors should be considered in establishing relative urgencies. As has been pointed out, urgency to the Munitions Board was chiefly a function of two things: (1) the degree of completion of the objective for a material, and (2) the degree to which a material was strategic, meaning the extent to which the material was normally produced in areas assumed to be inaccessible in wartime. Procurement was urgent if the percentage of completion was relatively low and/or if the material was highly strategic. These were the principal ingredients in the Board's urgency formula. Practically everyone but the Munitions Board believed another factor was relevant: the intrinsic "essentiality" of the material.

The Munitions Board insisted that all materials on the stockpile list were "absolutely essential." Logically enough, since degrees of "absoluteness" are clearly absurd, the Board maintained also that they were "equally essential." Its reasoning was as follows: Essentiality can refer to either end-items or materials used in end-items. It would have to be assumed that all end-item requirements used in stockpile calculations were essential requirements, and equally essential. The relative essentiality of the materials used in the end-items was a matter of the degree to which other materials could be substituted. But substitution possibilities had already been considered in establishing the objective for each of the materials. To bring the question of essentiality into the evaluation of relative procurement urgencies would be to consider this question twice.[27]

To almost everyone outside the Munitions Board staff, the idea that there was no difference in essentiality between materials seemed mistaken if not preposterous. Surely copper and manganese were more essential than waterfowl feathers and down, hog bristles, and pepper. It seemed a truism, obvious to all sane men. The Munitions Board retorted that for certain uses these materi-

<hr/>

[27] Interview with Department of Defense official, former Munitions Board staff member, August 19, 1955.

als were indispensable: feather and down in Arctic sleeping bags, hog bristles in wool daubing brushes, pepper for the seasoning and preserving of meat.

It may be that the belief in essentiality differences stemmed partly from a suspicion that the Munitions Board had not fully considered substitution possibilities in establishing military requirements. It is apparently true that the military standards for substitution were quite high. There was room for suspecting that for some materials there might be substitutes that were just below the military performance standards. The believers in essentiality differences may have felt, for example, that in a pinch, the services could get along with cotton, wool, or feathers from home-grown fowl in their Arctic sleeping bags, or with oak bark instead of quebracho for tanning their combat boots.

They may have been aware of another weak spot in the Munitions Board's position—the assumption that all end-use requirements were equally essential. Granted that there was no substitute for quinidine in the treatment of auricular fibrillation (commonly known as irregularly beating heart), it might have seemed less disastrous for a few people to have to live with this condition for a few years (or even die) than for the nation to be without manganese to make steel. A number of American soldiers suffering from insect bite because of a lack of pyrethrum would probably not mean the end of the Republic.

The Munitions Board's belief in the equal essentiality of all stockpile materials was not generally shared by military men who were associated with, but not directly responsible for, stockpiling. The representatives of the Army, Navy, and Air Force on the Strategic Materials Committee were among the truest believers and most insistent advocates of essentiality differences. The Munitions Board at one point agreed to let them have a try at establishing a list of urgency ratings or priority assignments which would take into account differences in essentiality, and appointed them as a subcommittee for this purpose. The subcommittee met but could not agree. The stated reason for the lack of agreement was that each member had different ideas about what factors should be considered in determining the priorities, presumably the relative weight to be given to being "essential" as opposed to being "strategic." The real reason, however, was that each military service was inclined to attribute higher priority to materials which *it* used heavily than the other services were willing to concede.[28]

The question of essentiality differences and of urgency ratings —two separate but closely related matters—came up also in discussions with the Bureau of the Budget. It has been said that the principal criterion used by the Bureau in evaluating the budget requests for stockpiling was the availability of materials in the market. This yardstick was sufficient during the period prior to 1948, when practically everyone agreed that the stockpile had to take a back seat to the requirements of industry. But after the President had asserted the priority of stockpiling in July 1948, more attention had to be given to the question of urgency.

The Bureau needed some criterion by which to evaluate the urgency of the request for stockpiling relative to that of other programs competing for funds. Attempts to find such a criterion began in earnest in the fall of 1948 in the consideration of the fiscal 1950 budget and were repeated in subsequent years, without notable success.

The Munitions Board people who defended the request before the Bureau's examiners were baffled by the question: how urgent is this request, or what is the relative urgency of different parts of it? In their view, this was an unanswerable question. It was urgent that the stockpile be completed as soon as possible, they would say, because no one could predict when a war might occur. Until the stockpile was completed, the nation did not have security in the raw-materials field. If the Bureau would specify the date of M-day, one military officer stated, then the Munitions Board would be able to say how much would have to be bought each year in order to complete the stockpile by that time. But so

[28] *Ibid.*

long as this date was unknown, he added, there was no way of describing the urgency of annual budget requests except in terms of how much progress they represented toward completion of the stockpile.

Still frustrated, the Bureau examiners tried to persuade the Munitions Board to present "priority lists" or "urgency ratings" for the individual materials. The Munitions Board was reluctant to provide such ratings because it believed that to cut the budget request by simply chopping off the amounts for the supposedly "least urgent" items was nonsense. The Board's representatives argued that relative urgency had already been taken into account in the preparation of the request and that, at the margin, urgencies were equal. For example, it made no sense to say that procurement of aluminum was more urgent than purchases of hog bristles if the requirements for hog bristles had already been scaled down to the point where a dollar's worth of hog bristles had equal utility with a dollar's worth of aluminum at the margin. Therefore, the only rational kind of budget cut, if one had to be made, was an equal, across-the-board percentage cut.

To satisfy the Bureau, the Board did consent, reluctantly, to rate the individual materials according to relative urgency, but on the basis of its own procurement formula, which assumed equal essentialities. The Bureau made use of these ratings by cutting the request for the least urgent items more than for the others. However, the resulting division of funds did not become mandatory on the Munitions Board; when Congress appropriated the funds, the Board was free to allot the money as it pleased. Cuts in the request were taken as fixed-percentage reductions across the board. In other words, the rating list was simply a tool which the Bureau used to decide how much to cut the *total* request, or, perhaps more accurately, it provided the Bureau with a superficially plausible reason for its cuts, but otherwise it had no real operational effect.

Development of Domestic Sources

"BUY-AMERICAN" PRINCIPLE

The Stockpiling Act stated that stockpile purchases were to be made in accordance with the "Buy-American" Act of 1933. The latter Act required that only materials or other supplies produced in the United States were to be acquired for public use, unless this was "inconsistent with the public interest" or the cost was "unreasonable." One of the purposes of the Stockpiling Act was to "encourage the conservation and development of sources of these materials within the United States . . ." Domestic producers were to be allowed "a reasonable time (not to exceed one year)" to make delivery, and where "economically feasible" they were to be exempt from the usual requirement that producers give bond to guarantee delivery.

The Buy-American provision produced controversy from the moment the Stockpiling Act became law. When President Truman signed the bill on July 23, 1946, he issued a statement which some people interpreted as a directive to the Munitions Board to ignore the Buy-American requirement. The President stated that his "reluctance" to sign a bill containing this requirement had been overcome only by the overriding importance of having some stockpile legislation. He went on:

These provisions will not only materially increase the cost of the proposed stockpiles but will tend to defeat the conservation and strategic objectives of the bill by further depleting our already inadequate underground reserves of strategic materials. Furthermore, there can be a serious conflict between those provisions and the foreign economic policy which this Government is actively pursuing. It also seems to me that the application of the Buy-American Act may frequently hamper the effective achievement of the essential purpose of the legislation which is to enlarge the stock of vital raw materials available within our borders in time of possible emergency.

It was generally believed in the Munitions Board that the Department of State had prepared the statement. A spokesman for

the Board, Carl Rolle, later said that the message "was not generated or subscribed to by the War and Navy Departments."[29]
Elmer Pehrson of Interior said he thought it would do "more
harm than good."

Within the Munitions Board, the immediate effect was to raise
uncertainties. Which should be followed, the Stockpiling Act or
the President's statement? A statement by the President clearly
could not overrule an Act of Congress; yet the President was the
chief executive and he had stated his desires in unequivocal
terms. The matter was left dangling for a while, until domestic
producers started making offers which would have to be accepted under the traditional application of the Buy-American Act,
but would have to be turned down if the President's wishes were
followed. The congressional friends of the producers forced the
issue. Morgan G. Huntington, a manganese producer, com-
plained to Congressman Clair Engle of California that the Munitions Board had failed to act upon his offer of manganese. Engle
and Huntington went to visit Admiral Roger W. Paine, Executive
Secretary of the Board, and learned that action was being delayed because of the aforementioned uncertainty which was being studied by legal counsel within the military establishment.[30]
Engle, according to Paine, expressed "extreme disapproval" of
the President's statement and said decisions involving the Buy-
American principle should be controlled by a 1937 Treasury Department ruling that domestic bids should be accepted if their
price was not more than 25 per cent over the nearest foreign
bid.[31]

Following the visit of Engle and Huntington, the Munitions
Board received several letters, telegrams, and telephone calls
from mining-state congressmen, including Senators McCarran of
Nevada, Hatch of New Mexico, and O'Mahoney of Wyoming,
all protesting that the President could not override an Act of

[29] Senate Committee on Interior and Insular Affairs, *Stockpile Hearings,*
1953 and 1954, Part 2, p. 109.
[30] House Committee on Public Lands, *Stockpiling Hearing,* 1947, p. 138.
[31] Memo, Major General S. P. Spalding to Kenneth Royall, December 11,
1946. AGO File No. 400.13.

Congress. Senator McCarran warned that if the President's statement became policy, Congress might amend the Act, and pending the amendment might refuse to appropriate money for stockpiling.[32]

The congressmen also took their case to John Steelman, Assistant to the President. On January 6, 1947, Richard R. Deupree, Chairman of the Army-Navy Munitions Board, asked Steelman for a "clarification" of the President's statement. He pointed out that the War and Navy Departments in judging what constituted "unreasonable cost" had always allowed domestic producers the 25 per cent premium established by the Treasury.[33]

After consulting further with the ANMB and other agencies, Steelman laid down what amounted to a compromise between the principles expressed by the President and those of the Buy-American Act. He said it was not the purpose of the Buy-American Act to give domestic producers an "unnecessary bonus," when domestic and foreign supplies were selling on the American market for the same quoted market price. Therefore, he continued, the proper policy, where a material had a regularly quoted domestic market price, was to pay no higher than the market price. Because of the magnitude of stockpile purchases, some concession from the market price might even be expected.

If a material did not have a regularly quoted domestic market price, a domestic bid higher than the foreign bid should be accepted, Steelman said, only "if (1) it does not exceed the maximum allowable differential [presumably 25 per cent], (2) is justified by a prudent governmental buying policy, and (3) is reasonable in the light of relevant price factors.

"It is clearly unreasonable under the Buy-American Act . . . that a domestic producer should expect an award if he bids above the world market price, merely because he feels that the Government will be compelled to buy from him at a premium."[34]

[32] Telegram, McCarran to Spalding, December 12, 1946. AGO File No. 400.13.
[33] Letter, Deupree to Steelman, January 6, 1947, AGO File No. 400.13.
[34] Printed in House Committee on Public Lands, *Hearing, Strategic and Critical Minerals and Metals*, 1948, p. 1237.

The "Steelman letter" was not very satisfactory to mining-bloc congressmen, who claimed that it constituted an illegal modification of the intent and purpose of the Buy-American Act. The congressmen were of the opinion that any domestic bid less than 25 per cent over a foreign bid should be accepted regardless of the quoted market price; in other words, that the 25 per cent differential was an automatic premium to which all domestic producers of all materials were entitled.

Steelman's resolution of the dilemma apparently was satisfactory to the Munitions Board, for it was adopted and followed consistently until the Korean War. The amount of material purchased under the Buy-American price differential, that is, where domestic producers were given bonuses or premiums over the foreign bids, was relatively insignificant. By mid-1950, only small quantities of manganese, beryl, and chrome ore—valued at about $500,000—had been purchased domestically at prices over the world price. Yet all was bought that could be bought under the Steelman interpretation.[35] In the first two years domestic purchases were about 10 per cent of the total, and only a small portion of these involved the payment of any premium over world prices. The proportion of domestic purchases increased in subsequent years, to about 35 per cent in fiscal 1950. Yet on June 30, 1951, purchases since World War II of 39 of the 64 materials being stockpiled were entirely foreign in origin. Only 4 materials (sapphires and rubies, molybdenum, magnesium, and lubricant-grade flake graphite) were entirely domestic. Apart from the latter 4, the proportion of domestic materials exceeded 50 per cent for only 6 materials: aluminum, 99%; cadmium, 93%; bismuth, 77%; zinc, 74%; vanadium, 67%; and lead, 66%.[36] After 1953, when the stockpile program was transferred to civilian control, the percentage of domestic purchases increased dramatically— but we are getting ahead of the story.

[35] House Committee on Armed Services, *Stockpiling Hearing*, 1950, pp. 7534, 7537.
[36] President's Materials Policy Commission, *Resources for Freedom*, Vol. V, June 1952, p. 145.

There were two reasons for the large proportion of foreign purchases in the early years. The fundamental reason, of course, was that about two thirds of the materials on the list were not produced in the United States at all. The other reason was that strategic considerations dictated an emphasis on foreign procurement early in the program. The idea was to get at least some of the foreign-produced materials in the inventory to be ready for a sudden emergency.

Many of the materials on the stockpile list did exist in the United States, but the mining and processing of most of these was not commercially feasible. To have purchased them under the Buy-American Act would have required a price premium much greater than 25 per cent.

In sum, the Buy-American requirement was never very important in an immediate economic sense. It did not significantly increase the cost or hamper the accumulation of the stockpile. However, if Buy-American meant not simply the price premium, but the general requirement that domestic producers be preferred, it may have reduced raw-materials security by contributing to the depletion of domestic resources. When domestic producers could meet the foreign or world market price, they were practically always favored.

PRESSURE FOR DOMESTIC DEVELOPMENT

The stockpile program was under continuous pressure from a group of senators and congressmen interested in the development of the domestic mining industry. Predominant in this group were congressmen from Western mining areas, operating principally through the Public Lands Committees and later the Interior and Insular Affairs Committees of both houses.

Munitions Board officials were summoned before these committees several times to explain why such a small proportion of stockpiling funds was being spent for domestic materials. The congressmen always pointed out that the Stockpiling Act mentioned two purposes: "acquisition and retention" of a stockpile, and "conservation and development" of domestic sources of supply. They felt that the Munitions Board was not properly carrying out the intent of Congress with regard to "conservation and development." (To these congressmen, "conservation" did not mean what it usually does, namely, the preservation of existing supplies; it meant "efficient production and use.")

A "healthy, going, mining industry" was at least as important for national security as a stockpile, if not more so, it was said. If domestic mines were allowed to close down, they might not be available for production during an emergency at all. They might be flooded by underground water seepage or they might cave in, so that reopening them would be either impossible or prohibitively costly. Furthermore, getting them reopened or starting new operations on previously unworked deposits would take time, perhaps years, whereas the next war would be likely to start without warning and require maximum output and military effort from the beginning.

Related to this thought was the idea that the accumulation of a stockpile was not an end in itself, but merely a tool for stimulating expansion of the domestic industry. Representative Thomas Martin of Iowa said the Buy-American clause was put into the Stockpiling Act

on the theory that a healthy domestic mining industry was perhaps the principal objective for national defense purposes, that the stockpile itself might be a very necessary adjunct to that program, and we hoped it would be a tool or means of building a healthy domestic and, as nearly as possible, self-sufficient mining industry within our own country.[37]

Congressmen often asserted that buying predominantly from foreign sources was dangerous because it made us dependent on long, hazardous sea lanes and on sources which might be cut off during war. The usual reply of Munitions Board spokesmen was that the very purpose of buying foreign materials in peacetime was to make us *independent,* or reduce our dependence, on for-

[37] House Committee on Public Lands, *Hearing, Strategic and Critical Minerals and Metals,* 1948, p. 17.

eign sources in wartime. They might have said further that the sea lanes were not "hazardous" during the time the stockpile was being accumulated, and after it was completed, should war occur, the enemy threat to sources and sea lanes would have been largely insured against. Buying high-cost domestic materials would reduce progress toward wartime independence from foreign sources.

Sometimes the congressmen asserted that the stockpile program could not make more than a marginal contribution to raw-materials security; it was only "a drop in the bucket." The only significant alternatives were to develop domestic mining industries or not to do so. If it were decided not to, then complete disaster would occur when enemy action blocked sources of imports. Congressman Engle of California, deploring what he considered the State Department's policy of "importation while we lock up our reserves in the ground," remarked, "They do not realize, of course, that if we get into a war our importations probably will be cut off. So we will be sitting here without any manganese to make steel with."[38]

Yet the same congressmen who entertained the assumption that the stockpile could never make more than a minor contribution to raw-materials security (thus necessitating development of the domestic industry) also urged the establishment of very high stockpile objectives and more vigorous procurement as a *means* of stimulating domestic mining. Congressman Engle was one of the leaders in the drive of the House Public Lands Committee for higher stockpile goals, which is treated in Chapter IV. A specific reason why larger objectives were desired was that Engle and others hoped to get passed a bill subsidizing domestic mining producers, with the subsidized production going into the stockpile. In short, in their zeal to help the domestic mining industry, the congressmen involved themselves in a flagrant contradiction: an assertion of the necessary inadequacy of stockpil-

[38] *Ibid.*, p. 19.

ing, and the consequent need to "develop" domestic reserves, combined with a demand for a stockpile large enough to be more than adequate for wartime needs without any stimulation of domestic industry. The contradiction was largely the result of the complementary nature of the two alternatives: stockpiling and domestic development. Domestic stockpile purchasing developed domestic industry, but also, in the process, accumulated a stockpile. As the stockpile grew larger, domestic development became less and less necessary. An argument for substantial domestic development stimulated by stockpiling necessarily had to demand a large stockpile and simultaneously belittle its efficacy.

The Munitions Board witnesses stated that the great majority of the materials on the stockpile list were not produced in the United States at all, or only in very small quantities, and therefore had to be purchased from foreign sources. But the congressmen tended to focus not on what was *produced* in the United States, but on what was *potentially available* in the United States. They pointed out that the stockpile was importing many materials of which substantial unexploited reserves existed in this country. Since they were available here, why not buy them here? The Munitions Board people replied with an economic truism: these reserves were not being exploited because production costs were high in comparison with foreign costs. The chief reason production was costly was that the reserves were below industrial quality specifications and thus required considerable "beneficiation." The stockpile buyers had an obligation to accumulate the stockpile at the least possible cost.

The congressmen found it difficult to believe that United States materials were inferior to foreign; some of them asserted that the only reason domestic materials were more costly to produce was that foreign materials were produced by "sweated" or "slave" labor. Besides, wasn't it true that costs did not count where national security was concerned? And when did military men start getting so concerned about costs, anyway, in view of their past record of waste and extravagance?

Committee members suggested several times that the policies of buying principally from foreign sources, and the high specifications, were the result of the influence of the Department of State, which was interested in making more dollars available to foreign countries. Admiral Paine said decisions on sources of supply were taken without consideration of the State Department's views, adding that "the Munitions Board administers the stockpile from a strictly rigidly national security point of view."[39]

Spokesmen for the Munitions Board expressed sympathy for the general objective the congressmen had in mind, namely, the preservation of a healthy domestic mining industry or the maximization of United States self-sufficiency. It was obvious that any addition to domestic production did contribute to national security, they said. They were prepared, they added, to favor domestic producers whenever those producers could meet stockpile specifications and could produce and deliver on terms equal to those offered by foreign suppliers. They would give domestic producers a price advantage when this was justified under the "Steelman interpretation" of the Buy-American Act. But they could not and would not use stockpile funds to subsidize domestic producers indiscriminately. The point was well stated by Major General A. B. Quinton, Jr., Acting Director, Industrial Programs, Munitions Board:

It has been the position of the Munitions Board, supported by the Secretary of Defense in every instance, that we ought not to depart from our principal objective in respect to side objectives such as using extraordinary means to develop American mining industry, and so forth. We feel that helping to achieve a healthy mining industry is not the Munitions Board's primary objective, but that the stockpile as such—the funds for that—goes to the objective of securing materials, the methods being the direct methods, and if anything is to be done toward the help of American mining it should be done under a separate act.[40]

[39] *Ibid.*, p. 927.
[40] U.S. Congress, Senate, Subcommittee of the Committee on Appropriations, *Hearing, Independent Offices Appropriations for 1951*, 81st Congress, 2nd session, 1950, p. 747.

While being careful to say that they favored "conservation and development" of domestic materials, as one of the purposes stated in the Stockpiling Act, Munitions Board officials flatly denied that this was *their* legal responsibility, aside from what might accrue in this direction from their observance of the Buy-American principle. This objective of the Act, they declared, was entirely the responsibility of the Departments of the Interior and Agriculture, under Section 7 of the Act, which authorized research by these departments in the mining, growing, and processing of domestic materials. They agreed that these activities did contribute to national security, since they tended, when successful, to reduce the necessity for stockpiling and also made more materials available for the stockpile. Thus the military departments had an interest in the development of the domestic mining industry, they said, even though they had no responsibility for doing anything positive in that direction. The following exchange between Admiral Paine and Congressman William Lemke of North Dakota is illuminating.

MR. LEMKE   I might say that I am satisfied that this committee is willing to recommend a greater appropriation than the amount you have asked now, provided we can be assured we will get a sufficient stockpile and also develop our own industry at the same time to supplement the foreign purchases.

ADMIRAL PAINE   Mr. Chairman, I would like to say that the feeling of the Munitions Board is founded very largely on the idea that it is the duty and responsibility of you gentlemen and not the Board to determine whether a subsidy should be paid to any particular segment of American industry.

MR. LEMKE   May I suggest, we say an incentive be given so the domestic mining industries can compete with slave labor and low standards of living abroad.

ADMIRAL PAINE   That is all right. I accept that, sir, but I would like to make the point that we do not believe ourselves that we in the Board are smart enough to make the determination of how one segment of American industry should be favored as against another and we try to keep out of that religiously. But, you take a bill like Mr. Russell's; if in your wisdom you thought that was a good thing to legislate, and that it was a fair thing to do to all of industry and you did it of your own volition, we in the Board would like the bill because it would enable us to develop sources perhaps that are not available at the present time. But, I would like it clearly understood that we can't support, or at least that is the opinion of the Board, and they have expressed it again and again, that we should not support a subsidy for one section of industry as against another.

We would prefer infinitely to keep stockpiling on the basis of the national security interest only, and not allow it to become a political football in any way, shape or form. Have I stated the point, sir?

MR. LEMKE You have. I may say this, that in this subcommittee there are no politics. We are just a family of members who realize we have been elected by the people. Most of us forget our politics after the election and try to work for the best interests of the Nation.[41]

Paine's remarks paraphrased a policy memorandum which the Munitions Board had prepared for the use of its staff members in testifying before congressional committees or dealing with the public. They expressed the Board's view that domestic development through subsidies was outside the proper military role, quite apart from the question of legal responsibility. It was not simply that such programs were considered beyond the range of military skills (although Paine's disclaimer that the Board was not "smart enough" is suggestive—it suggests not that the technical aspects of subsidy programs were beyond military competence but that politics itself was considered a somewhat arcane activity which the militarily trained mind was not equipped to fathom). More interesting and important was the implied definition of politics as a struggle between competing subnational interests, and political decisions as decisions to favor one set of interests over another. On several occasions, military men representing the Munitions Board stated that premium prices paid under the Buy-American requirement did not constitute a sub-

[41] House Committee on Public Lands, *Hearing, Strategic and Critical Minerals and Metals,* 1948, pp. 925-926.

sidy (and were therefore nonpolitical) because *all* business concerns were eligible for Buy-American benefits. They pointed out that one reason why the "Steelman letter" ruled out the payment of premiums on materials which had a regularly quoted domestic market price was that such payment would have meant favoring some domestic producers over others who sold commercially at the market price.

A corollary of this attitude was the notion that the "national security interest" (Paine's phrase) was not properly subject to the vagaries of politics, but was a matter to be objectively determined by experts.

Admiral Paine suggested that the NSRB was the proper agency to decide whether and to what extent stockpile money should be spent for subsidies. Their job was to set the policies; the Munitions Board's was merely to administer them.

If, in their wisdom, they believe that we are not doing the thing as well as it should be done, unquestionably they will tell us and we will be in a position then to work on perhaps a different basis than we work on at the present time . . . they are the people that should state a national policy much more effectively than the Munitions Board could. We are a working factual organization, faced with the problem of doing a very difficult thing just as fast as we can do it.[42]

At least until the Korean War mobilization, the views of the NSRB appeared to be close to those of the Munitions Board on the question of whether stockpile contracting should positively support the development of domestic industry. NSRB Chairman Arthur Hill said in 1948 that stockpiling should be kept distinctly separate from the objective of developing domestic mining.[43] However, when the NSRB received specific responsibility for promoting domestic expansion after the outbreak of the Korean War, its views on this question began to diverge from those of the Munitions Board.

The Department of State consistently favored stockpile pur-

---

[42] *Ibid.*, p. 940.
[43] *Ibid.*, p. 966.

chasing from low-cost foreign sources over the stimulation of marginal domestic production. Stockpiling from domestic sources ran counter to the objective of national security, not only because it was often more costly, but also because it speeded the depletion of dwindling domestic reserves. In addition, special encouragement of domestic mining, via subsidies and other means, conflicted with the government's economic foreign policy of reducing barriers to the free flow of international trade.[44]

The position of the Department of the Interior—represented usually by officials of the Bureau of Mines—was that self-sufficiency in metals and minerals was desirable as a general objective. The dominant theme in their comments was that since United States reserves were decreasing, it was up to the government to provide incentives for the discovery and development of new reserves. Such incentives might include subsidies, higher tariffs, more research in processing and mining techniques by the Bureau of Mines and mapping and testing of deposits by the Geological Survey, and larger stockpile purchases.[45] Greater self-sufficiency was valued by Interior spokesmen as contributing not only to national security but also to the nation's economic strength and growth. By and large, they rejected the idea that greater domestic minerals production, by depleting resources, reduced national security.

Economic Cooperation Administration

The Economic Cooperation Administration was not particularly enthusiastic about its duties in the strategic-materials field. It was felt that these duties conflicted to some extent with the major objective of the recovery program: to build up the produc-

[44] See testimony of Willard Thorp, in U.S. Congress, Senate, Subcommittee of the Committee on Military Affairs, *Hearing, Stockpiling*, 79th Congress, 1st session, 1945.

[45] However, Elmer Pehrson, Interior's representative on the Strategic Materials Commitee, opposed the lowering of specifications and the payment of premiums for domestic materials.

tion and productivity of Western Europe. Purchases with counterpart funds tended to drain away usable or salable resources. Expansion of strategic-materials production was more in line with the over-all objectives of the program, but most potentialities for such expansion were in overseas possessions rather than in the European countries proper, and too much emphasis on the extraction of primary materials—as opposed to industrial development—tended to raise suspicions of "exploitation" and "imperialism."

By June 30, 1950, the ECA estimated that some $85 million worth of materials had been or would be delivered to the stockpile as a result of its activities. This included $61 million in purchases with counterpart funds, and $24 million in expected repayment for development loans. Repayments were to be made over a period of twenty years, but mostly within seven years, from the date of the contract. The counterpart commitments were spread out over about 20 materials, with the heaviest concentrations on rubber, sisal, industrial diamonds, and bauxite. Typical development projects were for lead in Morocco, chromite in Turkey, bauxite in Jamaica and Greece, tin in the Belgian Congo, industrial diamonds in French Equatorial Africa, cobalt in Northern Rhodesia, and nickel in New Caledonia.[46]

The rate of progress was considerably less than had been anticipated by Congress and the stockpiling agencies. ECA officials pointed out several reasons for the unsatisfactory results. In the first place, the European countries as a whole (including their dependencies, where most of the materials were located) had surpluses over their own requirements only in a limited number of items. Second, the availability of counterpart funds was poorly matched with the availability of materials. With certain exceptions, counterpart funds could be spent only in the country which provided them, and some of the countries which were rich in strategic materials, such as Belgium, received only loans, and no

[46] Economic Cooperation Administration, *Ninth Report to Congress*, November 17, 1950, p. 87.

grants, so they did not generate any counterpart funds. Such funds were available in sizable amounts in only three countries which controlled significant amounts of strategic materials—the United Kingdom, France, and the Netherlands.[47] By the end of 1949, purchases in the United Kingdom and British Empire alone accounted for about two thirds of total ECA procurement. Out of the $193 million in counterpart funds made available in the first year of operations, the ECA estimated that only $50 million would be spent.[48]

In some instances, countries which had surpluses were unwilling to sell them for their own currencies because they expected to be able to sell them for dollars. Producers demonstrated some reluctance to sell materials and expand their production for stockpiling purposes because they feared the potential depressive effect on market prices of a large United States stockpile.[49]

Faulty procedures in the United States stockpiling program had impeded its work in the field of exploration and development, the ECA claimed. For one thing, the Munitions Board was unwilling to place long-term procurement contracts of the kind required to support the ECA's development projects. Unless this was done, the ECA said, very little increased production could be expected. Many producers, according to the ECA, were not willing to start large expansion programs unless they were assured of a market over a sufficient period of time to enable them to amortize their investment.

Another complaint was that the Munitions Board had failed to provide guidance as to either long-term or short-term requirements for the stockpile. The Board aimed to complete the stockpile substantially in a five-year period (originally by 1951, although the completion date was later "stretched out"); therefore

[47] *Ibid., Third Report to Congress,* May 16, 1949, p. 58.
[48] U.S. Congress, Joint Committee on Foreign Economic Cooperation, *Report, ECA and Strategic Materials,* Senate Report No. 140, 81st Congress, 1st session, 1949, p. 33.
[49] Economic Cooperation Administration, *Third Report to Congress,* May 16, 1949, p. 58.

it was reluctant to state requirements beyond that period. This deadline hampered the initiation of expansion projects which would not yield materials within five years, it was said.[50]

ECA spokesmen also pointed out that they had lost several opportunities to acquire materials because of frequent and sudden changes in the Munitions Board's short-term procurement objectives.[51] Such changes in the purchase program constituted the sorest point in relations between the ECA and the Munitions Board.

The ECA stated also that it had had to pass up opportunities to purchase some materials because they failed to meet the high quality specifications established by the Munitions Board.[52] As a result of the ECA's urging, the Munitions Board did agree to take some materials which met "acceptance" specifications, though not "purchase" specifications. Acceptance specifications were those governing materials transferred, without charge to stockpile funds, from surpluses held by other agencies.[53]

The Munitions Board and the NSRB tended to blame the ECA's meager results in stockpiling on the ECA itself and on the Department of State, although they did recognize certain difficulties mentioned by the ECA, such as the lack of either counterpart funds or surplus strategic materials in some countries.

Thomas J. Hargrave, Chairman of the Munitions Board, told the House Committee on Appropriations in April 1948 that Secretary of Defense Forrestal had brought "very forcefully" to the attention of the Department of State the Defense Department's desire that the bargaining power of the aid program be used to

[50] U.S. Congress, Senate, Subcommittee on Appropriations, *Report, Strategic Materials Program of the Economic Cooperation Administration*, subcommittee print, 82nd Congress, 2nd session, 1952, pp. 6-7.
[51] Economic Cooperation Administration, *Seventh Report to Congress*, May 17, 1950, p. 63.
[52] *Ibid.*, p. 68.
[53] President's Materials Policy Commission, *Resources for Freedom*, Vol. V, June 1952, p. 126.

obtain a maximum of strategic materials.[54] Chairman Hill of the NSRB expressed complete agreement with the Defense position. Hill said he "had not obtained any results" from the ECA, but that the NSRB was using "every kind of persuasion we can upon them . . ."[55]

Hubert Howard, a later Munitions Board Chairman, said in 1950:

the State Department has been reluctant to use or apply the leverage of what we are doing for these countries to try to obtain these materials from them. They have felt that that was not the purpose of ECA or the Marshall Plan, and that that would interfere with their objectives under those plans . . . In my judgment, they have not used the force which a good, ordinary American businessman would use in the desire to acquire these materials if he had the same leverage that they have.

Howard said the Munitions Board had urged the State Department to try to get materials for the stockpile through the Point 4 program, but that State had "practically rejected the inclusion of any reference to getting materials" via this program. The State Department's objection, he said, was "a little hard to understand," but it apparently was that any attempt to get anything in return for foreign aid would "destroy the atmosphere." The Department of State had not actually hindered stockpiling by its attitude, Howard said, but it had not helped either.[56]

The ECA's strategic-materials program came in for considerable criticism from Congress. A subcommittee of the Senate Committee on Appropriations charged that ECA officials were "apathetic" toward their strategic-materials responsibilities, that they had "dragged their feet" in this program because they thought it interfered with their prime objective—the economic

---

[54] U.S. Congress, House, Subcommittee of the Committee on Appropriations, *Hearing, Military Functions Appropriation Bill for 1949*, 80th Congress, 2nd session, 1948, p. 83.

[55] *Ibid.*, p. 162.

[56] *Ibid.*, *Hearing, Supplemental Appropriation Bill for 1951*, 81st Congress, 2nd session, 1950, pp. 459-460.

recovery of Europe. The ECA had staged a "complete retreat" from the original intentions of the Executive Branch, the Joint Committee on Foreign Economic Cooperation asserted, adding that "the lack of speed with which ECA has operated with respect to obtaining some repayment in strategic materials against either loans or grants is in sharp contrast with its activity as a disbursing agency."[57]

Administrator Paul Hoffman testified in February 1950 that the ECA's strategic-materials program had become "rather secondary."[58] The outbreak of the Korean War in June changed the orientation, however, and the agency began pushing the program with new vigor. By January 1952 the ECA had spent a total of $109 million in loans to expand production, $84 million of which was in local currencies and $25 million in dollars. Purchases with counterpart funds totaled $81 million.[59]

Relapse, 1949-1950

In spite of continuing scarcities of many materials, stockpiling progress improved substantially during the last six months of 1948. The increased use of long-term contracts and the President's order in July that purchasing be accelerated no doubt contributed to this progress. Approximately $402 million was obligated during the period, compared with $127 million in the preceding six months.[60] By the end of 1948 the appropriated funds for fiscal 1949 had been virtually exhausted and more funds were urgently needed, all the more so because raw-materials markets were beginning to loosen up. Materials were becoming available

[57] U.S. Congress, Joint Committee on Foreign Economic Cooperation, *Report on Progress of the Economic Cooperation Administration,* Senate Report No. 13, 81st Congress, 1st session, 1949, p. 123.

[58] U.S. Congress, Senate, Committee on Foreign Relations, *Hearing, Extension of European Recovery, 1950,* 81st Congress, 2nd session, 1950, p. 32.

[59] Munitions Board, *Stockpile Report to the Congress,* January 23, 1952, p. 5.

[60] *Ibid.,* January 23, 1949, pp. 33-34.

as they had never been before, and prices were sliding. The 1949 recession was under way. Here was a golden opportunity to make up for lost time and justify the wait-and-see approach which had governed purchasing in the earlier months.

Here was a chance also to make progress in the direction of balancing the stockpile. Although materials behind schedule had been emphasized in the immediately preceding months, there remained vast discrepancies among the amounts of different materials. To state the extremes: on April 30, 1949, there was no Rhodesian refractory-grade chromite and no kyanite in the inventory, but the stockpile of Baddeleyite zirconium ores, because of the transfer of a large amount left over from World War II, stood at 1,378 per cent of its scheduled objective for that date. Some of the most strategic materials were among those furthest behind schedule; for example, coconut oil, kyanite, pepper, talc, mica, tin, chemical-grade chromite, and battery-grade manganese ore. On the other hand, some of the least strategic were over their *final* objective or were far ahead of schedule. Among the latter were agar, emetine, mercury, and vanadium.

On an aggregate basis, about 25 per cent of the total stockpile objective was on hand. (If the original schedule had been adhered to, roughly 50 per cent would have been purchased by January 1949.) The inventory was valued at $821 million, of which only $175 million represented postwar purchases, $580 million having been transferred from the World War II hoard and $66 million from the prewar stockpile.[61]

Such was the picture when the Munitions Board hopefully asked Congress for $835 million in new procurement authority in January 1949. Of this amount, $40 million in cash and $270 million in contract authority were requested as a supplemental appropriation for fiscal 1949, and $314 million in cash and $211 million in contract authority as a regular appropriation for fiscal 1950. In addition, Congress was asked to provide $250 million in cash to liquidate contracts already made under contract authority

[61] *Ibid.*, p. 7.

granted in earlier years. (Incidentally, the request for new contract authority in fiscal 1949 reflected a cut by the Bureau of the Budget of about $600 million below the amount initially requested by the Board.)

Congress at first was not unreceptive to the budget estimate, but it was not very speedy about taking action: the appropriation was not approved until late June. Meanwhile the stockpilers were forced to look on in agonizing impotence as tons upon tons of materials urgently needed for the stockpile went begging for purchasers.

This delay was frustrating enough, but just as the stockpilers were rolling up their sleeves and getting back into action, a new difficulty appeared: an "economy drive," aimed especially at "paring the fat" off defense expenditures. The movement had been building up all spring but until now the stockpiling appropriation had not been a target, possibly because it was nicely concealed in the appropriation bill for the Departments of the Treasury and Post Office. However, just as this bill was in the final stages of passage, the possibility of a cut in stockpiling was brought to the attention of the Senate Appropriations Subcommittee which was considering appropriations for the military establishment.

To most of the senators, it seemed that since prices had declined, the stockpilers could buy all they claimed was required with a smaller appropriation. In addition to the price consideration, they were able to think of other reasons why stockpile appropriations should be cut. One was that since international political tension had declined, progress in stockpiling was not urgent. Another was that stockpiling was one of the less essential aspects of national defense.

Following such reasoning, some members of the Subcommittee on Military Appropriations favored rescinding a portion of the stockpiling appropriation which Congress had already approved in the Treasury Department's appropriation bill. The question was debated at some length and witnesses from interested groups and agencies, including the Munitions Board, were heard at sessions of the Subcommittee and the full Appropriations Committee. Mining-state senators on the Committee were caught between their sympathy for the economy drive and their responsibilities toward their mining constituents. For Senators O'Mahoney of Wyoming and Hayden of Arizona, the latter came first; consequently they opposed the rescission. Senators McCarran of Nevada, Thomas of Oklahoma, and Gurney of South Dakota resolved their personal dilemma by supporting the cut, but proposing a rider to the effect that the reduction would be applied solely to procurement of *foreign* materials.

These senators also proposed, alternatively, that the cut be taken in the procurement of "least essential" materials, most of which, at least in the examples given by the senators, were conceived to be of foreign origin. For example, Senator Thomas questioned the urgency of stockpiling 25 million pounds of pepper and 15 million pounds of castor oil: "That may be very necessary. If they use the pepper first and the castor oil second, it might bring results. I am not sure about that."[62]

On the Administration side, the Departments of the Interior and State opposed the rescission, largely because of their domestic and foreign "constituencies." Both of these agencies probably would have favored an increase rather than a reduction in stockpiling appropriations in order to shore up sagging commodity markets. As usual, the Munitions Board was caught in the middle, between the economizers and the market stabilizers. General Leroy Lutes, Executive Chairman of the Munitions Board, stated the Board's position very succinctly:

During the past month, proposals have been made that stockpiling be reduced as an economy measure. During this period it has also been proposed that procurement of domestic materials for the stockpile be accelerated to give support to our domestic mining industry in a time of surplus. During this same period, it has been proposed that procurement of foreign materials be accelerated to ease the

[62] *Congressional Record*, 81st Congress, 1st session, 1949, p. 12249.

dollar shortages of our friends overseas. We have replied to each suggestion that stockpile procurement should be sustained at as rapid a rate as possible, but that purchases of each material—wherever produced—should be made in accordance with strategic priorities, to comply with the Act under which we operate.[63]

Ultimately, the Senate Appropriations Committee, by a divided vote, recommended a rescission of $275 million from the stockpiling funds already appropriated. The report accompanying the bill stated that "all strategic minerals and materials which are produced in the United States should be purchased here rather than from foreign sources." It continued:

The Committee directs that the Munitions Board exhaust every possibility of securing the needed minerals and materials in the United States, before looking to foreign sources. The Committee further directs that any foreign contracts entered into in the future should be for a short term and should contain language to allow such contracts to be cancelled, if that becomes necessary.[64]

When the House Appropriations Committee held preconference hearings on the military appropriations bill early in August, members from the Treasury Appropriations Subcommittee waxed indignant about the action of the Senate Committee, which, they said, has "usurped the authority of our subcommittee." The congressmen listened with sympathy to the complaints of the Munitions Board, which were directed principally at the Senate Committee's restriction on foreign long-term contracting.

The broad case against the Senate Committee's action was stated in a letter by Secretary of Defense Louis Johnson. The Committee's directive, Johnson said, "might work serious injury to the stockpile program by virtually stopping the placement of long-term contracts overseas for such materials as manganese, beryl, cobalt, long-fibre asbestos, corundum and refractory chromite." Of the 69 materials stockpiled, 42 were not produced

[63] Senate Committee on Appropriations, *Supplementary Hearing,* 81st Congress, 1st session, 1949, p. 28.
[64] U.S. Congress, Senate *Report No. 745,* 81st Congress, 1st session, 1949.

in the United States in any substantial quantities, he pointed out; furthermore, many of these 42 were behind schedule. Long-term contracts were essential to purchase them and stimulate their production.[65]

The House Committee voted to fight for the full appropriation and prepared for a stiff battle with the Senate.

The Senate upheld its Appropriations Committee and passed the military establishment appropriation bill, along with the $275 million stockpile rescission as a rider, on August 29, not without some opposition from Western senators, notably Hayden and O'Mahoney.

On the House floor, strong opposition to the rescission and the Senate report was expressed, chiefly by members of the Armed Services and Appropriations Committees. Representative George H. Mahon of Texas, Chairman of the Military Establishment Appropriations Subcommittee, could think of nothing "more crippling to national defense than to destroy our well-thought-out stockpiling program." Congressman Dewey Short, ranking minority member of the Committee on Armed Services, was "shocked" at the Senate's action. Representative Gordon Canfield of New Jersey declared that stockpiling was the "No. 1 item in national defense—not a bigger Air Force, because we are not going to have a bigger Air Force unless we build up this strategic stockpile." Canfield revealed that President Truman had personally urged the chairmen of both Appropriations Committees—McKellar in the Senate and Cannon in the House—to keep the stockpiling appropriations intact.[66]

When the military appropriation bill came out of the conference committee on October 12, it was found that the Senate and House managers had not been able to agree on two points: the stockpiling rescission and the Air Force appropriation. The House had voted funds to build a 58-group Air Force; the Senate

---

[65] U.S. Congress, House, Commitee on Appropriations, *Hearing, Military Establishment Appropriation Bill for 1950*, 81st Congress, 1st session, 1949, pp. 18-19.

[66] *Congressional Record*, 81st Congress, 1st session, 1949, p. 14154.

had approved the Administration's request for only a 48-group Air Force. The difference involved $741 million. From this point on, the Air Force issue and the stockpiling issue were linked.

A bipartisan committee consisting of Senators Lucas, the Majority Leader, McKellar, Chairman of the Appropriations Committee, Wherry, Minority Leader, and Gurney, former Chairman of the Armed Services Committee, met with the President, who suggested that a compromise be worked out, whereby the Senate would drop its stockpiling action and the House would agree to a 48-group Air Force.[67] Such a compromise would have affirmed the Administration's request for both items.

When the bill went to the conference committee again, a compromise was made, but it was just the reverse of the one which the President had urged. The Senate managers agreed to a 58-group Air Force, and the House side accepted a stockpiling rescission. However, the rescission was only $100 million, which, while substantial, was a good deal less than the Senate had proposed. More importantly, the committee repudiated the restrictive language in the Senate report, about which the Munitions Board had been extremely concerned.[68] The conference report was accepted by both chambers and became law on October 19.

Although the Munitions Board had reason to be moderately pleased with the result financially, the over-all effect of the congressional handling of stockpile appropriations during 1949 was to deal a severe blow to the program. Most serious, of course, was the delay of over nine months, while the appropriation request and then the rescission were being debated. During a period when stockpile buying should have been accelerated because of market conditions—the most advantageous since World War II —purchasing either was stopped entirely or was placed on a limited or sustaining basis. Moderate cash procurement had taken place in the four months since June, but long-term contracting had been held up while Congress deliberated about the rescission

[67] *Ibid.*, p. 14355.
[68] *Ibid.*, p. 14920.

in contract authority. When purchasing again moved into high gear in October, business conditions had begun to improve, industrial demand for materials was picking up, and prices were beginning to rise. The best procurement opportunities had passed.

By July 1, 1950, the stockpile on hand was valued at $1.6 billion and another $500 million was on order. This compared with an aggregate objective of approximately $4 billion.[69] The stockpile was still badly out of balance: objectives were completed for 19 materials, but a number of others were less than 20 per cent completed. In its report to Congress, at the end of the fiscal year (and incidentally after the beginning of the Korean War), the Munitions Board warned that unless procurement were accelerated, completion of the stockpile would be "dangerously deferred." Under the current rate of acquisition, it said, attainment of the goals could not be counted upon until 1956 at the earliest.[70]

[69] The increase from the $2.1 billion valuation at the beginning of the program was a combined result of price rises and increases in quantitative goals.

[70] Munitions Board, *Stockpile Report to the Congress*, July 23, 1950, p. 7.

IV

The Establishment of Stockpile Objectives

Although issues of procurement policy were more immediate and concrete, the question of stockpile "objectives" generated more controversy, at least in the pre-Korea period. The main issues were what materials should be stockpiled and how much of each should be acquired for the completed stockpile. Ultimate goals were of course not unrelated to current or annual purchase programs, for they provided an important part of the criteria for budgeting and procurement decisions, particularly when combined with a time schedule, such as the Munitions Board's original five-year deadline.

The most interesting aspect of the process of determining stockpile goals was the pervasive tension and interaction between logic and politics—between objective, technical calculations and pressures from interested groups both in and outside the government. Such tension is endemic in the making of defense policy generally, but it seems to have been particularly intense in stockpiling, a program which on the one hand is quite amenable to precise calculation, but on the other hand impinges sharply on agency and private-group interests.

Technical Calculus

Perhaps the best point of departure is to describe briefly the logic establishing stockpile goals. The stockpile was, and is, intended to help fill an expected deficit between total wartime requirements and available wartime supplies of certain materials essential to the war effort. The estimate of both supplies and requirements will vary, of course, with a variety of assumptions concerning the nature of a future war. How long will the war be? When will it begin? Will it be nuclear or conventional in nature? Even to ask such imponderable questions may seem absurd, but assumptions concerning them must be made and in fact have been made to establish a basis for stockpile goals. (During most of stockpiling history, targets have been calculated on the assumption of a five-year conventional war beginning on January 1 of the year following the establishment of an objective.)

.There are essentially three categories of requirements: military, domestic nonmilitary, and export. Military requirements are a function of the amount and kinds of weapons and other "end-items" which are planned to be produced during a future war, which in turn are related (logically at least) to the amounts of weapons and forces in existence at the outset, the planned rate of further buildup, assumed rates of attrition and combat consumption, and the general strategic plans for fighting the war as well as the assumed capabilities of the enemy. Domestic nonmilitary requirements are a function of the necessary supporting industrial economy and the degree of sacrifice to be demanded of the civilian population. Export requirements are calculated as "normal" peacetime exports to friendly countries, based on historical experience. They do not include any amounts directly required for the *military* effort of allies in war. Stockpiling for allied military requirements has been considered but rejected at various points in the history of the program.

Implicit in the determination of requirements are assumptions regarding the acceptable degree of substitution of inferior but plentiful materials for scarce ones, and an estimate of the availability of substitutes.

The estimate of supplies involves first an estimate of production from all sources, foreign and domestic, during the assumed war period. Then the question is: how much of these supplies will be available to the United States? This question brings up a host of subsidiary ones. Which foreign supply sources will be accessible to the United States during the war and for what period of time? To what extent will these sources be willing and able to supply us with materials? How much will be lost through enemy attacks on shipping? How much through enemy bombing of production facilities, transportation lines, power plants, ports, and so on? How much by sabotage and labor disturbances? How much shipping will be available to carry materials during the war? By how much can domestic production be increased? Such questions can be multiplied and applied commodity by commodity and country by country. Since the answers will be educated guesses at best, a final overriding question is: how much risk should be accepted? Should the assumptions be made deliberately pessimistic to hedge against possible errors? Or are we willing to accept a considerable risk in the raw-materials field in order to economize or to release more of the federal budget dollar for other defense and foreign-policy programs?

Several agencies and interagency committees are involved in the computation of stockpile objectives. Military requirements are generated from armed service schedules of the end-item production required to meet prescribed force levels. These estimates are then broken down by military logistics planners into simple components such as steel plates, sheets, and rods, and the Department of Commerce then breaks down the components into requirements for basic raw materials. In only a few cases are the military requirements stated by the Department of Defense in raw materials. The Department of Commerce also makes an estimate of essential civilian requirements and "war-supporting" needs. Export requirements are established by the Department of Commerce and the Department of State.

Preliminary estimates of available supplies from both foreign and domestic sources—that is, without any discounts for wartime risks—are prepared by the Departments of Commerce, the Interior, and Agriculture.

Supply-requirements data for particular materials are collated by the appropriate Inter-Agency Commodity Committee, whose chairman, representing the central stockpiling agency, discounts or adjusts the supply estimates to reflect some of the imponderables just mentioned. The difference between the requirements and the discounted supplies becomes the stockpile objective. The objective is then considered by the over-all advisory board (known before 1950 as the Strategic Materials Committee or the Interdepartmental Stockpile Committee), which recommends its adoption, perhaps after adjustment, to the head of the stockpiling agency. Before 1953 the central stockpiling agency was the Munitions Board, but objectives had to be approved by the Secretary of the Interior as well as by the Chairman of the Board.

Munitions Board vs. Interior Department

According to the Stockpiling Act of 1946, stockpile goals were to be established jointly by the Army and Navy and the Department of the Interior. This arrangement produced a good deal of friction during the first four years of the program, because Interior wanted the objectives to be about twice as high as the military departments thought necessary. An initial, rather dubious compromise was achieved by adopting two sets of goals: minimum objectives, which were worked out and preferred by the staff of the Army-Navy Munitions Board; and maximum goals, which were preferred by Interior. At 1946 prices the eventual cost of the minimum stockpile would have been $2.1 billion; the maximum goals would have cost $4.5 billion.

This truce soon collapsed because each side had different ideas about what the maximum objectives represented. For the Munitions Board people, the compromise had been necessary to get the program under way, but they were never really satisfied with the formula, for they felt that the idea of having dual requirements for a national security program was inherently absurd. They believed that national security in stockpiling logically could be expressed only in terms of one set of goals, based upon objective calculations of probable supplies and requirements in wartime. Any additional goals were extraneous and tended to cast doubt upon the correctness of the first set and the expertness of those responsible for their calculation. Consequently, the Munitions Board, in its public statements and its formulation of purchase policies, virtually ignored the maximum targets and acted as if the minimums were the only stockpile objectives. In the Board's view, the only function of the maximum figures was to legitimize the free transfer of surplus materials from other agencies to the stockpile, in those few cases where such transfers would raise the inventory of a material above the minimum objective.

Interior apparently had believed either that appropriated funds would be used for procurement toward the maximum goals once the minimum levels had been attained, or that the minimum targets would gradually be raised as progress was made in accumulating a stockpile. When it became apparent in 1947 that the Munitions Board had neither intention and was ignoring the maximum figures in developing its annual procurement programs, the Interior Department challenged the objectives and demanded that they be raised.

The ensuing dispute, beginning early in 1947 and continuing until 1950, revolved principally around the question: how much material from foreign sources should be assumed to be available to the United States during a general, global war? For estimating such supplies, the Munitions Board used a set of "strategic assumptions" provided by the Joint Chiefs of Staff. The JCS guidance could be categorized roughly under three headings: military accessibility, shipping losses, and concentration of supply.

Under military accessibility, the JCS simply stated which countries and regions would be accessible to the United States during the war and which would not. They judged that the Western Hemisphere, the Southwest Pacific, Southeast Asia, China, and all of Africa south of the Mediterranean littoral would be accessible. Europe, with the exception of one or two peripheral countries, was assumed to be inaccessible.

The estimate of shipping losses took the form of percentage reductions to be applied to the rate of normal peacetime shipments of materials from each accessible source. No discount for this factor was greater than 10 per cent. Apparently the JCS assumed merchant shipping losses and a naval convoy effort roughly similar to World War II.

Under concentration of supply, the JCS recommended that if all or nearly all of the supply of a commodity were concentrated in a single source outside the Western Hemisphere, that supply should not be counted on at all in wartime.

In general, the JCS postulated a "global" and "total" war, rather closely resembling World War II.

The JCS made no specific evaluation of nonmilitary factors which might limit the availability of foreign supplies during war. However, they did make allowance for political contingencies in a very general way, and some of their strategic assumptions were based on political premises.[1]

The Department of the Interior's representative in the process of establishing objectives was Elmer Pehrson, an official of the Bureau of Mines and onetime professor of mining engineering. Completely unintimidated by the mystique of military expertise in strategic matters, Pehrson launched a direct attack on the JCS

[1] The information on the strategic assumptions of the Joint Chiefs of Staff was obtained in interviews with officials of the Department of Defense and Office of Defense Mobilization during the summer of 1955.

strategic assumptions, which provided most of the rationale for the low objectives favored by the Munitions Board. He first challenged the assumption that some supplies would come in from non-Western Hemisphere sources. The Joint Chiefs were much too optimistic about this, Pehrson thought. He pointed to the high degree of vulnerability of merchant shipping to enemy sea and air action, and the uncertainty as to which, if any, of the strategic bottlenecks on the principal sea routes the United States Navy would be able to control.

Pehrson could cite, in support of his position, the experiences of World War II, when the Japanese conquest of Southeast Asia cut off the principal peacetime sources of tin, rubber, Manila fiber, and other materials; when the Mediterranean was practically closed to merchant ship traffic; and when other areas were inaccessible in varying degree. Because of the wide margin of error in any assumptions about the nature of a future war, Pehrson said, it would be wisest not to count on getting *any* supplies from overseas sources. Above all, while it might prove possible to get some supplies through with adequate military protection, why spend precious military power for this purpose? Why not store up enough materials in advance so that all our military power could be used for the main task of defeating the military forces of the enemy? Moreover, prices would be higher in wartime. Pehrson also pointed out the hazards of sabotage to producing and transportation facilities, and the vulnerability of congested foreign ports to enemy bombing.

Much the same considerations should apply to the Western Hemisphere, Pehrson thought, though in lesser degree. He mentioned the large shipping losses from enemy submarine action in the Caribbean during 1942 and 1943, which sent to the bottom substantial tonnages of bauxite, the principal raw material for the production of aluminum, and required the diversion of scarce labor and equipment to the mining of lower-grade domestic bauxite.

Pehrson also warned of the unpredictability of the political allegiance of foreign countries in the next war. He pointed to the volatility of Latin American politics and the success of Nazi fifth columns in some countries south of the border. Even Canada might decide to be neutral in the next conflict, and the possibility of a diplomatic break between the United States and Great Britain could not be ruled out.

Pehrson's conclusions were that no supplies should be expected from outside the Western Hemisphere in time of war and that normal supplies from that hemisphere should be discounted 75 per cent to take account of shipping losses, shortage of ships, and possible adverse political developments. Where foreign supplies came from a single source, such as nickel from Canada or quartz crystals from Brazil, security required that no imports be depended upon during the war period.[2]

In addition to challenging the strategic wisdom of the Joint Chiefs of Staff, Pehrson also made the following arguments in support of higher stockpile goals:

1. Strategic materials are the foundation of industrial and military strength. Their fundamental importance justifies a program of "100 per cent security" in stockpiling, that is, the elimination of all conceivable risk.

2. Accumulation of a large stockpile would cost nothing, in fact would be a profitable investment. Since materials, unlike weapons and munitions, are always salable in the commercial market, the stockpile should be considered not an expense but a capital asset. The only expense involved is administrative, including storage costs and losses on deteriorated materials. No interest charge would have to be counted, any more than it has to be counted on the large stockpile of gold held by the government. Since the long-run trend of minerals prices is upward, the sale of materials would yield a profit more than offsetting maintenance costs.

3. A large stockpile would reduce or eliminate the need to use

[2] Interview with Elmer Pehrson, Interior Department, July 15, 1954.

costly or inefficient substitutes for scarce materials in wartime production.

4. Maximum stockpiling in advance of war would release a maximum of energy, resources, and manpower from mining and transportation to the manufacture of weapons and other end-items during war. It would also release military forces from the job of guarding sea lanes and source areas.

5. A larger stockpile would provide more dollars to our friends and allies abroad, thereby strengthening their economies, which would contribute to our own national security.

6. A large stockpile, by stimulating the development of domestic mining, would contribute to United States self-sufficiency in strategic materials, also a military asset.[3]

There was undoubtedly another, unstated reason why Interior sponsored high stockpile goals. The mining industry was a major constituency of the Interior Department. Stockpile purchases naturally supported minerals prices, and higher goals would mean either a higher rate of purchase or purchases over a longer period of time. Higher objectives, combined with a longer term of procurement, would allow more placement of long-term contracts designed to stimulate expansion of domestic production.

By way of rebutting the Interior views, the Munitions Board argued as follows:

1. There was no justification for taking less "calculated risk" in stockpiling than in other defense programs. An attempt should be made to maximize the security yield of the national defense dollar, and this goal would not be served by spending money for strategic materials which would yield more security if invested in tanks or airplanes. Larger stockpile objectives logically would call for larger appropriations. Even though appropriations were made to the purchasing agency, stockpile budget estimates were carried in the national defense section of the Budget document and the President's budget message. In view of the practice of

[3] *Ibid.*, July 20, 1954.

establishing over-all ceilings for the national defense budget, every dollar requested for stockpiling would have to come out of some other military program. Therefore, reducing the risk in stockpiling would be likely to increase the risk in other areas of national security. Strictly speaking, the size of the annual appropriations requests did not have to be governed by the size of the stockpile objectives, but the Munitions Board was committed to a five-year completion target. To meet this schedule, an increase in objectives would call for an increase in yearly appropriations. The Munitions Board agreed with Pehrson *in the abstract* that stockpile purchases should not be considered expenses since the materials were salable assets, but the Board was painfully aware that the Bureau of the Budget and the congressional appropriations committees did not subscribe to this concept. The latter considered stockpile expenditures to be current costs, to be balanced and weighed against other current security costs. (Pehrson, of course, was less concerned with this practical problem since his department did not have responsibility for national defense. Moreover, raw-materials security probably loomed large in his mind in comparison with other national security programs because raw materials were "his job." Like many specialists, he tended to magnify the importance of his own specialty.)

2. Congress would be more likely to take kindly to the stockpiling program if it were presented in terms of moderate, "reasonable" figures. A $5 billion program would be reasonably certain of congressional support, while a $10 billion program might be considered extravagant.

3. The strategic assumptions of the Joint Chiefs of Staff and the Munitions Board were based on strategic plans for fighting the war. It followed that these assumptions represented the best possible military estimate of what the situation would actually be.

4. It further followed that it was unnecessary and illogical to stockpile more than was necessary on the basis of the JCS plans and assumptions.

5. Acquisition of a stockpile of the size proposed by Interior would have a damaging inflationary effect on the national economy.

6. The existence of such a large stockpile would cause considerable uncertainty and instability in world commodities markets.

Other agencies became involved in the dispute through their advisory membership on the Strategic Materials Committee. In several meetings during 1947 and 1948, the Committee debated the issues and eventually reached the point of taking a formal vote on the percentage discounts to be applied in estimating probable wartime supplies from foreign countries. A vote was taken for each source area, and in almost every case Pehrson's views favoring maximum discounts had the majority. He usually had the support of the Minerals Division of the Commerce Department, the Procurement Division of the Treasury Department (the stockpile buyers), and the Army, Navy, and Air Force. On the other side, favoring the Munitions Board's position, were usually the Department of State, the Department of Agriculture, and the Office of Materials Distribution in the Commerce Department, which reflected the interests of industrial consumers.

The result of the voting was a set of supply discounts from various areas which gained the support of the majority. There were to be no supplies assumed during wartime from any source outside the United States, Canada, and Mexico. The Munitions Board and the State Department member protested vigorously against the total write-off of supplies from South and Central America but apparently were only mildly opposed to the 100 per cent discounting of Eastern Hemisphere supplies.

A small discount was voted for Canada. This was the only area where the Munitions Board view had a majority. Interior preferred a larger write-off of Canadian supplies, and State favored none at all.

A larger discount was assigned to prospective supplies from Mexico. The Interior position carried here, with the Munitions

Board favoring a lesser discount and the State Department, again, no discount.

Any decisions of the Strategic Materials Committee were not, of course, authoritative. Nevertheless, the net effect of the discussions and the voting was to strengthen the position of Interior and put the Munitions Board on the defensive, especially with the representatives of the three armed services all voting with Interior and against their "own" mobilization agency, the Munitions Board.

It may be interesting to speculate a bit about the reasons and interests behind the positions taken by some of the agencies. The views of the main protagonists, Interior and the Munitions Board, need no further explanation. The views of the State Department can be related in part to its international orientation. A large stockpile perhaps smacked too much of self-sufficiency and economic nationalism. The Department may have feared a disruptive effect on world materials markets of heavier stockpile buying. Like the Munitions Board, the State Department tended to view the stockpile program within the larger context of overall national defense capabilities and budgets and felt that a stockpile of the size implied by the Interior assumptions would represent a disproportionately high degree of security in the materials field, when compared to the level of security implicit in more important national defense programs—the military forces in being. Finally, and probably most important, the State Department regarded the function of making strategic assumptions as logically within the field of expertise and responsibility of the Munitions Board and the Joint Chiefs of Staff. On that ground alone, State felt that the military views deserved support.

Probably a good part of the reason why the armed services disagreed so sharply with the Munitions Board is that they did not feel a responsibility for measuring the security yield in stockpiling against that in other programs: they did not feel called upon to balance marginal utilities across the entire national defense budget, as did the Board. Thus they were freer to indulge whatever feeling they had along the lines of "the more security the better." There was still another reason: the military representatives were conscious of the fact that there were other important uses for military equipment and manpower in wartime besides maintaining and gaining access to raw materials. They felt that one purpose of stockpiling in peacetime was to free a maximum of military power for use in activities more directly related to defeating the enemy. The representative of the Air Force, Col. C. C. Segrist, was the principal advocate of this view. He emphasized that the next war was likely to begin without much warning and that all military power in being would be urgently needed immediately on the fighting front. The sudden beginning would also mean that war production would have to get started in a very short time, and this fast start would be facilitated by having a large amount of materials on hand, ready to be fed into production lines. Procuring and storing materials in advance of war not only insured availability but also saved time and released labor which might otherwise be used for mining the materials after the beginning of the war.[4] This argument—that the stockpile was not just a pile of materials, but was also a stockpile of time, labor, facilities capacity, transportation, electric power, and so on— was also used by Pehrson and other advocates of the large stockpile.

The Commerce Department had two votes: that of its Minerals Division, whose representative consistently supported Interior; and that of the Office of Materials Distribution, which was just as consistently cast on the side of the Munitions Board and the Department of State. This anomaly is best explained in terms of the personal background of the individuals concerned and their conceptions of their subagency's interests. Walter Janssen, the Minerals Division representative, was a mining engineer; his support for a large stockpile probably reflected to some extent a partiality toward his own field of professional activity and knowl-

[4] Interview with Department of Defense Official, former Munitions Board staff member, July 9, 1955.

edge, as well as, perhaps, some sense of agency responsibility for the welfare of the domestic mining industry. Miss Marion Worthing, representing the OMD, more accurately spoke for the agency interests of the Commerce Department and those of its major constituency, the materials-consuming industries. Higher stockpile goals, to the extent that they stimulated more strenuous purchasing, would raise materials prices and generate an inflationary impact on the economy; and one of the principal objectives of the Department of Commerce in 1947 and 1948 was to counter inflationary tendencies. At this time, the OMD actually was authorizing the release of large amounts of materials from the leftover wartime stockpile for this very purpose.

Interior also acquired an ally on Capitol Hill, the Mines and Mining Subcommittee of the House Committee on Public Lands. The Subcommittee was interested in getting a domestic mining subsidy bill passed. The bill under consideration would have authorized a resurrection of the premium-price plan which had been in effect during the war. The subsidized production was to go into the stockpile. Naturally, the Subcommittee (heavily packed with representatives from Western mining states) wanted high stockpile objectives so there would be room in the stockpile program for a maximum amount of subsidized production. The Subcommittee actually prepared a set of stockpile goals with extremely pessimistic strategic assumptions to justify the goals.[5]

Whereas the Munitions Board's stockpile plans were based on the assumption of a war lasting five years, the Subcommittee preferred to think in terms of eleven. This would include eight years of actual fighting plus a three-year "postwar emergency period" during which supplies would be scanty because of war damage. The Subcommittee assumed that all sources of supply outside the Western Hemisphere would be closed off during the eight years of war and that destruction of mine, port, and rail facilities would prevent shipments from being resumed from these sources

[5] House Committee on Public Lands, *Hearing, Strategic and Critical Minerals and Metals*, 1948, pp. 942 ff.

in substantial quantities for at least three more years. In addition, it was assumed that bomb or sabotage damage to production and power facilities, and enemy submarine action, would reduce supplies from South America to one half the peacetime levels.

Applying these assumptions, the Subcommittee came up with a proposed objective for copper alone of $2,881 million, which was about $200 million higher than the current Munitions Board objectives for all of some 35 minerals and metals on the stockpile list! Objectives for manganese would have taken thirty-two years to accumulate at the then current rate of acquisition.

The Subcommittee attempted to sell this program to witnesses from the Munitions Board, the NSRB, and the Department of the Interior. Rear Admiral Roger W. Paine of the Munitions Board did not appear disturbed about the Subcommittee's excursion into the field of military strategy or their implied criticism of the strategic wisdom of the Joint Chiefs of Staff, but simply pointed out that the Subcommittee's proposal would require many times the funds which the appropriations committees and Congress were likely to make available for stockpiling.[6] Arthur Hill, Chairman of the NSRB, politely stated that assumptions about the nature of future war should be left to the "specialists in that field"—namely, the Joint Chiefs of Staff.[7] On the other hand, James Boyd, Director of Interior's Bureau of Mines, expressed sympathy with the Subcommittee's proposal and said its strategic assumptions were "reasonable."[8]

After the Strategic Materials Committee had taken its vote on supply discounts late in 1947, the results, favoring the Interior position, were submitted to the Joint Chiefs for comment. The reasons for this move are obscure. Interior may have believed that the JCS, when confronted with alternative assumptions supported by a majority of the Committee, would revise their own

[6] *Ibid.*, p. 944.
[7] *Ibid.*, p. 966.
[8] *Ibid.*, p. 57.

assumptions to bring them closer to those advocated by Interior. More likely, the Munitions Board may have sought to buttress its position by getting a fresh statement of the military point of view from the fount of strategic wisdom. At any rate, the Chiefs, replying in the spring of 1948, indicated their disapproval of the Committee's figures by simply ignoring them and by issuing a new set of strategic assumptions which differed in no significant respect from those already in use. Pehrson and his superiors in Interior were unimpressed and refused to back down.

Then, in an attempt to reach some sort of compromise, the Munitions Board prepared an "interpretation" of the new JCS assumptions which, in effect, changed them considerably in the direction of the views of Interior. The JCS judgment about which countries would be militarily accessible was unaltered, except that certain areas, about which the Joint Chiefs had been equivocal, were considered totally inaccessible. Where a single source accounted for more than half of the total accessible supply of a material, supplies from that source were discounted completely if outside the Western Hemisphere, and fractionally if in South America or the Caribbean area. For purposes of making this concentration discount, a source was defined not as a country, but as an area, such as Southeast Asia. This definition meant of course that discounts for concentration were considerably larger than under a strict application of the JCS formula, not only because they were applied for a considerably lesser degree of concentration but also because the area considered in establishing whether concentration existed was larger. To illustrate hypothetically, Indonesia might provide 40 per cent of United States rubber supplies and not be eligible for discount if considered by itself. But if lumped with Malaya, the percentage would approach 100 per cent and the entire Far Eastern rubber output could be written off.

In addition, the interpretation called for a further partial discount of all remaining Asian supplies because of the uncertainty as to whether such supplies would be available, even if militarily accessible. Furthermore, shipping losses considerably larger than those estimated by the Joint Chiefs were assumed.[9]

This interpretation added up to an assumption of far less foreign supplies being available in wartime than would be assumed under a literal application of the JCS guidance. The new formula gained the approval of the Munitions Board and, somewhat surprisingly, of the Joint Chiefs of Staff. But Pehrson quickly made known that it was not acceptable to Interior.

It was now Pehrson's turn to appeal to higher authority. He persuaded the Secretary of the Interior, Julius Krug, to broach the subject with the Secretary of Defense, James V. Forrestal. Late in the summer of 1948, Krug wrote to Forrestal, urging him to find some way of getting the stockpile objectives raised to the level favored by the majority on the Strategic Materials Committee, without explicitly contradicting the strategic assumptions of the Joint Chiefs of Staff. Krug did not spell out how this might be done, but hinted that further discounts might be applied for risk factors not specifically covered by the JCS guidance.

Forrestal was not a stockpiling enthusiast; he was having trouble squeezing military requirements under national defense budget ceilings and regretted that stockpiling took up any room at all under those ceilings. Far from being sympathetic, Forrestal was trying to get the stockpile program out of the Department of Defense and the defense budget. So Krug got no satisfaction from the Secretary of Defense.

At this point, the situation was one of complete stalemate. There was only one way to get an authoritative decision: by appeal to the stockpile "review agency," the National Security Resources Board. The Munitions Board resisted this move, first because current procurement could still go forward without Interior's concurrence on the eventual goals, and second because it was uncertain where the NSRB stood on the question of goals. However, when all other members of the Strategic Materials Committee voted for the appeal, the Board acquiesced.

[9] Interview with former Munitions Board staff member, July 7, 1955.

It should be pointed out to the NSRB, the Committee agreed, that the JCS-Munitions Board assumptions would provide "reasonable" national security, with a certain "calculated risk," while Interior's formula would provide greater security at greater cost. The NSRB was to be told also that rates of acquisition in the near future would be the same under both plans, since these rates would be governed by availability of funds.

John Steelman, Acting Chairman of the NSRB, announced the decision late in September 1948, in favor of the Munitions Board and the Joint Chiefs of Staff. In a supporting statement, Steelman indicated that making strategic estimates, in stockpiling as elsewhere, was a military responsibility. The clear implication was that Interior had no business attempting to make strategic assumptions or challenging those of the Joint Chiefs, although its concurrence on stockpile goals was still legally required with respect to the nonmilitary aspects of their formulation.[10]

Nonstrategic Assumptions[11]

The way was now cleared for a review of stockpile goals by the Munitions Board and the Strategic Materials Committee. It was felt that many of the prevailing objectives were obsolete since they dated from 1944. Actually, a "provisional" review had begun during April 1948, and had gone forward slowly under the insistent prodding of the NSRB.

The process of reviewing the objectives revealed additional differences between the Munitions Board and the Department of the Interior, on questions not strategic in character. The chief issues were: (1) the degree of wartime expansion of production, and (2) the level of civilian requirements.

The Munitions Board proposed that estimates of wartime pro-

[10] Interview with Department of Defense official, former Munitions Board staff member, July 20, 1954.

[11] Where not otherwise noted, material in this section was obtained principally from interviews with officials in the Interior and Defense Departments during the summer of 1955.

duction assume some extraordinary expansion beyond the peace-time norm, but not subsidized expansion. The proposed criterion was the degree of elasticity of supply for the commodity in question. If a small increase in price would bring forth a relatively large expansion of production, considerable expansion would be assumed. If the level of production of a commodity tended to remain relatively stable, regardless of price changes, less expansion would be expected.

Pehrson argued that expansion of production during war should not be counted on at all, except in special cases. Why spend valuable energy, resources, and manpower building new production facilities when there was a war to be fought? Also, there was a good chance production would be reduced rather than expanded because manpower might have to be taken out of the mines and processing plants to meet an extraordinary military crisis, such as a parachute invasion. Production or transportation facilities in the United States or elsewhere might be knocked out by enemy bombing or sabotage. Pehrson also thought the Munitions Board was not giving sufficient weight to the probable depletion of United States minerals reserves in advance of the war.

On the requirements issue, the Munitions Board proposed that military requirements generally should be one third higher than the peak year of World War II, multiplied by five, for the entire assumed war period. Whenever possible, however, military requirements were to be estimated directly from strategic plans for World War III. Requirements for war-supporting industries similarly were to be one third higher than during World War II. Civilian requirements were to be established generally at the World War II level of civilian consumption (not peak year plus one third), with an addition to take account of population increase.

Pehrson had no quarrel with the criteria for calculating military requirements, but asserted that civilian requirements, as outlined by the Munitions Board, were much too low. World War II was not a good standard for civilian requirements, he argued, because essential civilian production in that war had been cut back too severely and the scrap drives, gasoline rationing, and other conservation measures had had a demoralizing effect on civilian morale. He proposed that stockpile goals be based on the assumption that no essential civilian use of a material would be reduced more than 50 per cent.

Finally, Pehrson wished to assume that the next war would begin in the year 1970. The Munitions Board preferred to use the year just following the year in which an objective was reviewed. Here again, Pehrson's preference would have meant higher stockpile objectives; the use of a distant date like 1970 would have increased requirements by an amount commensurate with economic and population growth, while reducing estimated supplies by taking account of considerable depletion of domestic reserves.

The upshot of the discussions was that the Interior view prevailed on the disputed points, except for the assumed date of the outbreak of war. It was decided that expansion of domestic production during a future war was not to be assumed, except for certain materials which were expected to be required in amounts much greater than during peacetime, and whose reserves were large. The Interior language on civilian requirements was also agreed to in large part. Estimated reductions in essential civilian requirements during war were generally to be not more than 50 per cent of these requirements for the latest peacetime year.

With these issues out of the way, the review proceeded smoothly. In February 1949 the aggregate stockpile objective was valued at $3.7 billion at current prices, which roughly represented the difference between estimated wartime requirements of $12.4 billion on the one hand and estimated domestic supplies of $4.5 billion and assumed imports of approximately $4.2 billion on the other hand. The effect of the review by June 30, 1950, when it was nearly completed, was to raise the value of the overall objective to $4 billion. New objectives had been established for 34 materials, and staff work had been completed on 20 more.

In 26 instances, an increase was established or recommended, 13 goals were decreased, 10 remained unchanged, and 5 materials were removed from the stockpile list.[12]

Development of the Factoring System

The experience of working with the strategic assumptions of the Joint Chiefs of Staff led to increasing civilian dissatisfaction with those assumptions as the sole basis for foreign supply discounts. One source of annoyance was the ambiguity and rather oracular tone which the civilians thought they detected in the Joint Chiefs' statements. The statements were terse and succinct but also ambiguous and cryptic. A certain country or area might be considered accessible at the beginning of the war but not during the war. Just when the "beginning" stopped and the "during" began, the Joint Chiefs did not say. There were numerous statements of the on-the-one-hand-this-but-on-the-other-hand-that variety. The phrase "partial accessibility" turned up now and then with no definition. The Chiefs never explained precisely what they meant by "accessibility." The words "unless," "if," and "possibly" were used frequently. Such ambiguities were almost always pessimistically resolved by the Munitions Board; for example, if a country was declared "partially accessible" by the JCS, the staff considered it completely inaccessible.

The principal complaint was directed at the Joint Chiefs' rather arbitrary handling of nonmilitary factors. As mentioned earlier, the JCS recommended that where virtually all of the supplies of a material were concentrated in a single source outside the Western Hemisphere, those supplies should be discounted entirely. The main purpose of this discount was to offset the risk of political and economic contingencies which might reduce supplies available to the United States, even though the sources were "militarily accessible." According to the Joint Chiefs, such factors were unpredictable, so that the only practical course was

[12] Munitions Board, *Stockpile Report to the Congress*, July 23, 1950, p. 7.

to make sure that unfavorable political or economic developments did not deprive us of our entire supply of a material.

The critics from the civilian agencies felt that although such matters *were* difficult to predict with a high degree of precision, they were predictable enough to justify an attempt to assess each variable separately. They wanted to take separate account of such contingencies as breakdown of government and civil order in a source country, sabotage, labor disturbances, political alignments with the enemy, or vulnerability to enemy influence which might result in the refusal to sell materials to the United States.

The Joint Chiefs gave no weight at all to differences in political and economic tendencies among source countries. It seemed obvious to the civilian critics that vast differences did exist. Was not the danger of sabotage or an unfriendly political attitude much less from Australia than from, say, India or Guatemala? The JCS concentration factor applied only to the Eastern Hemisphere, so the danger of adverse political developments in South America—a very real possibility with respect to some countries— was not considered at all.[13]

Occasionally in the past the Munitions Board and the Strategic Materials Committee had given special consideration to obviously important nonmilitary factors in source countries. But the procedure had been highly informal and haphazard, and the assessments had been very general in nature. A movement toward more system and precision developed during the full-dress review of stockpile goals which took place in 1949 and 1950. One reason was that the exercise of actually applying the assumptions to the supply data stimulated thought about the factors and procedures involved and revealed defects in the formula. A second

[13] The information about the strategic assumptions of the Joint Chiefs of Staff and the civilian agency reaction to them was obtained during the course of several interviews with officials of the Departments of State, the Interior, and Defense, the General Services Administration, and the Office of Defense Mobilization. A very general discussion is to be found in the President's Materials Commission, *Resources for Freedom,* Vol. V, June 1952, 143-144.

reason was the increased influence of the NSRB in the stockpile program generally. By 1949 the NSRB had taken hold of its legal responsibilities and had accumulated an energetic staff of economists and administrative experts whose natural and professional tendencies were to tidy up the system. There were others on the NSRB staff who were not so interested in precision as in getting an increase in stockpile goals. Both groups were critical of the JCS assumptions but for different reasons.

Pressure for more precision emanated also from the Bureau of the Budget. The Bureau had natural inclinations toward precision, first because of its responsibility for promoting administrative efficiency, and second because the size of stockpile goals was relevant to judgments about the urgency of annual appropriations requests.

The Munitions Board, in the early years of the postwar program at least, had tended to agree with the Joint Chiefs of Staff that the variables in question were so nebulous that attempts to assess them accurately were useless. It was felt that the calculation of stockpile objectives was far from being an exact science and that attempts to make the calculation more exact than the information warranted were misguided. By and large, the staff members were less impressed by the need for precision than by the value of having *a* formula, uniformly applied across the board, to insure consistency in evaluating the several materials. Later, however, the staff recognized that more precision, within limits, was necessary.

Significantly, the Department of State was not an active advocate of refining the system, despite the fact that the slighted factors were largely political in nature. This was partly because the Department, like the Munitions Board, preferred a small stockpile. Supply discounts for additional risks would tend to raise the objectives. Also, the Department did not feel that it had a positive role in the establishment of goals; this was considered an administrative matter under the primary jurisdiction of the Munitions

Board and the Department of the Interior. The Stockpile Act gave this job specifically to Interior and the military while State had only an advisory role. Department of State representatives refrained from injecting political considerations into the calculation of objectives unless asked, and they were never asked. Such political assumptions as were made, were made by the Joint Chiefs of Staff and the Munitions Board.

While the concentration factor reflected the Joint Chiefs' unwillingness to evaluate political factors in detail, the Chiefs nevertheless *did* make certain broad political assumptions in arriving at their judgments about military accessibility. A basic political assumption was that the enemy would be the Soviet Union. This assumption was not made explicitly but was nevertheless obvious. They also made assumptions about which countries would be certain to ally themselves with the United States, and commented upon the possible neutrality or unfriendly attitude of other countries. But the analysis of political orientation was not complete; it did not cover all countries of the world. When such judgments were made, they were not labeled as political judgments but rather as aspects of "military accessibility."

Besides these specific predictions of political alignments, the JCS made statements about internal political instability in various countries and about the East-West ideological struggle generally, all of which were accounted for by the above-mentioned blanket discount for concentration.

The Department of State never protested that such appraisals constituted an unwarranted extension of the military role. Even when the judgment of the Joint Chiefs was obviously faulty, as when they estimated in the spring of 1949 that the southern part of China would be militarily accessible to the United States in war, nothing was heard from the Department of State. The State Department's explanation is that, at the time, the review of stockpile objectives had not yet reached those materials for which China was a major source, most prominently tungsten and antimony, so there was no occasion for bringing the matter up. Yet, this assumption *was* pounced on by Pehrson of Interior as evidence that the strategic guidance was too optimistic.

In general, the Department of State took an extremely passive attitude toward the establishment of stockpile goals. It seems that this attitude resulted not only from deference to military leadership, but also from a feeling that the military assumptions were about as good as any that could be devised. The assumptions necessarily had to be arbitrary in view of the lack of data from which to make definite predictions, the Department felt; although there was nothing very profound to be said in justification of those made by the Joint Chiefs, it would be difficult to improve upon them.

At length the advocates of increased precision were able to persuade the Munitions Board to take up the subject with the Joint Chiefs of Staff. The Board did so and asked for another set of assumptions providing a somewhat more specific evaluation of nonmilitary contingencies. In May 1950 the Joint Chiefs returned a document which included only an appraisal of military accessibility and shipping losses. In addition, the Chiefs stated that their appraisal did not include political considerations and other factors relating to conditions within source countries, and that in the future they would avoid evaluating such factors.

This communication left a void which had to be filled. A subcommittee of the Interdepartmental Stockpile Committee was appointed to work out a set of assumptions covering nonmilitary risks. Its membership was one representative each from the Department of State, the Department of Commerce, and the Central Intelligence Agency, with the State Department man, Harlan Bramble, serving as chairman.

Bramble drew up the basic framework, setting out four categories of considerations: general political orientation, sabotage, labor dependability, and governmental stability, plus a set of instructions which outlined the reasoning process to be used in the evaluation. Besides the Commerce and CIA members of the subcommittee, Bramble also recruited an operations officer and an intelligence officer from State. Each of these men, working independently, applied Bramble's categories and instructions to every country which had been declared militarily accessible by the Joint Chiefs. The results were collated and reconciled by Bramble.

In this manner the subcommittee devised a set of "dependability ratings" for about thirty countries. The ratings were arrived at in the following fashion: Each country was rated for each of Bramble's categories on a scale from 0 to 100. The numbers represented not "discounts" as in the assessment of shipping losses, but rather the converse of discounts. That is, a rating of 100, say, for political orientation, meant unequivocal alignment with the United States, while a rating of 80 signified a somewhat lesser probability that the country would be a reliable friend and/or the degree to which such unreliability might be expected to reduce shipments of materials. The over-all dependability rating for a country was simply the lowest rating in any of the four categories. For example, if a country had a rating of 100 for political orientation, 50 for sabotage, 80 for dependability of labor, and 90 for internal governmental stability, its over-all dependability rating was 50.

Since the Joint Chiefs were no longer suggesting a discount for concentration of supply, it was necessary for the Bramble subcommittee to assess this factor also. The subcommittee proposed discounts, varying by region, for concentration of more than half of the available supply of a commodity in a particular region. This factor could not be estimated as precisely as, say, shipping losses or even political dependability, since it was not at all in the nature of a prediction, but was simply an extra discount taken to offset the extra risk involved in relying on a concentrated supply. If a country which previously had been declared militarily accessible were in fact overrun by enemy forces, and if that country produced a large proportion of a certain material, we would be in much worse shape with regard to that material than with some other materials which that country supplied, but which had other major sources. In short, the concentration discount was a partial hedge against the possible incorrectness of the military and political assumptions.

The subcommittee went further and proposed an additional discount representing the extent to which the United States was dependent upon foreign sources generally for a commodity, or conversely the degree of United States self-sufficiency.

The over-all risk was whittled away further by a "contingency factor," which was nothing but a kind of catchall discount designed to offset miscellaneous risks not covered adequately by the rest of the system. The major risk was possible insufficient shipping to carry extremely bulky commodities, such as bauxite and manganese ore. Whereas the shipping-losses factor of the Joint Chiefs covered only the percentage of loss of *attempted* shipments, the contingency factor covered the chance that it would prove impossible or undesirable to attempt movement of all the available supplies.

Obviously the work of the Bramble subcommittee amounted to a complete revamping of the basic supply assumptions. The "strictly military" assumptions of the Joint Chiefs were left intact, but Bramble's group had to make sure that their assumptions and the Joint Chiefs' were rationally integrated and that the combination of the two took into account all major variables. One factor which almost fell between the political and military stools was the vulnerability of foreign production and transportation facilities to enemy bombing. Bramble felt that bombing was a military consideration which his team was hardly competent to estimate. He thought that an appraisal of this kind could most properly be made by the intelligence services of the Department of Defense. But when he asked Defense for aid on this matter, he was turned down. So his subcommittee went ahead and assessed the possible bomb damage, lumping it with sabotage on its rating sheets. Although by this time the Soviet Union had exploded an atomic weapon, the bomb-damage discount apparently reflected conventional bombing of a type and scale similar to that of World War II.

The weight given to the bomb-vulnerability factor varied inversely with distance from the Soviet Union and directly with the degree of vulnerability of production and transportation facilities within the country. In practice, it was applied only when there were serious potential bottlenecks, for example, in India, where a single railroad was relied upon to carry manganese ore from mine to port. Relatively isolated power dams and bridges were also considered vulnerable, justifying a lower rating. Consideration was given to the amount of time it would take to get a damaged facility back into operation.[14]

Bramble and his associates labored on through the summer of 1950. Their deliberateness was irritating to those who were more interested in getting the situation resolved than in precise computations. The outbreak of the Korean War added a new urgency and increased the irritation. The NSRB, in particular, now headed by Stuart Symington, pressed for a quick decision. Although the NSRB had earlier been impressed with the need for getting more accuracy and precision in the supply estimates, it now proposed a system of its own which was even more general in nature than the JCS formula. It assumed that no supplies would be available from outside the Western Hemisphere except from Australia, New Zealand, and Africa; it discounted supplies from the latter three areas by 75 per cent; discounted supplies from the Western Hemisphere, except the United States, Canada, and Mexico, by 50 per cent; and counted on full supplies from the latter countries, except for materials whose production was especially vulnerable to sabotage or bombing.[15] The NSRB formula would have eliminated the Joint Chiefs' guidance entirely,

[14] The material on the work of the Bramble subcommittee was gleaned largely from interviews with officials of the Departments of State and the Interior, and the ODM during the summer of 1955.

[15] Interview with Office of Defense Mobilization official, former NSRB staff member, July 9, 1955.

unlike the Bramble plan, which merely supplemented the JCS assumptions. Also, it would have raised the stockpile objectives substantially.

The NSRB made the point that even if the Joint Chiefs' assumptions proved accurate as predictions, there was no assurance that the materials which did come in would go as far as they did in World War II. The Joint Chiefs were implicitly assuming that the mobilization-control system in World War III would be as efficient as it was in the last war, or efficient enough to channel into military hands all the materials needed for military requirements, and enforce the maximum possible civilian belt-pinching—a dubious assumption, according to the NSRB. The latter took the position that in a war which might begin with an all-out atomic attack on the United States, if a control system were possible at all, it would have to be very loosely organized and administered. A large amount of supplies could be expected to slip though the controls and go into the black market or into nonessential civilian consumption. Therefore it made sense, according to the NSRB, to stockpile larger amounts than the calculations called for.

Incidentally, this was the first apparent consideration, in stockpiling, of the possibility of nuclear war involving attacks on the United States. By this time, the Soviet Union had exploded an atomic bomb, an event which led to a thorough reexamination of United States national security policy at the higher levels of government.

This review produced not only a decision to go ahead with development of the hydrogen bomb but also an important National Security Council document, NSC-68, which recommended a substantial increase in conventional armed forces. Since the chairman of the NSRB was a member of the National Security Council, it was natural that the NSRB should be the first to introduce the contingency of nuclear war into the stockpiling discussions. Also, NSC-68, which implicitly revised upward the estimate of the Soviet threat and the urgency of defense preparedness generally, may have contributed to the more active role which the NSRB now assumed in stockpiling and to its advocacy of higher stockpile goals, sharply contrasting with its earlier support of low stockpile objectives in resolving the Interior-Munitions Board dispute.[16]

Apparently the NSRB only partially assessed the possible consequences of nuclear war, failing to consider, for example, the probable reduction of requirements because of destruction of materials-consuming facilities and large population casualties, or indeed the possibility that a nuclear war might be so damaging as to preclude any war production at all in the conventional sense.

In urging adoption of its system, the NSRB was careful to point out to the Munitions Board that it did not intend to question the professional expertness of the Joint Chiefs of Staff, nor was it presuming to make any judgments about military strategy. All it wanted to do was to take out a little more insurance than the Joint Chiefs and Munitions Board were willing to buy. Its proposal was based on a value judgment, not an expert assessment. According to ex-NSRB people the Munitions Board and the JCS accepted this line of argument as valid and did not accuse the NSRB of attempting to step over the boundary between military and civilian expertise and responsibility.[17] By contrast, they were resentful of Interior's approach, which featured a frontal attack on the strategic assumptions of the Joint Chiefs of Staff.

When the Bramble subcommittee finally reported in September 1950, the Interdepartmental Stockpile Committee thus had two systems to choose from. Adoption of either of them would

[16] For an analysis of NSC-68, see Paul Y. Hammond, "NSC-68: Prologue to Rearmament," in Warner R. Schilling, Paul Y. Hammond, and Glenn H. Snyder, *Strategy, Politics, and Defense Budgets* (New York: Columbia University Press, 1962).
[17] Interview with Office of Defense Mobilization official, former NSRB staff member, July 16, 1955.

cause an increase in stockpiling objectives, but in varying degree
—the Bramble plan less, the NSRB system more. After some vigorous discussion the Committee voted to accept the Bramble
plan, with minor changes. It had the support of the Munitions
Board and the Bureau of the Budget, as well as the Departments
of State and Commerce, and the Central Intelligence Agency. Interior naturally lined up with the NSRB in advocating a simpler
system, more pessimistic assumptions, and higher stockpile goals.

The formula which emerged became known as the "factoring
system." There were four major factors, with subfactors under
some of them. In outline form, the system looked something like
this:

A. Military accessibility and shipping losses
B. Political dependability
   1. General political orientation
   2. Sabotage (including aerial bombing)
   3. Labor dependability
   4. Governmental stability
C. Concentration of supply
   1. Concentration by region
   2. Total dependence on foreign sources
D. Contingency factor

The procedure for applying the factors was as follows: first,
countries judged militarily inaccessible by the JCS were eliminated. To the normally available supplies from the remaining
sources, the discounts for shipping losses, political dependability,
concentration, and contingencies were then applied cumula-
tively; that is, the result of the first discount became the base for
the second, and so on.

With the adoption of the factoring system, another major review of stockpile objectives was conducted during the last six
months of 1950; all but 10 of the objectives were increased, 3 materials were added to the list, and 3 were deleted. On December
31, 1950, the total value of the aggregate objective was $8,870

million, an increase of more than 70 per cent from the July total, after correcting for the general rise in prices which occurred after the beginning of the Korean War.[18] This was a substantial rise, and it seems to have been accounted for in large degree by the initiation of the new supply discounts under the factoring system. Some of it resulted from the fact that the JCS assumptions which were issued just before the Korean War were somewhat more pessimistic than previous assumptions about the military accessibility of sources in the Far East.

It is noteworthy that the factoring system was adopted in a period of high international tension following the outbreak of the Korean War, although work on it was begun before the war. It took account of factors which Interior had always pushed for consideration, and the resultant increase in objectives no doubt was gratifying to Interior after its own proposals for raising the objectives had been turned down by the NSRB before the war. Now it was the NSRB which had taken the lead in pressing for a bigger stockpile, more than coincidentally perhaps at about the time Congress was granting large supplemental appropriations for stockpiling and calling for a stepup in stockpile buying. One might speculate that the objectives tended to follow the appropriations and the sense of urgency, and the calculating formula was simply adjusted to fit the demand for higher objectives and more active procurement. If this is so, the outbreak of the Korean War affected stockpiling policy more or less as it affected general military doctrine and planning. In the latter realm, NSC-68, with its recommendation for greater military forces in being, was roughly parallel to the earlier Interior proposal to raise the stockpile objectives. Both proposals failed of adoption in the relatively placid period of early 1950, but were adopted a few months later in somewhat different form after the Korean aggression had broken the inertia and provided the necessary sense of urgency.

[18] Munitions Board, *Stockpile Report to the Congress*, January 23, 1951, p. 1.

The procedure for applying the factoring system remained about the same as it had been when the Joint Chiefs' guidance alone was used. The principal difference was that the discounting of supplies no longer rested exclusively on JCS guidance. Although the mechanics were carried out by the Munitions Board staff as usual, the Department of State now had responsibility for evaluating political and economic developments in source countries and making appropriate changes in the discounts. Discounts for concentration of supply became the responsibility of the Munitions Board.

Although some of the stockpilers on the Munitions Board tended to scoff at the factoring system because it seemed to introduce a spurious degree of precision into a process which, as one of them put it, was really "a form of crystal-gazing," the system nevertheless was administratively and politically useful. It provided a uniform, across-the-board procedure for supply discounting which assured consistent calculation of objectives for all materials. It explicitly took account of several types of considerations which previously had been left to "judgment" or "intuition." By thus reducing the range of uncertainty and freedom of choice, the system reduced the vulnerability of the stockpile program to pressures from special interests. When challenged or urged to change its policies by Congress, another government agency, or private groups, the Board could defend itself by invoking the objective "system." Finally, by actively involving the Department of State in calculating goals, the new system not only relieved the Board and the JCS of the responsibility for making political and other nonmilitary judgments in estimating supplies, but also made the State Department a more active and influential ally in the recurring battle with the big-stockpile extremists in Interior and other agencies.

Nevertheless, while the system provided a useful façade of precision and objectivity, the Munitions Board did occasionally deviate from it. The deviations were occasionally the result of a sort of visceral feeling that the results cranked out by application of the factoring system were not in fact correct or did not give adequate weight to some special consideration. In other cases they seemed to represent capitulation to political pressures which the Board found impossible to resist. Sometimes both factors may have been involved.

The case of manganese is instructive. According to ex-members of the Munitions Board staff, application of the formula produced an objective which seemed low to all concerned. The objective was increased by a large amount because it was thought that the large proportion of imports in the estimated wartime supplies constituted a special risk for a material of such vital importance. Also, there were some doubts that sufficient shipping would be available to move the large assumed imports of this bulky material. However, some cynics allege that the real reason for the deviation was to placate Interior, which had long stressed the hazard of relying on imports from India and Africa, or to satisfy the congressional friends of the domestic manganese producers.

Another case in point was wool. Farm-state congressmen urged that wool, cotton, and a few other agricultural commodities be purchased for the strategic stockpile (as distinct from the "stockpile" of surplus agricultural commodities held by the Commodity Credit Corporation). The Munitions Board for a time resisted this demand, on grounds that sufficient wool or acceptable substitutes would be available from domestic and accessible sources during war, that what the services needed was a stockpile of wool cloth rather than wool, that expenses of maintenance and "rotation" would be too high, and generally that "a dollar invested by the Government in the stockpiling of wool was considered to yield much less protection than the same dollar invested in 71 other materials being stockpiled."[19] However, wool was finally

[19] Munitions Board, *Statement on Wool*, circa October, 1950, printed in U.S. Congress, Senate, Preparedness Investigating Subcommittee of the Committee on Armed Services, "Agricultural Products and the Mobilization Program," *Investigation of the Preparedness Program, 3rd Report,* Senate Document No. 3, 82nd Congress, 1st session, 1951, pp. 21-22.

placed on the stockpile list in the latter part of 1950, following
issuance of a sharply worded report from the Preparedness Subcommittee of the Senate Committee on Armed Services, headed
by Senator Lyndon B. Johnson of Texas, criticizing the Munitions Board's failure to stockpile wool and long-staple cotton.[20]
Long-staple cotton was placed on the list at about the same time.

What Quality?

One aspect of the determination of stockpile objectives was
the establishment of quality specifications. In practice, this meant
specifying minimum percentages of various impurities which
stockpiled materials might contain. During the early years of
postwar stockpiling, the Munitions Board insisted that all materials for the stockpile had to meet the highest quality standards in
use by industry, even though some lower-grade materials could
be used or in fact were being used in some manufacturing processes. The principal rationale of this policy was as follows: the
greatly expanded materials requirements in wartime would force
industry to make use of some low-grade domestic ores; a stockpile of very high-grade material, when mixed with the low-grade
domestic production, not only would increase the average quality
of all supplies, but also would maximize the amounts of domestic
ores which could be used. In addition, it was argued that the
output of smelters and processing plants decreased with the use
of lower-grade materials, that low-grade materials would require
changes in industrial equipment and practices and would result
in inferior end-products, and that the cost of "beneficiating" low-
grade materials would have to be added to the cost of acquiring
them.

In establishing the "specs," the Munitions Board consulted
with its industry advisory committees. Naturally enough, the advisory committees (which included consumers as well as producers,
and chiefly high-grade producers) recommended the qualities

[20] *Ibid.*

which were considered most desirable by industry and which industrial equipment was presently set up to use. The Munitions Board usually accepted without question the standards recommended by the advisory committees, although it reduced the standards somewhat on materials which were difficult to procure. On the civilian side, there was some disagreement with the Munitions Board's preference for the highest qualities. When the initial postwar stockpile objectives were established in 1944, Secretary of the Interior Harold Ickes put in a stiff protest against the Munitions Board's specifications, arguing that they would "discourage the utilization of domestic ores, particularly those of a marginal character."[21] The purchasing agents also tended to press for somewhat lower specifications. Their motive apparently had little to do with any special feeling for the domestic producers, but was simply to ease the problem of meeting purchase schedules for scarce materials. Widening the range of acceptable qualities would tend to increase the supplies available for stockpile purchase.

The Munitions Board's quality standards were criticized severely in Congress. Mining-state legislators on the Public Lands committees sometimes accused the Board of deliberately setting the specifications high in order to bar domestic materials from the stockpile. It was charged that specifications were written to favor the large domestic producers over the "little fellows." Some congressmen were convinced that an irrational military preference for nothing-but-the-best had something to do with it.[22] If the Board had been less particular about quality, it was said, more progress could have been made in accumulating the stockpile. The Preparedness Subcommittee of the Senate Committee on Armed Services accused the Munitions Board of "rigidity" in requiring that all deliveries of tungsten to the stockpile meet the minimum purity standards for *all* end-uses. In practice, the Sub-

[21] Letter, Ickes to Forrestal, January 5, 1945. National Archives, Special File No. 401.1.
[22] House Committee on Armed Services, *Stockpiling Hearing*, 1950, p. 7513.

committee said, tungsten for use in tool steels did not need to be
free from molybdenum content, since molybdenum often was
added to the alloy anyway. On the other hand, some other impurities not desirable in making tool steels were acceptable in
other uses. By insisting on the principle of "universal application"
rather than stockpiling various qualities for a variety of end-uses,
the Board had unnecessarily limited the amount of domestic
tungsten which could qualify, the Subcommittee asserted.[23]

Just as the Munitions Board tended to invoke the military wisdom of the Joint Chiefs of Staff or the objectivity of the factoring
system when the size of stockpile goals was under fire, it invoked
the expertise of its industrial and technical advisers when quality
standards were criticized. Quality specifications were established
in the first instance by the Board's industry advisory committees
and reviewed by governmental industrial specialists, it was said.
The Board simply followed the advice it received from these
sources since it did not itself command the technical competence
to make such judgments.

The principle of universal application indicated flexibility rather than rigidity, Munitions Board officials declared—flexibility,
that is, in the usefulness of the stockpile during wartime. To have
different quality standards for different end-uses would require
earmarking portions of the inventory for particular end-uses. If
the advance estimate of requirements for particular uses should
turn out to be wrong, part of the stockpile might lose some of its
utility or might require expensive processing. However, the Munitions Board somewhat relaxed its general insistence of high
quality as it gained experience with stockpiling. In January 1950
the Board reported that it had revised some specifications to permit acceptance of materials from new sources and also had encouraged research to determine the utility of grades of materials
produced domestically when the customary source was foreign.[24]

The relaxing tendencies continued during the Korean War

[23] Senate Preparedness Subcommittee, *Twenty-seventh Report, Tungsten,*
committee print, 82nd Congress, 1st Session, 1951, pp. 14-17.
[24] Munitions Board, *Stockpile Report to the Congress,* January 23, 1950,
p. 19

under pressure of greatly increased stringency of supply. The purchasers in the General Services Administration were given authority to deviate, within limits, from established specifications when it was necessary to acquire scarce materials.

What Form?

Another issue concerned the form in which the materials should be stockpiled. The ruling philosophy in the first two years of the program was that materials should be stockpiled in the form of raw ore or after having been subjected to a minimum of processing. The Munitions Board defended this policy on three grounds: (1) Stockpiling funds were limited; therefore they should be spent for security against only the most serious contingencies. (2) The worst contingency, because it was the least correctible during war, was to be cut off from overseas sources of *raw* materials. (3) The higher the degree of processing to which the materials had been subjected, the greater the danger of obsolescence from technological change.

The Munitions Board pointed out that pig aluminum cost four times as much as bauxite, ferro-vanadium twenty times as much as vanadium ore, and ferro-manganese twenty-two times as much as manganese ore. Moreover, aluminum, ferro-vanadium, and ferro-manganese could always be produced in the United States, provided the ore was available. The Munitions Board admitted that processing of materials would involve wartime expenditure of valuable time, labor, and energy, but reasoned that to bear such costs was infinitely better than to risk not having the raw materials. It was the ore which had to come from distant places and through dangerous waters. The "most security for the money" clearly called for giving priority to those raw materials for which the United States was dependent on foreign sources.

While such simple metal forms as ingots and bars were not likely to become obsolete because of technological change, further processing to such forms as forgings, shapes, and sheets did raise this danger because they sharply narrowed the range of uses to which the metal could be put (without melting and re-shaping). Hard experience increased the Munitions Board's sensitivity to this factor when the development of a new military watch by one firm made part of the stockpile of jewel bearings obsolete.[25] After this experience the Board decided to provide for security in jewel bearings by maintaining a pilot plant for their production, rather than by stockpiling.[26]

Privately, Munitions Board people had another reason for opposing the stockpiling of processed and fabricated materials: letting in such materials would open the door to stockpiling "everything but the kitchen sink" and maybe even that, depending on the political influence of the sink manufacturers.

The idea of stockpiling processed materials had a greater appeal among the civilian agencies, principally Interior and the NSRB. As early as 1944 the Department of the Interior had attempted to get aluminum and other refined metals on the stockpile list. The attempt had been initiated by one of Interior's bureaus, the Bonneville Power Administration, which marketed power to aluminum plants in the Northwest and feared that demand for electric power in this area would fall off considerably after the war with the decline in war production. Bonneville was supported by some people in the Bureau of Mines who reasoned that a stockpile of processed metals would tend to make more domestic low-grade materials eligible for purchase; if the materials were not usable in their raw state, they could be processed into higher forms.

The prevailing view of the Munitions Board, however, was that the proper way to make "prior provision" for security in processed materials was to plan for quick expansion of processing facilities after the outbreak of war, and in some cases to maintain standby plants.[27]

[25] President's Materials Policy Commission, *Resources for Freedom*, Vol. V, June 1952, p. 141.
[26] Munitions Board, *Stockpile Report to the Congress*, August 10, 1953, p. 15.
[27] House Committee on Public Lands, *Hearing, Strategic and Critical Minerals and Metals*, 1948, pp. 990-991.

The principal argument of Interior and the NSRB was that a stockpile of processed metals was not only a stockpile of the metal itself, but also of the time, labor, resources, electric power, and plant capacity necessary to refine it. Thus, the extra cost was more than justified by the extra security obtained by shifting resource expenditures out of the war period, or, to put it another way, by releasing resources for other wartime uses. Another argument was that processing facilities, for example, aluminum plants, being small in number and large in size, were strategic bottlenecks in the national productive system. A stockpile would insure against the possibility of these bottlenecks being plugged by sabotage or enemy bombing.

The Munitions Board recognized the validity of these arguments in the abstract but not in the context of the small amount of funds available for stockpiling. Eventually it might be desirable to stockpile higher forms, but the problem of insuring geographic availability of the raw materials would have to have first priority. For their part, Interior and the NSRB recognized the sense of the Munitions Board's first-things-first view as long as appropriations were limited; *but*, they asserted, the Board itself must answer for the paucity of funds, for it was responsible for the preparation and defense of the budget estimates. They urged that more funds be requested to allow the purchase of refined and processed metals and the processing of ores already in the stockpile. The Munitions Board insisted, naturally enough, that Congress was responsible for the lack of sufficient funds. Admiral Paine lectured the House Public Lands Committee as follows:

If you have a small amount of money to work with, you would buy the raw materials. Say we are talking about aluminum. If we want to stockpile—aluminum, not bauxite, is what we should have. We do not buy aluminum; if we buy aluminum we are stockpiling labor and time. We would love to be able to do it, but you gentlemen have got to give us a lot more than you have given us so far before we can even talk about such a thing.[28]

Much of this debate was generated by strong pressure from

[28] *Ibid.*, p. 927.

several sources to stockpile aluminum. Stockpiling of this metal was urged repeatedly from 1945 to 1949 by the Department of the Interior, the Surplus Property Administrator, and the Aluminum and Magnesium Industry Advisory Committee. Interior's interest, as explained above, was stimulated by the Bonneville Power Administration. The Surplus Property Administrator had to dispose of surplus aluminum plants, built at government expense during the war; an increase in demand for aluminum would enhance the possibility of an advantageous sale. The Civilian Production Administration and the Commerce Department were not interested; they were busily selling off the sizable stock of aluminum left over from the wartime stockpile. Two of the aluminum producers on the Industry Advisory Committee, Reynolds Metals Company and Kaiser Aluminum and Chemical Corporation, were playing it both ways: while they took what they could get from the war-surplus stocks to satisfy their current fabricating needs, they supported their future as small but growing primary aluminum producers by urging an aluminum stockpile, piously arguing before congressional committees the vulnerability of aluminum plants to enemy bombing. The largest producer, the Aluminum Company of America, while it also purchased from the government surplus stocks, was at least consistent in that it opposed a stockpile. Its main reason, however, was that it feared a stockpile's depressive effect on the market. The Munitions Board resisted all this pressure, believing that aluminum wartime needs could be met by expanding domestic production and curtailing nonessential consumption.

In April 1949 the Air Force member recommended to the Strategic Materials Committee that aluminum be placed on the list, presenting in support a sharply increased estimate of military requirements. The Committee approved the recommendation and established a tentative objective. Action was held up by the Munitions Board pending the outcome of an NSRB study of the feasibility of the new military requirements. Meanwhile, Congress had moved in to provide a meaningful nudge. The Federal Property and Administrative Services Act, setting up the General Services Administration, was passed on June 30, 1949, with a provision authorizing the GSA to accept strategic materials in lieu of rental, or principal and interest payments, on leases or sales of government surplus property. The provision was inserted by the conference committee without discussion, either before or after conference, on the floor of either house. It may be nothing more than a "funny coincidence," but it is worth noting that three of the five Senate conferees—McClellan of Arkansas, Hoey of North Carolina, and Ives of New York—came from states which contained primary aluminum producers and/or standby surplus aluminum facilities.[29]

The passage of this bill was a bonanza for the producers, especially Kaiser and Reynolds, who already had taken over some of the surplus aluminum plants and were in the market for more, if suitable terms could be arranged. They trooped in to the GSA and the Munitions Board, offering aluminum ingots which the Board could hardly refuse, since to do so would have been to flaunt the will of Congress. Besides, the acquisitions were not to be charged to stockpile appropriations.

Although the congressional action no doubt helped to remove the Munitions Board's last hesitancies, it probably was not the decisive factor, which was the size of the new military requirements. By August the NSRB had decided that the wartime requirements could not be met by current producing capacity plus potential wartime expansion. The result was that aluminum, on November 17, 1949, was placed on the purchase list and plans were started under NSRB sponsorship for further expansion of the aluminum industry.[30]

The decision to stockpile aluminum did not eliminate the need

[29] Public Law 152, 81st Congress.
[30] Information on the aluminum decision comes chiefly from interviews with officials of the Office of Defense Mobilization, the Department of the Interior, the Department of Defense, and the Reynolds Metals Company, and from the Munitions Board's *Stockpile Report to the Congress*, January 23, 1950, pp. 20-21.

for a stockpile of bauxite. Since the stockpile objective for aluminum represented only a minor portion of total wartime needs
and since the shipment of bauxite supplies from South America
and the West Indies was subject to enemy interruption, the raw
material continued to be stockpiled.

By June 1952, 13 of the 30 metallic minerals being stockpiled
were carried in the form of metal ingots and 17 in the form of
ore, concentrates, or other simpler forms. Aluminum-bauxite was
apparently the only case of stockpiling more than one form of the
same basic mineral. The principle of the "highest homogeneous
form" was stated as a general guide. According to this principle,
materials were to be stockpiled in the highest possible form without committing them to a specific end-use, provided processing
costs were not too high.[31] However, this principle was applied
very conservatively and not across the board.

The factoring system in its initial formulation took no account
of the vulnerability of concentrated domestic processing facilities. The omission seems conspicuous in retrospect, particularly
since the Bramble subcommittee did give some weight to bomb
damage in foreign sources. The Department of the Interior and
the NSRB urged consideration of this factor in connection with
projections of domestic production, and received some support
from other civilian agencies, but the Munitions Board resisted.
Although mining facilities were not particularly vulnerable,
transportation lines and processing plants were, Interior and the
NSRB pointed out. The argument was especially valid for metals
which were processed in a few large installations. Four or five
well-placed atomic bombs could take out most of the country's aluminum production, for example. Production of molybdenum, of
which the United States produces about 90 per cent of the
world's supply outside the Soviet Union, is largely concentrated
at a single operation in Colorado. Aside from this specific kind of
vulnerability, a nuclear bombing attack would be likely to cause

[31] President's Materials Policy Commission, *Resources for Freedom*,
Vol. V, June 1952, pp. 140, 146.

enough general disruption of industrial and economic processes to reduce supplies of all materials considerably.

In rebuttal, the Munitions Board pointed out that consuming facilities also were vulnerable to bombing. If an attack occurred, materials *requirements* would be reduced as well as supplies, and no one could predict which would be reduced more. Who could say how the Russians would distribute their bombs as between aluminum plants and airplane factories? Since prediction was impossible, it was best not to consider the matter at all, according to the Munitions Board.[32]

The Board's attitude was implicitly criticized by the President's Materials Policy Commission, which recommended in June 1952 that vulnerability of producing and processing facilities in the United States and other Western Hemisphere countries be "fully evaluated" in establishing stockpile objectives.[33] The Department of Defense, along with all other interested agencies, concurred in this recommendation. A report to the Commission asserted that "stockpiling of materials at somewhat higher stages of fabrication, consistent with wide usefulness . . . would help to shift the expenditure of labor, electric power and other general resources from a future war to the present."[34]

However, the Munitions Board steadfastly resisted all pressures to stockpile metal in forms higher than ingots, primarily because of cost but also because of the obsolescence risk. The Board also refused to consider the contingency of nuclear attack on the United States in estimates of stockpile needs, for reasons already mentioned. It did, in some cases, discount projections of domestic metals production, especially when production was concentrated in one or a few plants, but this discounting was intended only to hedge against the danger of sabotage, not nuclear attack.

[32] *Ibid.*, p. 144.
[33] *Ibid.*, Vol. I, p. 163.
[34] *Ibid.*, Vol. V, p. 149.

V

Stockpiling in Partial Mobilization, 1950-1953

The mobilization effort touched off by the Korean War affected profoundly the stockpile program and its administrative framework. Until then, stockpiling had been the primary economic arm of national defense. During the Korean War the stockpile program became submerged in the larger mobilization; it became only one public claimant for scarce resources among many. It had to compete not only with greatly increased demand for materials and weapons but also with a vast program for building new production facilities for a variety of "defense-supporting" products. The rate of stockpile accumulation was determined no longer by the size of congressional appropriations and the degree of buying aggressiveness of the stockpilers, but by the decisions of a new set of civilian mobilization agencies concerning the relative urgency of stockpile accumulation compared to other defense programs.

The situation was complicated by the fact that the Korean mobilization was only partial. The problem was not one of organizing production and distribution toward the single overriding objective of victory in all-out war, but rather of allocating resources so as to achieve the desired level of defense capability while preserving a maximum of peacetime values and comforts. In other words, it was a multiple-value, as opposed to a single-value, mobilization. To a much greater degree than in a full war mobilization, the problems concerned value choices rather than pure "efficiency." How much national security is worth how much sacrifice of comfort and convenience in private automobile transportation? That was the kind of question the Korean War mobilizers had to answer; whereas the parallel problem faced by their World War II predecessors was more like: How many cars should be produced to maximize the national power in war? Questions of equity, among persons and groups affected by the mobilization, loomed almost as large as questions about rational distribution of resources from the broad national point of view. All these were ticklish choices, carrying a high degree of political potency. As will be shown, the stockpile served to make some of the choices less difficult.

The limited nature of the mobilization raised problems more directly related to stockpiling. Did the Korean War constitute the kind of national emergency in which, according to the Stockpiling Act, materials were to be sold from the stockpile to further the defense effort? Or, by increasing the probability and imminence of all-out war, did the Korean War increase the urgency of accelerating stockpile acquisition and holding on tight to what had been acquired? Neither question was answered unequivocally, and the compromise which evolved first stimulated confusion about, and then considerable rethinking of, the purpose and nature of stockpiling.

The outbreak of the Korean War on June 25, 1950, found the stockpile only two fifths complete, although four years of the original five-year program had slipped by. Goals for 9 of the most strategic items were less than 20 per cent complete. The Munitions Board, with the aid of its various interdepartmental committees, had just finished a meticulous review of stockpile objectives which raised the planned cost of the completed stockpile to $4 billion. Some $1,600 million worth of materials were on hand, and another $500 million were on order.[1]

The outbreak of a shooting war introduced a greater sense of urgency into the stockpile program. Was this the prelude to World War III? Were the nation's raw-materials security measures again going to be too little and too late? No one knew, of course, but an acceleration of procurement seemed to be called for.

Urgency was heightened further when stockpile objectives were nearly doubled late in the summer. The increase, to a total valuation of $8,870 million, reflected some rise in prices, but was mostly the result of the introduction of the formal factoring system, which lowered the estimates of wartime supplies from overseas sources by the application of discounts for a wider range of contingencies than had been considered previously.[2]

Signals from Capitol Hill also indicated a stepup in stockpiling efforts. The congressional attitude was expressed in two ways: by a huge increase in stockpile appropriations, and by sharp criticism of the Munitions Board for not having made more progress.

The $500 million requested in the regular budget for fiscal 1951 was granted without change. Then in September 1950 Congress appropriated another $600 million, and in January 1951 $1,800 million more. In total, Congress appropriated $2,900 million in about six months—more than three times the funds it had made available in the previous four years!

The newly formed Preparedness Subcommittee of the Senate Armed Services Committee, headed by Senator Lyndon B. Johnson of Texas, led the congressional attacks on the Munitions Board's past performance. In a rapid-fire series of reports, the Subcommittee charged that the Munitions Board's rubber stockpiling program was "meagerly conceived and meagerly executed,"

---

[1] Munitions Board, *Stockpile Report to the Congress*, July 23, 1950, p. 1.
[2] For a more extensive discussion of the factoring system, see Chapter IV, pp. 122-136.

that the Board had shown "abysmal lack of foresight" in the stockpiling of certain agricultural products, and that it had been "timid" and "complacent" in stockpiling nickel.[3] Conveniently forgotten were Congress's earlier warnings against stimulating inflation and its failure to provide appropriations when supplies were plentiful during 1949. The Munitions Board had blundered; the Munitions Board must now make amends.

Thus fortified by ample funds, stimulated by a new sense of urgency, and smarting under the congressional whiplash, the stockpilers turned to their job with vigor and determination. The Munitions Board directed the purchasers to "drastically accelerate" acquisition, to emphasize materials from Far Eastern sources, and not to worry much about prices.

Although they had plenty of money to work with, the buyers were unable, in the last six months of 1950, to achieve this drastic acceleration. They placed contracts worth $430 million, which was just a shade more than the $401 million placed in the first half of the year. The Munitions Board, in its report to Congress in January 1951, said that this rate of progress was "not considered satisfactory."[4]

The chief reason why more progress was not made was that stockpile acquisition collided head-on with a greatly increased private demand for materials and a stepped-up armament program, both touched off by the Korean War. The increase in the defense effort of the United States and its allies did not have much *direct* effect on the materials market during the fall of 1950, but the announced plans, with their portent of severe shortages and higher prices to come, greatly stimulated private buying. Speculators and industrial buyers, whose inventories had been generally low prior to the war, jumped into the market and bought wildly. Materials became scarcer and scarcer, and prices

[3] See the first four reports of the Subcommittee, Senate Documents Nos. 230 and 240, 81st Congress, 2nd session, and Senate Documents Nos. 3 and 4, 82nd Congress, 1st session.

[4] Munitions Board, *Stockpile Report to the Congress,* January 23, 1951, p. 13.

moved steadily upward. Prices of rubber and tin—to select the most prominent examples—more than doubled in the last half of the year.

Meanwhile the government had acquired new powers to control the situation. These powers, and the administrative changes which went along with them, were to have a profound effect upon the stockpile program.

Defense Production Act

Congress passed the Defense Production Act on September 8, 1950. In essence, the Act authorized government action to divert scarce resources into the production of military weapons and other essential programs, including stockpiling; to expand production of needed materials, equipment, and components; and to minimize the economic impact of the defense buildup. The President was given broad powers to issue priorities, allocate materials, prevent hoarding, control prices, buy and sell materials for current use, and offer incentives to expand production. The legislation was based on studies which the NSRB had prepared prior to the outbreak of the Korean conflict, and to a high degree it reflected the experience gained and lessons learned during the industrial mobilization of World War II.[5]

Although the powers probably were sufficient for the regulation of an all-out mobilization, the mobilization under way and planned was only partial. The prevailing view of the Administration was that the controls should be minimal and that they should be applied with a minimum of change in the existing governmental organization. In line with this philosophy, President Truman at first decided to parcel out the powers among the existing agencies and not to set up a new and centralized mobilization organization. For example, most of the powers to allocate materials and assign priorities to essential uses went to Secretary

[5] Public Law 774, 81st Congress. For a more extended analysis of the Act, see A. L. Scanlan, "The Defense Production Act of 1950," *Rutgers Law Review*, Spring 1951, pp. 518-529.

of Commerce Charles Sawyer, who vested them in a new bureau in his department, the National Production Authority. Other functions were vested in the General Services Administration, the Department of Interior, and other agencies. The stabilization of prices was made the responsibility of the new Economic Stabilization agency and its subordinate agency, the Office of Price Stabilization.

The NSRB received the job of coordinating this sprawling organization. Although the NSRB's new powers were quite insubstantial in a literal sense, they did serve to enhance its prestige and influence.[6] Long-range mobilization planning, which had been the NSRB's main concern prior to June 1950, necessarily became subordinated to the new and more urgent role.

The NSRB's increased stature tended to strengthen its position in the stockpile program. The NSRB had much to do with the preparation, and justification before the President, Bureau of the Budget, and Congress, of the large supplemental appropriations requests of September 1950 and January 1951. Chairman Symington took the lead in defending these requests in Congress, thus establishing himself in the eyes of congressmen as the head man in stockpiling. In recommendations to the President, the NSRB urged faster stockpile acquisition, most notably of rubber.

The NSRB also led moves on related fronts which indirectly helped the accumulation of the stockpile. Such other measures included reactivation of government-owned standby plants for producing aluminum, synthetic rubber, nickel, and magnesium; a comprehensive rubber security program, including—besides reopening of the synthetic plants—conservation controls and an expanded program for growing rubber in the Western Hemisphere; and general action toward expanding production of scarce and strategic materials.

[6] Briefly, the NSRB was to resolve interagency disputes, prescribe directives which the President had approved, obtain information, take measures to obtain coordination, and advise the President on the progress of defense production. Clearly, the NSRB was still essentially a staff adviser to the President. Executive Order No. 10161, September 9, 1950.

While the NSRB was eroding the Munitions Board's stature and influence "from the top," that is, at the policy-making level, the Munitions Board was also forced to give ground at the lower, or operational, end of the stockpile decision-making process. Al Walsh, the head buyer and chief of the Emergency Procurement Service, the GSA's stockpiling division, had always fretted under the restraints imposed by the Munitions Board. He now demanded that the Board release him from the requirement of clearing with the Board all contracts for a longer term than a year, and drop the practice of giving him annual purchase directives. Walsh had the strong support of GSA Administrator Jess Larson and NSRB Chairman Symington. It was Symington who finally persuaded the Munitions Board to give Walsh his freedom.

The principal reason why the GSA and the NSRB wanted this change was that the Defense Production Act had just given them the job of administering—the NSRB as general supervisor and the GSA as operating agency—a vast new program of production expansion and government purchase of materials. The GSA needed more flexibility in stockpiling so as to be able better to coordinate its operations in this field with the new, broader program. The Munitions Board had been given no role in the new mobilization program, but its policy role in stockpiling, along with its tendency to make decisions without regard to other related activities, made it a potential source of trouble and friction in the new industrial-mobilization effort. Hence the civilian top and bottom of the stockpile decision-making hierarchy combined to minimize the role of the military middle although they could not, of course, eliminate it so long as the Munitions Board bore the legal responsibility for stockpiling.

On October 30, 1950, the GSA was authorized to contract for deliveries more than a year in the future without reference to the Munitions Board, and to exercise its own judgment as to prices. The emancipation was virtually completed when the Munitions Board, late in the year, sent Walsh an "expanded" purchase directive. This directive was not limited to the current fiscal year; it simply stated the ultimate objectives of all the materials and the approximate date on which the Board felt each of them should be completed. The pace of acquisition was left entirely to the buyers.

The NSRB was just beginning to get the mobilization program organized, starting first with a firm determination of military, defense-supporting, and civilian requirements, when events wrought another drastic change in its role. The entrance of the Chinese Communist armies into the Korean War on November 26, 1950, created the distinct possibility of a much larger conflict and thus increased the urgency of the mobilization. This event indicated to many people, including the President, that a further centralization of mobilization responsibilities was called for. On December 16, 1950, the President declared a national emergency and created two new agencies, the Office of Defense Mobilization and the Defense Production Administration. Charles E. Wilson, president of General Electric Company, was made head of of the ODM. His duties were to "direct, control and co-ordinate all mobilization activities of the executive branch of the government, including, but not limited to, production, procurement, manpower, stabilization and transport activities."[7] This grant of power was as great as, if not greater than, that enjoyed by any of the mobilization agencies of World War II.

The Defense Production Administration was established as a "central programing" agency under the ODM. Within policies established by the ODM, it was to make the basic decisions concerning expansion of production and allocation of scarce materials among competing claimants, civilian and military. The "line" mobilization agencies, such as the National Production Authority, were responsible for carrying out in detail the decisions made by the DPA.[8]

Creation of these two agencies rendered the NSRB's current mobilization functions superfluous, so that agency was stripped of all its new powers under the Defense Production Act. Much of its staff was transferred to the new agencies, and the NSRB re-

[7] Executive Order No. 10193, December 16, 1950.
[8] Executive Order No. 10200, January 3, 1951.

verted to its earlier role of planning for the effective use of the nation's resources in the event of all-out mobilization. Eventually, even this function was taken over by the ODM, and the NSRB was abolished in April 1953.

Mobilization Policy

As Wilson saw it, the mobilization program had four major objectives: (1) to insure quick and orderly production of weapons and supplies ordered by the armed forces; (2) to build an adequate industrial "mobilization base," meaning the productive capacity needed for a quick shift to full-scale mobilization should all-out war occur; (3) to expand the country's basic industrial capacity to the point where it could support both the expanded military effort and an adequate level of civilian production; and (4) to minimize the "dislocation" of the civilian economy resulting from the pursuit of the first three objectives.[9]

According to the plan, defense spending and production would increase gradually during 1951 and 1952 and then level off early in 1953, on a plateau of spending at the rate of approximately $42 billion a year. During the buildup period, industrial facilities and materials production would be expanded, so that when the plateau of defense production was reached, there would be enough capacity and material to maintain indefinitely a high level of military production plus roughly the same level of civilian production that had existed just prior to the Korean War. The expansion program thus reflected both the limited and the long-run nature of the mobilization: since it did not carry the urgency that would have accompanied an all-out effort and since it was to be relatively permanent, provision had to be made for easing quickly the sacrifice of normal comforts and values. The expansion would deprive civilians of a few more comforts during the period of the buildup, but would ease the sacrifice over the long run. From

[9] U.S. Congress, House and Senate Committees on Banking and Currency and Small Business, *Joint Hearing, Production and Allocations*, 82nd Congress, 1st session, 1951, p. 3.

another point of view, the expansion program would reduce the time period during which economic controls would have to be imposed, although it tended to increase their stringency while they were in effect. This get-the-pain-over-with-quick philosophy seems to have originated with Wilson, although it was widely shared throughout the mobilization community.

The second objective listed above—building a mobilization base—was really the expansion objective looked at from the security rather than the economic point of view, plus the provision and maintenance in standby condition of certain specialized equipment and facilities, and the continued accumulation of a stockpile of raw materials. Its purpose was to have an economy that could be converted rapidly and smoothly to large-scale production of military equipment, should limited war or cold war explode into full-scale hot war. It reflected the general belief of the time that a war with the Soviet Union would be a long struggle between conventional armies and navies, more or less on the model of World War II. Although the Soviets had exploded a nuclear weapon in 1949 and the United States had developed a considerable nuclear force, the notion of a short, highly destructive nuclear war, which might make irrelevant any prewar plans and capacities for production of conventional equipment during the war, had hardly penetrated into defense planning outside of certain avant-garde Air Force circles.

Stockpiling was affected by three different aspects of the Korean War mobilization: allocation of scarce materials among competing programs, expansion of materials production, and international factors. The discussion which follows is divided along these lines.

Controls and Allocations

The actions taken by the new defense agencies under their authority to allocate materials had a two-edged effect on stockpiling. Measures to reduce industrial usage in civilian goods production made it easier for the GSA to buy materials. However, the mobilizers used their powers also to restrict the flow of materials to the stockpile.

The earliest control orders were of the first type. During the fall of 1950, the National Production Authority issued a series of directives limiting the use in nondefense production of certain basic and scarce materials, such as aluminum, copper, zinc, nickel, tin, and rubber, to stated percentages of manufacturers' consumption in a specified base period. The NPA also established a simple priority system to go along with the cutbacks. It delegated to the Defense Department and other agency claimants the authority to issue a "DO" (Defense Order) priority rating to contractors producing military weapons and other products essential to defense. These ratings were "tickets" which gave their holders first call on available materials. Although stockpile purchases were not assigned a priority rating, the cutbacks in nonessential uses assertedly did take into account stockpile needs, and there was no limit on amounts that could be acquired for the stockpile as long as willing sellers could be found.

As rearmament orders began taking a larger share of materials supplies early in 1951, stockpile acquisition came under stricter control by the civilian control agencies. The Defense Production Administration set up a system of direct quantitative allocation of the scarcest materials to all claimants, including the stockpile.

For assistance in evaluating and scaling down claims, the DPA established a Vital Materials Co-ordinating Committee, later succeeded by the Defense Materials Operating Committee, which brought together representatives from all agencies concerned with materials aspects of the defense effort. Most of the agencies also were represented on the Interdepartmental Stockpile Committee, often by the same persons. The DPA representative acted as chairman of the Committee, and since the Committee was only advisory, the DPA retained the power of decision.

The DPA and the Committee decided upon broad allocations of materials to the various essential programs, including stockpiling. For some of the scarcest and most urgently needed materials, such as copper, aluminum, and cobalt, purchase of the allotted quota for the stockpile was aided by the NPA's direct allocation orders requiring producers and importers to deliver materials to the stockpile. But as of September 30, 1951, only 13 of the 70-odd stockpile materials were under such detailed control. The remainder had to be purchased without any special assistance from the NPA.[10]

With the inauguration of this system, effective control of the rate of stockpile buildup for each material passed into the hands of the civilian mobilizers. In the general schedule of priorities which they established, stockpiling ranked behind military production requirements of the United States and its allies, requirements of the Atomic Energy Commission, essential exports, defense-supporting industries (railroads, electric power, and so on), and essential consumer-goods production. There were variations among individual materials, of course; *some* stockpile acquisition of materials lagging far behind their procurement schedules was given precedence over some essential consumer goods and exports.

The DPA began restricting the rate of stockpile acquisition during the second quarter of 1951. As one of its first actions, in April, it ordered a reduced rate of rubber stockpiling along with an increase in allotments for civilian products. This was done over the protest of John D. Small, Munitions Board Chairman. The Senate Preparedness Subcommittee declared that in making this decision, the DPA had allowed "private groups" to advance their interests "at the expense of the nation's defense."[11]

In spite of these restraints, the stockpile buyers accelerated enormously their placement of contracts during the first half of 1951. They committed themselves to purchase $1,646 million

[10] U.S. Congress, Joint Committee on Defense Production, *First Annual Report*, Senate Report No. 140, 82nd Congress, 1st session, 1951, pp. 22-23, 189.

[11] Senate Preparedness Subcommittee, *Twenty-Ninth Report, Rubber*, 1951, p. 37.

worth of materials, almost four times their obligations of the preceding six months.[12] The primary reason for the stepped-up rate was the large appropriation which Congress had granted in January. Another reason was that most of the funds were obligated under long-term contracts, for delivery of materials in subsequent periods. Such contracts skirted the scramble for materials in current markets, and were not affected by current DPA quotas, although some deliveries might be barred by quotas in effect when the contracts matured.

The DPA's control had a much greater effect on stockpiling during the last half of 1951, largely because the military rearmament program began to take a much larger bite out of the available materials supplies. Contract placements dropped to $588 million, and expenditures for deliveries fell to $357 million. The stockpile lost $120 million worth of materials through diversions to industry of pending stockpile deliveries of aluminum, columbite, copper, acid-grade fluorspar, lead, manganese ore, nickel, tungsten, and zinc.[13] Deliveries of copper were stopped entirely in July, of aluminum in October, and were not resumed for many months.

What was perhaps more significant, the mobilization agencies caused the actual withdrawal of materials from the stockpile. Unlike diversions of pending deliveries, withdrawals required Presidential action, under the Stockpiling Act. Upon the recommendation of the ODM and the DPA, President Truman ordered the release of 10,000 tons of aluminum, 55,000 tons of copper, and 30,000 tons of lead, having a total value of more than $40 million.[14] Informed guessers said the copper withdrawal represented about 10 per cent of the copper inventory.[15] Diversions and withdrawals continued during the first half of 1952 although at a somewhat reduced rate.

At mid-1951 the percentage of fulfillment of individual material objectives varied from 0 to 184. The DPA's policies threw the stockpile further out of balance. In general, the items which the

---

[12] Munitions Board, *Stockpile Report to the Congress*, July 23, 1951, p. 11.
[13] *Ibid.*, January 23, 1952, p. 9.
[14] *Ibid.*, p. 10.
[15] *Business Week*, August 11, 1951, p. 134.

stockpile most urgently needed, chiefly metals and minerals, were also those for which the acquisition quotas were relatively low and which were diverted and released from the stockpile. Allocations were ample for "soft" items like oils, fibers, drugs, and rubber, the inventory of which, in most cases, was already in good shape.[16] The reason was fairly obvious: metals and minerals, for which the stockpile objectives were relatively high and which had always been the hardest to buy at scheduled rates, were at the same time the items most in demand for the current arms buildup.

Discussions about stockpile quotas at meetings of the Vital Materials Co-ordinating Committee were along lines somewhat similar to those which had taken place between the Munitions Board and the Bureau of the Budget. Whereas, before the Korean War, appropriations had been a major limiting factor on the acquisition rate, now the rate was set by quantitative quotas. The mobilizers were no more satisfied with the Munitions Board's justification of its claims than the Bureau of the Budget had been. As before, the Board's request was based largely upon its urgency formula, in which the major factors were size of the objective, inventory on hand, wartime accessibility and reliability of major sources, and the target date for completion of the stockpile. The Board again justified its request in rather absolute terms: The United States would not have security in raw materials until the objectives were reached; therefore it was necessary to proceed as fast as possible toward completion of the objectives. Like the Bureau of the Budget, the DPA wanted the request supported in more meaningful terms. The mobilizers mistrusted the Board's urgency formula and the related formula for calculating stockpile objectives because they seemed rather arbitrary, mechanical, and abstract—not sufficiently based on empirical data and differences among materials.[17] The formulae did not throw much light on the urgency of proposed current rates of ac-

[16] Munitions Board, *Stockpile Report to the Congress*, January 23, 1952, p. 11.
[17] Interview with John D. Morgan, ODM, former DPA staff member, July 10, 1955.

quisition. DPA officials wanted to know just how safe we would
be at this or that level of accumulation of this or that material.
The Board persistently answered that security would be assured
only when the whole stockpile was in the warehouse. Finally, the
DPA asked the Board to formulate a set of "peril-point" objectives, that is, objectives which it was "absolutely necessary" to
reach before all-out war. The Munitions Board met this request,
but with great reluctance since it believed the existing objectives
represented no more than minimum insurance against wartime
shortages. The Board feared that any lower, rock-bottom objectives would come to be interpreted by the mobilizers as *the* objectives; that once these targets were reached, further progress
would not be considered urgent.[18]

The Munitions Board recognized that the DPA, as the central
allocating authority, had a perfect right to set limits on stockpile
acquisition. Nevertheless it did not approve of the place assigned
to stockpiling in the hierarchy of priorities, and its representative
said as much at meetings of the VMCC. The feeling was that the
DPA did not give enough consideration to the security value of
stockpile acquisition, that it treated the stockpile program as a
mere "residuary legatee," which was to get materials only after
the requirements of other programs, for which the DPA was
more directly responsible, were satisfied.

The Munitions Board thought the DPA placed far too much
civilian production and use of materials in the "essential" category, thus giving it priority over stockpiling. They noted with annoyance, for example, that during the period from October 1951
through April 1952—when the stockpile was on austerity rations
and suffering withdrawals of copper, aluminum, and other metals
—the automobile industry received enough copper, aluminum,
and steel to produce cars at a rate equal to the 1947-1949
average.[19] In the first quarter of 1952, the period of greatest strin-

[18] Interview with Department of Defense representative, former Munitions Board staff member, June 30, 1955.
[19] Director of Defense Mobilization, *Defense Mobilization—The Shield
Against Aggression: Sixth Quarterly Report to the President,* July 1, 1952,
p. 24.

gency, manufacturers of consumer durable goods received 50 per
cent of their pre-Korea requirements of copper and aluminum.
By substituting other metals, drawing down inventories, and getting "hardship allotments" over the basic allotment, manufacturers of consumer durables were able, from October 1951 to
April 1952, to produce at a rate 4 per cent higher than the
1947-1949 rate.[20] When more copper and aluminum became
available for the second quarter of 1952 than had been anticipated—mainly because of a "stretch-out" in military requirements
and a reduction in inventory buildup—the windfall was distributed entirely to nondefense claimants, including an allotment to
the automobile industry to enable it to produce 120,000 more
cars that had been scheduled under the original allocation, "because of the high unemployment rate in the Detroit area." Over-
all, nondefense allocations of aluminum in the second quarter
were increased by 12 per cent and of copper by 3 per cent.[21] But
none went to the stockpile. In fact, the copper stockpile was
drawn on in June to offset losses from strikes and a reduction in
shipments from Chile following that country's termination of a
copper trade agreement. Then on July 1 allotments of copper to
defense-supporting and consumer durable-goods industries were
increased "to encourage the importation of copper" under a new
trade agreement with Chile.[22] In the third quarter, more copper
and aluminum were made available for "decorative purposes on
consumer goods" and other civilian uses.[23]

In the view of the Munitions Board, such decisions showed
clearly that the mobilizers were biased in favor of civilian comforts. In protesting at interagency meetings the relatively low
priority assigned to stockpiling, the Board repeatedly pointed out
that what was being denied to the stockpile was going into consumer goods. It was not a question of stockpiling vs. military
production, or stockpiling vs. expansion programs, but of stock-

[20] *Ibid.*, p. 24.
[21] *Ibid., Fifth Quarterly Report*, 1952, p. 22.
[22] *Ibid., Sixth Quarterly Report*, 1952, p. 24.
[23] *Ibid., New Resources Bring New Opportunities: Seventh Quarterly Report to the President*, October 1, 1952, p. 22.

piling vs. civilian comforts. Stockpiling, a national security program, was being sacrificed for such frivolities as passenger cars, radios, and television sets.

The Munitions Board recognized that in a partial or "guns-*and*-butter" mobilization it was necessary to maintain the civilian economy at a "healthy" level. As one Board official put it, "over the long pull, one aim of the enemy is to weaken the United States through industrial bankruptcy."[24] However, members of the Board believed that a good many persons in the mobilization agencies, because of their business background, were inclined to overestimate the amount of butter necessary for health. They thought also that many of the mobilizers were unfitted for the measurement of security needs because of their lack of military expertise.

The Board protested most vigorously when materials were withdrawn from the stockpile. Withdrawals were entirely different from diversions, for the diverted materials were not yet in the stockpile.[25] Diversions were simply an application of the allocating authority. But materials to which the stockpile purchasers had already taken title represented security for all-out war, all purchased and salted away, and should be held for that contingency. The Board's representatives also argued that releases from the stockpile would create fears of government "price breaking" among producing industries and consequently would discourage the expansion of production.

In the latter view, the Board had some support on Capitol Hill. Some congressmen were dubious about the precedent being set, even though they recognized that the releases from the stockpile probably would have little depressing effect on the market prices, given the tremendous demand. There was some feeling in

[24] Interview with Department of Defense representative, former Munitions Board staff member, July 20, 1954.

[25] In some cases, the difference was not apparent to the naked eye. Some "diverted" materials were delivered to stockpile sites and held in a "reserve" for later transfer to industrial users. But they were not officially part of the stockpile because the GSA did not take title to them.

Congress, especially among friends of the mining industry, that the President might have exceeded his authority in releasing materials short of all-out war.[26] Senator George Malone of Nevada said the President had interpreted the word "emergency" in the Stockpile Act to include "political emergency" when he ordered the withdrawals, and thus was able to "manipulate the market." The stockpile, he said, should be held for a "real emergency." (Somewhat inconsistently, Malone also scolded the Administration for calling the Korean War a "police action"; he repeatedly referred to it as "World War III.")[27]

The Department of State also supported the Munitions Board's position against withdrawals of materials during a limited emergency. In private conversations State officials spoke of the withdrawals as "raids" undertaken chiefly to appease domestic political pressures. An official statement of the Department, published in December 1952, mentioned "possible disastrous decisions as to the disposal and use of resources that should be held for extreme emergency."[28] The Munitions Board had the sympathy and at least tacit support of the other stockpile agencies from the "old regime," the GSA and the NSRB. Jess Larson, GSA Administrator, declared in September 1950:

My personal feeling is . . . that it is to the best advantage of this government from a defense standpoint to create our stockpile as quickly as we can, as cheaply as we can, and put our arms around it and not let anybody take an ounce of it away, unless it is very dire circumstances.[29]

[26] See testimony of Representative Thomas E. Martin of Iowa in U.S. Congress, Senate, Subcommittee of the Committee on Interior and Insular Affairs, *Hearing, Stockpile and Accessibility of Strategic and Critical Materials to the United States in Time of War*, 83rd Congress, 1st and 2nd sessions, Part 2, p. 9.

[27] *Ibid.*, Part I, p. 236-237.

[28] National Security Resources Board, *The Objective of United States Materials Resources Policy and Suggested Initial Steps in Their Accomplishment*, USGPO, 1952, p. 84.

[29] U.S. Congress, House, Subcommittee of the Committee on Armed Services, *Hearing, Stockpiling of Strategic and Critical Materials*, 81st Congress, 2nd session, 1950, p. 7688.

In support of their decisions vis-à-vis stockpiling, the mobilizers made several points. One was that the actions were made necessary by events over which they had no control and which they could not have foreseen. The withdrawals of copper, it was said, were made necessary largely by strikes in the copper mines of Utah and Chile. The withdrawals and stoppage of stockpile deliveries of aluminum were partly the result of power losses in the Pacific Northwest and the Tennessee Valley.[30] Another factor was that United States price ceilings, often being lower than world prices, tended to discourage imports of some of the scarcest materials, particularly copper.

The mobilizers pointed out that the materials expansion programs would begin bearing fruit in a year or two and would make plenty of materials available for all uses, including stockpiling, so that the current stringency was only temporary. They noted that some of the diverted materials were not forever lost to the stockpile, for the producers had had to promise, via an amendment of their stockpile contract, to pay back the stockpile in the future. (Contracts for some of the diverted materials were simply canceled, however.) A similar argument was applied to the withdrawals: they were "loans" which would be repaid when materials became more plentiful.[31]

These statements were all true and valid, and, as far as they went, they supported the mobilizers' position. But they did not deal with the main issue, which was: If something had to be sacrificed now in order to have more security and comfort later, why did it have to be the stockpile rather than the production and consumption of nonessential goods? As was mentioned above, producers of nonessentials *were* put on a short diet of aluminum, copper, nickel, and a few other materials, but a lot of nonessential production continued. The reduced consumption of these materials was not very noticeable in display windows and

[30] U.S. Congress, Joint Committee on Defense Production, *Hearing, Defense Production Act Progress Report No. 21*, 82nd Congress, 2nd session, 1952, p. 13.
[31] Office of Defense Mobilization, *Press Release No. 54*, August 17, 1951.

on department-store counters. As Defense Mobilizer Wilson put it, it was "still a pretty fat, luscious economy for the civilians."[32]

Mobilization policy reflected the peculiar nature of the project on which the mobilizers were engaged. Since they were not mobilizing for short-term war but for long-term peacetime security, it was necessary that a "healthy economy" be preserved. In practical terms, this meant that individuals and groups could not be made to sacrifice beyond the level of political feasibility, and this level was determined in turn by the level of perceived threat to the security of the nation, which was only moderate. It was a multi-value mobilization, in which the most difficult problems were political, rather than technical or economic. One aspect was that the mobilizers could not, as in full-scale war, make their allocation decisions entirely according to comparative contributions to the national security. One of the most important values which had to be protected was "equity." It would not do to make Peter suffer more than Paul just because Paul's product was more essential. As DPA Administrator Manly Fleischman said: "The man who is unemployed in a jewelry factory is just as unfortunate in his situation as the man who is unemployed in Detroit in the automobile industry."[33] With automobile companies getting enough materials to produce 930,000 cars in the first quarter of 1952, it would not be fair, Fleischman declared, to inflict severe deprivations even on the "least essential" industries.

A procedural factor was important in the decisions to release materials from the stockpile, and possibly also in the diversions. Allocations were issued by three-month periods and necessarily had to be based on advance estimates of available supplies. If anything occurred during the period to throw off the supply estimate in considerable degree, planned allocations would not jibe with available supplies and production schedules would in turn

[32] U.S. Congress, House, Subcommittee of the Committee on Appropriations, Hearing, Department of Defense Appropriations for 1952, 82nd Congress, 1st session, 1951, p. 244.

[33] U.S. Congress, Joint Committee on Defense Production, Hearing, Defense Production Act Progress Report No. 16, 82nd Congress, 2nd session, 1952, p. 844.

be thrown out of kilter. This was especially true after the inauguration in the latter months of 1951 of the "controlled materials plan," under which almost the entire production economy was brought under control through precise allocations of steel, aluminum, and copper to each user. When the copper strikes and the abrogation of the trade agreement by Chile occurred in the spring of 1952, the DPA was forced to go into the stockpile in order to make good on the CMP allotment tickets it had already issued. Fleischman said that such occurrences were "acts of God, in the sense that no one can foresee them in planning this arrangement."[34]

The mobilizers did not include the building of a stockpile among the major objectives of their program. Although they made occasional reference to it in their public statements, it was certainly not emphasized, at least not until the latter part of 1952, when the materials pinch had eased and military production and expansion programs were well under way. Until then their focus was on production: production of the scheduled requirements of military end-items and expansion of capacity to produce basic materials, supplies, components, and weapons, along with the negative objective of preventing dislocations in the civilian economy.

In explanation, it should be noted first that stockpiling was not part of the explicit legal responsibility of the mobilization agencies, even though they did substantially control the program through their allocating authority. As Fleischman said: "We consider our mandate from Congress to be to operate, first, the military programs at their screened requirements, and secondly, accomplish an industrial expansion program."[35] Stockpiling, although run by a military agency, did not fit clearly into the category of military requirements, which the mobilizers had vowed to fill before looking to other needs. The stockpile was to provide for civilian as well as military needs in all-out war. Moreover, stockpiling was not production, and as the mobilizers conceived

[34] *Ibid.*, p. 827.
[35] *Ibid.*

it, their job, above all else, was production: planning and scheduling current production and expansion of future production. To
a degree, the mobilizers looked upon the stockpile as a reserve to
be drawn on to advance other security programs, not as a security program in its own right.

Another contributing factor may have been that the mobilizers
tended to concentrate on the short-term aspects of their job, that
is, the military buildup and the installation of new producing facilities. By identifying "urgency" with "immediacy," they might
have tended to slight such essentially long-term programs as
stockpiling.

Pressure from Congress was also important. Congressional sentiment for easing consumer and business inconveniences was related to the decline of the sense of urgency during 1951 as the
limited nature of the Korean War was recognized. Ironically, the
military program, which had been kicked off at the height of the
war scare in the fall of 1950, did not begin to cut deeply into civilian supplies until the public's sense of urgency had worn off.
There is no "lead time" in public opinion. The public's willing-
ness to sacrifice decreased while the military share of resources
increased, thus squeezing the available supplies from both sides.

The main sources of congressional pressure were the Small
Business Committees and senators and congressmen from predominantly industrial areas. Senator Ferguson of Michigan, for
example, was very much concerned about unemployment in the
automobile industry which he believed was the result of copper
shortages. Senator Sparkman of Alabama demanded that the
stockpiling of aluminum be reduced to help small fabricators.[36]
Senator Benton of Connecticut urged that the copper stockpile
be tapped to alleviate unemployment in Connecticut brass
mills.[37] The Small Business Committees, supported by the Inter-
state and Foreign Commerce Committees, spoke up for the "least

[36] *The New York Times,* June 21, 1951, p. 1.

[37] Letter, Senator Benton to Henry Fowler, Director of Defense Mobilization, May 14, 1952. Printed in U.S. Congress, Senate, Committee on Banking and Currency, *Hearing, Nomination of Henry H. Fowler,* 82nd Congress,
2nd session, 1952, p. 24.

essential" users, principally small firms who flooded their congressmen with letters protesting their relatively low allotments. The Committees repeatedly urged diversions and withdrawals from the stockpile to bring relief.

The Armed Services Committees, especially the Senate Preparedness Subcommittee, as has been mentioned, urged more aggressive stockpiling in the early stages of the Korean War, but did not have much to say about it in the latter part of 1951 and early 1952 when scarcities were at their worst. The Interior and Insular Affairs Committees, heavily loaded with mining-state congressmen, were, as usual, interested in a maximum of purchasing from domestic sources, but their attention had shifted largely to the purchase and expansion programs under the Defense Production Act as better vehicles for realizing their objectives. All in all, stockpiling—at least stockpiling of scarce materials—had a minimum of support in Congress during the shortage period of the mobilization.

Materials started becoming more plentiful in the second quarter of 1952, partly as a result of the expansion programs, and stockpile acquisitions picked up accordingly. The trend continued in the ensuing six months as materials production increased, military and industrial demands leveled off, and prices of many commodities fell. Withdrawals and diversions continued but at a greatly reduced rate. Although aluminum, copper, and nickel were still not available for stockpile purchase, the Munitions Board noted a "marked improvement" in the general supply picture, which allowed some progress in improving the balance in the stockpile inventory.

The Board reported that by December 31, 1952, the inventory of 38 of the 76 materials on the stockpile list had reached 60 per cent or more of their ultimate objective, and for 18 items the goals were completed. Twenty-four of the materials for which the goals had not been reached were nonetheless on hand in such quantities that, given strict wartime economic controls, the war mobilization needs could be met "without serious danger to national security." Acquisition of these items, the Board said, was no longer of the highest urgency. Their acquisition would proceed at a gradually declining rate so as to withdraw gradually, rather than suddenly, from the market. On the other hand, the targets for half of the materials were still less than 60 per cent fulfilled.[38]

Controls and allocations were gradually relaxed and removed during the latter part of 1952 and during 1953. In 1953 the controlled-materials plan was first open-ended, that is, relaxed to allow free market distribution of some of the materials supply, and then replaced by a simpler system—the Defense Materials System. This system allocated steel, copper, and aluminum only to military, atomic-energy, and stockpile programs. Special controls continued in effect for some other scarce materials, but by October 1, 1953, most of these had been eliminated.[39]

Expansion of Production

Prior to the Korean War, the Munitions Board had resisted pressures to use stockpile money for the primary purpose of stimulating expansion of production by creating a market, by making advances on contracts, or by other forms of aid or subsidy. It was willing to stimulate expansion of production via long-term contracts (up to five years) for materials the stockpile urgently needed. The purpose of these contracts, however, was not primarily expansion but acquisition of more materials for the stockpile. Moreover, the financing method was orthodox in the sense that no money was handed over until the material was delivered, and quantities and times of delivery were specified. The price paid was almost always the market price at the time of delivery.

When expansion of materials production became a primary goal of mobilization policy during the Korean War, the mobiliza-

[38] Munitions Board, *Stockpile Report to the Congress,* August 15, 1952, p. 3.
[39] Director of Defense Mobilization, *Defense Mobilization, Report to the President,* October 1, 1953, pp. 20-21.

tion agencies exerted pressure to make the stockpile funds do double duty—not only acquire materials but guarantee a market for the output of new and expanded facilities. To those who advocated it, this seemed a legitimate demand—the stockpile needed materials, and one purpose of the expansion program (though not the major purpose) was to make more materials available for the stockpile. Since the expansion programs were helping the stockpile program, it seemed only fair that the stockpilers should return the favor.

After the outbreak of the war, the NSRB urged the Munitions Board to place more emphasis on expanding domestic production. In particular, the NSRB wanted stockpile funds used to aid the reactivation of government-owned standby aluminum, nickel, magnesium, and synthetic rubber plants. The Munitions Board did give in somewhat to this demand: by mid-1951 some $26 million in stockpile funds had been made available to rehabilitate and modernize such plants.[40] Most of this amount went into a nickel plant in Cuba and several magnesium plants in the United States. The reactivation of these plants resulted in some deliveries to the stockpile.

The case of aluminum was different in that it was proposed to use stockpile funds, not for the direct expense of reactivation, but to guarantee a market for the production, after the plants were leased or sold to private operators. The "Big Three" aluminum producers—the Aluminum Company of America, the Kaiser Aluminum and Chemical Corporation, and the Reynolds Metals Company—were to participate. The stockpile needed aluminum, but the contracts which were negotiated (chiefly by the NSRB and the GSA) contained a number of features previously frowned upon by the Munitions Board. In the first place, they were "contingent" contracts: the stockpile was to take whatever production could not be sold commercially, which meant, of course, that the future intake for the stockpile was dependent on business condi-

[40] Munitions Board, *Stockpile Report to the Congress*, August 15, 1952, p. 9.

tions. This feature was tempered by another clause, which gave the stockpile the right to "take" a certain minimum amount regardless of industrial demand. At least one of the contracts called for premium prices to offset high power costs. Another required a change in stockpile specifications to allow acceptance of aluminum sheets as well as ingots.[41]

The Munitions Board looked askance at such unorthodoxies, but finally agreed, after being subjected to strong pressure from the top, bottom, and side of the stockpiling hierarchy. The leading promoter of the deal was Stuart Symington, Chairman of the NSRB, supported by his staff. According to some observers, the main reason for Symington's enthusiasm was that, when Secretary of the Air Force, he had developed a special feeling for aluminum which he carried with him to the NSRB. It might have seemed to him that a larger aluminum stockpile and a larger producing industry would increase the economic base for aircraft production. The Senate Preparedness Subcommittee, under Lyndon Johnson, strongly supported Symington.

Although the Emergency Procurement Service tended to agree with the Munitions Board that stockpile funds should not be committed under indefinite contracts and should not be used primarily to promote expansion, its parent agency, the GSA, had custody of the aluminum plants and thus was responsible for getting rid of them and getting them back into operation. Jess Larson, GSA Administrator, also was a close friend of Symington. So Larson combined with Symington and Johnson, and the three of them were able to exert the required amount of persuasion.[42] Almost coincident with the negotiation of these contracts, the Munitions Board also raised the stockpile objective for aluminum. This action also had been urged by Symington.

The Munitions Board successfully resisted pressure from the NSRB and Congress to stockpile synthetic rubber as a stimulus

[41] Interview with Nathan Reingold, Historian of the Emergency Procurement Service, GSA, August 18, 1955.
[42] Ibid.

to the expansion of synthetic production. The Board felt that stockpile funds should be used only for natural rubber, since this was the type of rubber for which the United States was totally dependent upon distant imports. The synthetic rubber plants were reactivated without stockpile assistance.

The Defense Production Act of 1950, as amended in the following year, provided vast new authority to encourage expansion of both foreign and domestic production capacity and supplies. The government could make loans for this purpose, specifically including the "exploration, development and mining of strategic and critical metals and minerals." Agencies designated by the President could guarantee private loans. Most importantly, the Act conferred almost unlimited powers to purchase, store, and sell raw materials. Specific authority was given to make advance payments and to pay premium prices and subsidies. Loans and purchases under the Act were to be financed by borrowing from the Treasury. There were no restrictions on the disposal of the materials purchased.

The new legislation did not affect directly the stockpile operations by the Munitions Board and the GSA. These continued to be governed by the Stockpiling Act of 1946. The Defense Production Act actually set up a second stockpile program, although it was not called by that name. Even though this second program did involve the purchase and storage of materials, it differed sharply from the original, strategic stockpile program with respect to the *purpose* of these operations. Whereas the purpose of the Stockpiling Act was simply to acquire a hoard of materials for use in wartime, the aim under the Defense Production Act was to provide a guaranteed market for the additional materials to be produced under government-sponsored expansion programs. It was just one of many implements in the kit of tools which the government had acquired under the Defense Production Act to stimulate the production of scarce materials. Expansion was the aim; government purchase of materials was instrumental. It was expected that most of the materials acquired would be sold either to private industry or to the Munitions Board's stockpile. The expansion programs and the strategic stockpile program served the same ultimate end—national security—by expanding the nation's wartime mobilization base. The expansion program served the additional value of economic welfare, however, since more supplies would ease the consumer and business sacrifices implicit in projections of greatly increased defense budgets.

Obviously, the two programs were highly complementary, even though their immediate objectives differed. Expansion projects, when completed, would increase materials available for the stockpile; and materials held in Defense Production Act stocks, even if not transferred to the permanent or strategic stockpile, provided just as much "materials security" as did materials in the latter. At the same time, strategic-stockpile purchase contracts were an important stimulant to production expansion. As production capacity grew—especially domestic production—stockpile objectives could be lowered.

Two programs so obviously related seemed logically to call for a considerable degree of administrative integration. Some degree of coordination was achieved at the operational level. The General Services Administration, the stockpile purchasing agency, was also given the job of buying materials to support expansion programs under the Defense Production Act. The latter operation involved much more flexible ground rules than stockpile purchasing—specifically the use of such incentives as advance payments, guaranteed floor prices, fixed premium prices, and outright subsidies. Jess Larson initially encountered some difficulty in coordinating with the Interior Department, which administered a "grub-stake" subsidy program to encourage domestic minerals prospecting and also participated in the negotiation of DPA purchase contracts for domestic minerals. There was also a problem in coordinating with the ECA, which purchased foreign materials with counterpart funds, both for the permanent stockpile and in support of DPA-authorized production expansion programs overseas. These difficulties were corrected in August 1951, when the Defense Materials Procurement Agency was created to handle all buying for the DPA account, both foreign and domestic, and to act as custodian of the stockpile thus acquired. Since Larson was appointed to head the new agency, while retaining his post at GSA, he was in a good position to coordinate buying for the stockpile and for the DPA account, so far as was possible, considering the continued separation of policy making for the stockpile and the DPA expansion programs at the higher levels.

At the policy level, however, relations between the Munitions Board and the Defense Production Administration continued to be characterized by tension and disagreement about the proper use of stockpile funds. Bending under pressure from the mobilizers, the Board did allow the commitment of some stockpile appropriations for Defense Production Act expansion contracts. However, in the majority of such cases, stockpile funds were limited to those portions of the contracts which were certain, that is, not contingent on future market conditions, and which did not involve subsidies. For example, the subsidy aspects of the aluminum contracts were transferred to the DPA account. In purchases of several grades of materials, stockpile funds were committed only for that portion which met stockpile specifications.

Still, the pattern was not entirely uniform. Some stockpile funds, though a small amount, were paid out for premium-price purchases. Some stockpile contracts were made at fixed prices, or floor prices, and the market price at time of delivery was below the contract price. Premium prices as such did not constitute a radical departure from previous stockpiling policy, for premiums had always been paid to domestic producers who qualified under the Buy-American Act, and long-term contracts, even before the Korean War, had sometimes carried floor-price clauses. What was new was the increased proportion of long-term contracts and the size of the premiums. Prior to the Korean War, Buy-American premiums had been limited to 25 per cent over the lowest foreign bid. On August 10, 1950, John R. Steelman, Assistant to the President, presumably speaking for the President, authorized the Munitions Board to pay premiums above this ceiling when justified by "urgent national security need."

In short, the Munitions Board did make concessions, but by and large it was able to do so in a manner which minimized the compromise of its principles. High premium prices could be viewed as an application of the Buy-American rule. The stockpile funds which were used for reactivation of standby plants were placed in a separate account, thus keeping the regular stockpile account free from taint. Making contracts, including contingent contracts, in support of expansion programs was justified by calling them temporary loans of funds. The aluminum contracts had some dubious features, but they did include definite "take" rights for the stockpile, and the subsidy aspects eventually were transferred to the DPA account.

Whatever movement there had been toward stockpile support of expansion programs was stopped and reversed by the Bureau of the Budget in mid-1952. Several long-term stockpile contracts were switched to the DPA account. Most of the transferred contracts were rather shaky or carried contingent or subsidy features. The stockpile account kept the sound, orthodox contracts. Many delinquent stockpile contracts, which had been let during the exuberant period early in 1951, were canceled. The Bureau of the Budget established the policy that stockpile funds were no longer to be used to make long-term contracts for materials covered by a DPA expansion program.[43] Such contracts were to be covered exclusively by DPA financing. Henceforth, the bulk of stockpile contracting was to be short term—for delivery in 12 to 18 months.

One concern of the mobilization agencies was to make sure that stockpile objectives were high enough to include all the materials they might have to buy under their own contracts. When, for example, the DPA approved a chrome expansion program, it recommended to the Munitions Board that it increase its stock-

[43] Munitions Board, *Stockpile Report to the Congress*, August 15, 1953, p. 3.

pile objective.[44] In October 1952 the ODM stated that "stockpile objectives shall provide a firm basis for commitments to expand supply."[45]

Thus, not only did the mobilizers attempt to use the *means* of stockpiling in support of their own ends, they also attempted to influence the *ends* of the stockpiling program. But it was not simply, as might be inferred from the discussion so far, that they were trying to use another agency's authority to advance their own program. They did take an interest in the stockpile program on its own merits, even though they gave it a lower priority than the Munitions Board thought proper. The stockpile was clearly a part of the mobilization base for all-out war which the mobilizers were seeking to establish. It was separate only in an administrative sense; logically, stockpile planning and programing could not be carried on rationally as a separate program. Stockpile goals had to reflect expansion goals, and the means available to both programs inevitably contributed simultaneously to both sets of goals. Expansion programs had to take into account the size of the stockpile on hand, projected future stockpile requirements, and the foreseeable capacity of the market to satisfy those requirements. In view of this situation and of the overriding powers which had been granted to the ODM, it is not surprising that the mobilization agencies tended to take over stockpile policy making.

The Munitions Board made no comparable attempt to influence the expansion program. In the first place, it had no legal authority for doing so. Second, it did not feel that expansion of production per se was a proper subject for military concern. According to Chairman Small: "It is not a military decision as to whether they expand a great many of these things . . . It is a civilian job—not a military job. . . . And I, for one, do not want

[44] U.S. Congress, House, Subcommittee of the Committee on Interior and Insular Affairs, *Hearing, The Defense Minerals Production Program,* 82nd Congress, 1st session, 1951, p. 233.
[45] Office of Defense Mobilization, *Defense Mobilization Order No. 22, Program to Minimize Prospective Full Mobilization Deficiencies of Strategic and Critical Band I. Materials,* October 17, 1952, p. 1.

the military running our country."[46] Small went on to say, however, that there were gradations of military interest and proper military participation in expansion programs. It depended upon the degree of the shortage. Where there was enough of a material to take care of military needs and the expansion program was directed entirely toward providing increased supplies for the civilian economy, the military had no interest and would not participate in the decision. On the other hand, if supplies of a material were not sufficient to fill even military requirements, then "we could get up on our hind legs and holler," Small declared. Or if the material or product in question was "strictly military," then a "direct recommendation" (as opposed to "advice") would be made.

Small indicated that the civilian agencies were anxious to get the stamp of Munitions Board approval on all expansion programs, even those directed primarily to the filling of civilian requirements. "The civilian agencies would like to have the military sponsor everything," he declared. "That is a normal human thing."[47]

In formulating its stockpile policy, the Munitions Board did not take special account of materials which were expected to come into the DPA stockpile in the future. It was expected that much of this intake would be turned over to the permanent stockpile, but since the amounts were indefinite, the Board did not feel justified in basing its current plans on prospective future supplies from this source. The purchasers simply were told how much was needed according to the usual calculations; where they got the material was up to them.

The mobilization agencies had made contracts for expanding production to the tune of $6,500 million in gross transactions by March 31, 1953. However, only $600 million of this sum was considered as "probable ultimate net cost" to the government, since

[46] U.S. Congress, House, Subcommittee of the Committee on Appropriations, *Hearing, Department of Defense Appropriations for 1952*, 82nd Congress, 1st session, 1951 p. 221.
[47] *Ibid.*, pp. 220-221.

loans were expected to be repaid and the materials purchased were to be resold. New capacity for the production of end-products, components, electric power, and other essentials was included in this figure, but the great bulk of the commitment was for materials. Aluminum accounted for almost $1 billion; and copper, rubber, and nickel another $2 billion. In all, production of 27 of the 75 materials on the stockpile list was being boosted by DPA contracts. By 1955 domestic copper production was expected to increase by 10 per cent over 1951; zinc, 18 per cent; cobalt, 50 per cent; fluorspar, 30 per cent; and nickel, 30 per cent. Aluminum output was to be expanded to more than double 1950 production. The Munitions Board reported that these expansion programs had begun to make a "major contribution" to the acceleration of stockpile accumulation in the first half of 1953.[48]

Under the DPA expansion programs, the materials delivered were either sold to the permanent stockpile or to private buyers, or held in a separate, temporary inventory by authority of the Defense Production Act. Distribution in most cases was governed by DPA-NPA allocations. Sales were made at the prevailing market or ceiling prices.

During 1951 and 1952, materials moved in and out of the DPA stocks rather quickly. By 1953, however, the completion of many expansion projects, combined with reduced demand, increased the flow of materials into government hands and in effect created a second stockpile of rather substantial size.

The expansion programs included foreign as well as domestic transactions, but the emphasis was definitely domestic. Domestic producers also were given the best price terms, as indicated by the fact that domestic manganese was purchased for $2.30 a ton in early 1953, when equivalent foreign materials could have been bought for $1.15 a ton.[49] Similarly large domestic premiums were being paid for tungsten, chrome, and other materials.

[48] Munitions Board, *Stockpile Report to the Congress*, August 15, 1953, pp. 8-9.
[49] Senate Committee on Interior and Insular Affairs, *Stockpile Hearing*, 1953 and 1954, Part 1, p. 63.

By 1953 there was evidence that some of the expansion programs had been carried too far. Expansion goals had been exceeded for some materials. Some prices, notably for lead and zinc, were falling, and materials were pouring into the GSA and the DMPA under the purchase programs and contingent contracts.[50] Congressional sentiment was strong for continuing the DPA purchase programs beyond established expiration dates in order to keep new and expanded facilities in operation. Such pressure resulted in passage of the Defense Minerals Program Extension Act of 1953, extending for another two years all domestic purchase programs for the DPA account.[51]

International Materials Conference

The International Materials Conference was an organization which allocated several scarce materials among countries of the free world during the peak months of the Korean War mobilization. The buying scramble and price inflation of late 1950 turned many minds on both sides of the Atlantic in the direction of some form of international allocation. A primary motive of the European advocates undoubtedly was to place restraints on the enormous buying power of the United States. The Europeans tended to believe that the principal cause of the price boom was United States "hogging" of materials and, more particularly, unrestrained buying for the stockpile.[52] The charge against the stockpile was mistaken or at least grossly exaggerated. The inflation was primarily the result of frantic speculative buying and inventory accumulation by private importers and manufacturers. Stockpile purchases increased only 7 per cent during the last half of 1950 and accounted for only 17 per cent of the total United States

---

[50] Office of Defense Mobilization, *Seventh Quarterly Report,* October 1, 1952, p. 3.

[51] Public Law 206, 83rd Congress.

[52] *The Economist,* a responsible British publication, declared in August, 1951, pp. 439 ff. (referring specifically to United States stockpiling), that ". . . it should clearly not be left to the wisdom of one government to take decisions of world-wide effect . . ."

purchase of strategic materials. Materials inventories in United States manufacturers' hands increased three times as much as did the stockpile holdings during this period, when most of the price increases occurred.[53] Nevertheless, probably because of considerable publicity given to it at the time, the stockpile was considered by the Europeans to be the main culprit. The IMC was established partly to appease their complaints, although other, more generally shared motives of equity and control also contributed.

The IMC consisted of seven Commodity Committees and a Central Group. Twenty-eight nations and two international organizations—the Organization for European Economic Cooperation and the Organization of American States—representing between 80 and 90 per cent of the production and consumption of the materials allocated, participated in the Commodity Committees. The Central Group, consisting of the United States, the United Kingdom, France, Australia, Brazil, Canada, India, and Italy, and OEEC and OAS, provided the secretariat and coordinated the work of the Committees.

The materials under study by the seven Commodity Committees were copper, zinc, and lead; manganese, nickel, and cobalt; tungsten and molybdenum; wool; cotton and cotton linters; pulp and paper; and sulphur. Of these 14, only the first 9 were being stockpiled by the United States.

United States representation on each of the Commodity Committees was provided by the Defense Production Administration. Each representative was advised by an interagency committee, which included the Munitions Board as the claimant for stockpiling needs.

The IMC began recommending allocations of tungsten, molybdenum, and sulphur in the third quarter of 1951; and copper, zinc, nickel, and cobalt in the fourth quarter. The remaining commodities were found not to require international allocation, but were kept under review by their respective committees.

[53] President's Materials Policy Commission, *Resources for Freedom*, Vol. V, June 1952, p. 148.

The committees recognized three categories of needs: current defense, stockpiling, and essential civilian consumption. The defense requirements of all participating countries were met in full when possible. Further allotments were made for strategic stockpiling "when feasible," and the material remaining was allocated for essential civilian consumption on the basis of each country's record of past consumption.[54]

The above statement indicates that stockpile needs were given preference over all essential civilian consumption. This was not the case; some civilian consumption took precedence over any stockpiling. In fact, the United States representatives had difficulty persuading other countries that stockpiling should be included at all. Supported and prodded by the Munitions Board, the DPA was able to get recognition of stockpiling "in principle" as a legitimate requirement. The allocations of copper, zinc, and cobalt in the fourth quarter of 1951 included a small "special allowance" for stockpiling, but those for tungsten, molybdenum, and nickel provided nothing for stockpiling. No amounts of any material under IMC control were allotted for stockpiling in the first and second quarters of 1952. Stockpile allowances were gradually resumed when the shortages began to ease after mid-1952.[55]

Within the United States government, interagency discussions took place in two stages: *before* the IMC negotiations commenced, when the problem was to determine the acceptable range of the United States allotment, for bargaining purposes; and *after* the IMC committee had recommended an allotment, when the issue was whether the United States should accept the allotment.

These discussions generally were amicable and free from serious controversy. However, the Munitions Board did keep pressing for higher stockpile allowances in the first stage and usually had to be satisfied with smaller ones than it desired. The Board made at least three appeals to the ODM, protesting the stockpil-

[54] International Materials Conference, *Report on Operations,* 1951-1952, pp. 22-23.
[55] *Ibid.,* pp. 24-25.

ing allowance, but was overruled each time by ODM Director Wilson.[56]

The Munitions Board differed with the State Department on the principles and criteria which were to guide the allocation decisions. In the interagency discussions prior to the actual organization of the IMC, everyone agreed that defense needs of the participating countries would have to be satisfied first, but there was some question about how to divide the remaining amounts as between stockpiling and civilian consumption and how to determine which civilian requirements were "essential."

State Department thinking supported the principle of "equality of sacrifice" as a guide for allocating materials for nondefense needs. This principle seemed to mean that the United States would take a greater relative cutback in nonessentials than other countries because the United States started from a higher level of civilian consumption. One document stated:

The United States can better afford to eliminate certain civilian uses of raw materials than can most of our allies, because the United States has a higher standard of living, more adequate supplies of consumer goods, and a wider range of uses of raw materials in less essential fields. Nearly all of our allies have been experiencing severe shortages of convertible currencies ever since World War II, and have been operating their economies in many respects on a minimum requirements basis, especially where raw materials from hard-currency areas are concerned.[57]

The Munitions Board took issue with the concept of "equality of sacrifice." Commenting on the State Department memo just quoted, the Board declared that the United States should not accept proportionately greater sacrifices in civilian consumption than other countries. Since the United States was carrying most of the burden of the free world's arms buildup, it was important that its economy not be "disturbed too severely." Also, United

[56] Interview with Frederick Winant, U.S. Representative on IMC Central Group, July 1954.

[57] Unsigned State Department memo, quoted in U.S. Congress, Senate, Subcommittee of the Committee on Interior and Insular Affairs, *Stockpile Hearings,* 1953 and 1954, Part 4, p. 208.

States stockpiling should be given higher priority than allied civilian consumption or export production.[58]

According to the Department of State and the ODM, the Munitions Board did not press this point of view once the IMC got well under way. These agencies interpreted this early statement as simply a case of the Munitions Board having to "go on record" with its "agency views"; having done so, it proved to be generally cooperative. Still, the Munitions Board never was satisfied with the IMC stockpiling allotments and continued to press for larger ones. The prevailing view on the Board was that the organization did act as a limiting factor on stockpile acquisitions and on total supplies available to the United States.

The Board had support for this view in Congress. Representative Carl Durham of North Carolina charged that the IMC had "suspended the stockpile program without any authority whatever to do so."[59] Congressman Thomas Martin of Iowa stated that the organization "had subordinated American needs to the international picture."[60] Senator George W. Malone of Nevada devoted an entire hearing of his subcommittee of the Senate Interior and Insular Affairs Committee to an attempt to prove that the IMC was an attempt to get part of the proposed International Trade Organization "in the back door."[61] Senator Homer Ferguson of Michigan charged that the IMC was directly responsible for the shortage of copper which, he alleged, was causing unemployment in the Detroit automotive industry.

Felix Wormser, Assistant Secretary of the Interior, agreed that the IMC had caused a "serious shortage" of copper in the United States and stated further that no international group "should be armed with the power to tell the American people how much copper, lead, zinc or any other material they should use."[62]

The Department of State and the mobilization agencies vigor-

[58] *Ibid.*, pp. 219-220.
[59] *Congressional Record*, 82nd Congress, 2nd session, p. 7633.
[60] *Ibid.*, p. 7634.
[61] Senate Committee on Interior and Insular Affairs, *Stockpile Hearings,* 1953 and 1954, Part 4.
[62] *Ibid.*, Part 1, p. 25.

ously rebutted these views. The copper shortage of late 1951 and early 1952, they asserted, was a consequence simply of the huge demand for the material plus United States price ceilings, which discouraged importing at the higher world prices. During the peak period of shortage, the United States did not purchase its full IMC allotment of copper because of this price factor. Aside from the price limitation, the rebuttal continued, allocations to the United States rested, in the last analysis, on a prior decision by the DPA as to the amount this country could legitimately take, considering total defense requirements of the free world. The IMC only recommended, and its recommended allocation to the United States was always at least equal to minimum requirements, as presented by the DPA.

The charge that the IMC restricted stockpiling was met with similar arguments. Stockpile acquisition quotas were determined by the DPA; the IMC allotments for stockpiling merely put these prior DPA decisions in an international context. Thus the Munitions Board's criticism of the IMC was misdirected, according to this view.

These statements seem beyond dispute. Whatever influence the IMC exerted upon United States supplies and stockpiling would have to be attributed to more subtle factors. It is possible that experience in international negotiating may have made the DPA more conscious of, and responsive to, other countries' needs. Perhaps the other countries' antipathy to United States stockpiling reinforced the DPA's own tendency to place stockpiling rather low on its scale of priorities. When reductions were taken from the initial statements of the United States requirements, most of the cut was often charged against stockpile requirements.[63]

Some of the more general effects of the IMC allocations probably worked to the advantage of United States stockpiling. Ad-

[63] See testimony of Al Walsh, Director of Emergency Procurement Service, in Senate Committee on Interior and Insular Affairs, *Stockpile Hearings, 1953 and 1954*, Part 2, p. 74.

ministrative allocations reduced market competition and tended to hold prices down, thus increasing the yield of the stockpiling dollar. The mere fact of the existence of the IMC tended to dampen speculation in commodities. According to State Department sources, participation in the IMC negotiations helped to educate foreign countries as to the purposes and processes of United States stockpiling and thus to reduce foreign criticism of the program.[64]

The IMC allocations were gradually discontinued during 1953 as shortages eased. By the end of September the organization had ceased to exist, except that the Central Group remained formally on a standby basis.

Conclusion

The Korean War mobilization had two major effects on the stockpile program: one concerning administration, the other concerning policy. Administratively, policy control slipped out of military into civilian hands. The fact that this shift was unaccompanied by any change in the formal administrative structure for stockpiling created an anomalous situation, with a military agency bearing the formal and public responsibility for stockpiling progress, but with a set of civilian mobilization agencies having real policy control. In a way, this anomaly merely continued the trend begun before the war with the grant of increased discretion for the GSA's buyers and the gradual assumption of *de facto* policy control by the NSRB. The Korean War developments further eroded the Munitions Board's power from both the bottom and the top: the buyers got an even freer hand, and the new mobilization agencies took over policy control to a much greater degree than the NSRB had ever attempted.

The rate of acquisition—the real core of stockpile policy—was

[64] Where not otherwise stated material for this section was obtained from interviews with several officials in the Department of State and the Office of Defense Mobilization during the summer of 1954.

now entirely controlled by the mobilizers. The GSA made decisions on individual offers without reference to the Munitions Board and controlled the ratio between long- and short-term contracts. Under pressure from the mobilizers, the Board had been forced to compromise the long-standing principle that stockpile funds should not be used to support expansion of production and should be committed only for definitely scheduled deliveries. About all there was left for the Board to do was to establish objectives and quality specifications. But the mobilizers had potential authority even to set the objectives and, as with aluminum and chrome, did not hesitate to assert their influence. Partly as a result of allocation decisions of the mobilizers, the Board to some extent lowered its specifications in order to increase the supplies of material which could qualify for the stockpile.

The stockpile program was subject to two separate lines of authority. One line—the pre-Korea line—ran down from the President to the NSRB to the Munitions Board to the GSA. The other ran from the President to the ODM to the DPA to the DMPA. The lines were joined at the top by the President and at the bottom by Jess Larson, who took orders from two sets of masters. At the level of the "central staff agencies"—the Munitions Board and the DPA—where the important decisions were made, there was duplication of activity because the two agencies worked with roughly similar data. There was conflict because the two agencies tended to focus on different time periods—the DPA on the short term and the Munitions Board on the long term—and because they held different views concerning the proper role of stockpiling in the over-all mobilization function.

It is not surprising, therefore, that the top Munitions Board officials began to wish to get rid of their stockpiling responsibilities. There had always been some feeling in the Department of Defense that the stockpile program was a sort of unwanted stepchild, chiefly nonmilitary in nature and politically controversial to boot, and the recent developments made it seem even more so. Some members of the Munitions Board staff wished to hold

CONCLUSION

on to the program, however, in the belief that the civilian mobilization agencies eventually would fade out of the picture, thus
enabling the Board to reassert its control and to adjust stockpiling policy according to criteria of strict "national security rationality."

Chairman Small made the first move toward relinquishing the
program in the fall of 1951. He sent a memo to the Secretary of
Defense suggesting that the program be transferred to the DPA.
The Secretary agreed and so recommended to the President. The
move got as far as a draft reorganization plan, when someone
suggested that the plan be discussed privately in advance with
the Armed Services Committees of Congress. When the Committees were informed, they both indicated strong disapproval,
so the plan was dropped.[65] Undoubtedly, the reason the Committees balked was that a transfer to civilian control would have
also removed the stockpiling program from their jurisdiction.

In terms of policy, the stockpile was used increasingly during
the Korean War as a cushion to absorb frictions, mistaken estimates, and irreducible demands in other programs, which carried
not only more political support but more administrative rigidity.
On the one hand, the mobilizers viewed the stockpile, in part, as
a reservoir to absorb unsalable materials resulting from production expansion programs. On the other hand, they drew upon the
stockpile to meet shortages in other programs, including consumer-goods production. Part of the reason for these developments
was the nature of stockpiling itself: it was the most flexible element in the mobilization program. Other programs, civilian and
military alike, were so rigidly planned and controlled and so dependent upon interlocking production processes that they were
not nearly as susceptible to short-term manipulation as was the
stockpile. It was easy to use the stockpile to meet "acts of God,"
because all that had to be done was to move the stuff from warehouse to railroad car or change a few words in a contract. More-

[65] Interview with Department of Defense representative, former Munitions Board staff member, July 25, 1955.

over, with the stockpile it was possible to be selective. If copper was short, it was a much more precise and neat operation, and also much less disruptive to the economy generally, to take it out of the stockpile than to reduce, say, production of automobiles. The latter action would increase supplies of not only copper, but also steel, lead, chrome, rubber, and a host of other materials which might not need to be increased, not to speak of the increased complaints of the auto workers, auto manufacturers, and auto consumers which could be expected to reverberate loudly in the halls of Congress. In a sense, one might say that the stockpile was used as a sort of lubricant to ease the administrative and political frictions in the cumbrous mobilization machinery, or more precisely to fill the gap between the uncontrollable factors on the one hand and the planned programs on the other.

These two trends, toward civilian control and toward use of the stockpile program as a "buffer stock," continued in the next period of stockpiling history.

VI

The Eisenhower Stockpile Program

The Republican Administration which took office in 1953 initiated some fundamental changes in the stockpile program. As one of several steps to consolidate the organizational structure for mobilization, the program was transferred to a civilian agency. While the national security objective ostensibly was still paramount, other values and objectives, which formerly were only tangential, were now given more prominent consideration. After 1953 the stockpiling program became, in substantial degree, a program for economic stabilization—supporting materials prices on the one hand and relieving shortages on the other. As the organizational changes reduced the administrative frictions which formerly characterized the program, the policy changes tended to decrease the political frictions. The various groups, congressmen, and agencies with an interest in stockpiling, with the significant exception of the Department of Defense, all appeared to be more satisfied with the program's new orientation. However, as the following description and analysis attempt to show, the increased satisfaction of the particular interests was secured only at some cost to the over-all national interest, and the stockpile program grew increasingly out of harmony with both the Administration's military strategy and its fiscal policy.

Reorganization

Reorganization Plan No. 3, effective June 12, 1953, established a "new" Office of Defense Mobilization, which took over functions previously performed by the Defense Production Administration and the NSRB, both of which were abolished. It also received the stockpiling program from the Munitions Board. The Munitions Board was abolished by Reorganization Plan No. 6, effective June 29, 1953, and its duties were assigned to a new Assistant Secretary of Defense for Supply and Logistics.

In presenting Plan No. 3 to Congress, the President noted that stockpiling had been subject in considerable measure to the authority of the mobilization agencies and that transfer of the program to the ODM would thus "correct the present undesirable confusion of responsibilities," and integrate stockpiling with other mobilization planning and operations.[1] Arthur S. Flemming, formerly the ODM's Assistant Director for Manpower, became the new Director of the ODM. He was advised by an interdepartmental committee known as the Defense Mobilization Board.

Stockpiling procedures remained pretty much as they had been except that a different agency was giving the orders. The GSA continued to purchase the materials and manage the inventory. The Department of Defense became one of the advisory agencies, its function being primarily to present military requirements and, along with the other advisory agencies, to cooperate with the ODM in establishing stockpile goals.

The obvious virtues of the reorganization, aside from the simplification of administrative structure, were that decisions in stockpiling and in closely related programs were now to be made by the same people and that *de facto* and *de jure* authority over

---

[1] *Congressional Record,* 83rd Congress, 1st session, p. 2717.

stockpiling, previously separated, were joined. The reorganization stilled the criticisms of persons, inside and outside the military establishment, who had always felt that a military agency had no business running a program which provided for both military and civilian needs. It consolidated long-term planning with current operations.

The Long-Term Stockpile Program

One of the major problems facing the mobilizers of the new Administration was the plight of the domestic mining industry, which was suffering a bad hangover from the exhilaration of the Korean War. With the end of that war, some of the rosy glow disappeared from business expectations and activity, and military and industrial demand for raw materials declined. Most important of all, by 1953 some of the materials expansion programs inaugurated during the war began to produce substantial additional supplies. It soon became evident that some of these programs had been carried too far and that the market could not absorb all the output at prices anywhere near Korean War prices. Low-priced imports from foreign sources (whose production had also been stimulated by United States government "incentives") began taking a larger share of the market.

Zinc and lead producers were the most "distressed." Zinc prices dropped from 19½ cents a pound in May 1952 to 10 cents in October 1953. Lead declined from 19 to 13½ cents in the same period. Mines began to close down, causing unemployment. By 1954 domestic production of lead and zinc had declined to the lowest level in twenty years.[2]

One result of the price declines was a flood of zinc, lead, and other materials into government hands under contingent purchase contracts signed earlier, as market prices dropped below contract floor prices. The floor prices, in effect, became premium

[2] Office of Defense Mobilization, *Stockpile Report to the Congress*, January-June 1955, p. 6.

prices. On May 30, for example, lead was selling in the open market at about 13 cents a pound, while the government was taking it at 17 cents. When tungsten was selling privately at from $34 to $38 per 20-pound unit, the government had to pay $63.[3]

The problem was twofold: first, what to do with the surpluses being acquired by the government; second, what, if anything, to do for the domestic mining industry. Selling the government's stocks would only depress the prices further. An obvious solution was to put the stocks in the permanent stockpile, but the goals for lead and zinc were completed. As for the larger problem of the mining industry, the most obvious solution—higher tariffs—conflicted with the new Administration's firm policy of reducing tariffs as part of a drive for world-wide lowering of trade barriers.

Friends of the mining industry in Congress were highly vocal in demanding tariff rises and other aid, including continued government purchasing. They were successful in getting approval of a bill extending for two years the government's special purchase programs for tungsten, manganese, chromite, mica, asbestos, beryl, and columbium-tantalum. Another bill, which failed to pass, would have forced an increase in stockpile objectives for certain materials. The main drive was for higher tariffs, especially for a sliding-scale tariff, highly favored by the mining industry, under which tariff rates would automatically move up as prices moved down. Several delegations of congressmen descended on the White House demanding succor for the lead and zinc miners.

The mining industry also had its friends in the Executive Branch—notably Douglas McKay, Secretary of the Interior, and George M. Humphrey, Secretary of the Treasury. These men persuaded President Eisenhower to appoint Felix Wormser, president of the Lead Industries Association and vice president of the St. Joseph Lead Company, as Assistant Secretary of the Inte-

[3] *The Wall Street Journal*, September 25, 1954, p. 1.

rior in charge of all minerals programs. At the hearing prior to confirmation of his appointment, Wormser asserted that for reasons of national defense, "it is inescapable we must have a lead and zinc mining industry."[4] When he assumed office, Wormser told his Interior Department colleagues that he intended to press for a comprehensive "national minerals policy" which would assure national security in minerals and an economically healthy mining industry.[5]

Wormser's campaign showed its first results when President Eisenhower, on October 26, 1953, appointed a Cabinet Committee on Minerals Policy. Douglas McKay was made chairman. The other members were John F. Dulles, Secretary of State, Sinclair Weeks, Secretary of Commerce, and Arthur S. Flemming, Director of Defense Mobilization. Significantly, the Department of Defense was not represented. In appointing the Committee, the President referred to depressed conditions in the mining industry and specifically mentioned lead and zinc producers.

The President charged the Committee with the following tasks: (1) to make sure the United States had available mineral raw materials to meet any contingency during the "uncertain years" ahead; (2) to make sure the United States could meet the ever-growing minerals requirements of an expanding economy; and (3) to preserve the added economic strength represented by recent expansion of facilities by the domestic mining industry, through policies that would be consistent with other United States national and international policies.[6]

George M. Humphrey, Secretary of the Treasury and formerly president and chairman of the board of M. A. Hanna Company, a holding company for various mining enterprises, sat with the Committee as a consultant, as did Joseph M. Dodge, Director of the Bureau of the Budget. Wormser attended virtually all the

[6] President's Cabinet Committee on Minerals Policy, *Report*, November
[4] U.S. Congress, Senate, Committee on Interior and Insular Affairs, *Hearing, Nomination of Felix Edgar Wormser*, 83rd Congress, 1st session, p. 14.
[5] Interview with Interior Department official, August 17, 1955.
30, 1954.

meetings and played a very active role in preparing background studies and proposals. Mining-area congressmen were consulted freely.[7]

As between two obvious alternatives, higher tariffs or increased stockpiling, Wormser was inclined to prefer tariffs—both if possible. He recognized that more stockpile buying would raise prices but probably also would attract more imports. Humphrey also preferred tariff increases, but Dulles vigorously dissented on the ground that a tariff rise would impair relations with other minerals-producing countries, especially Canada and Mexico, the major foreign producers of lead and zinc. The dispute was taken to the President, who supported Dulles, indicating that he would reject an anticipated recommendation by the Tariff Commission for higher duties on lead and zinc.[8]

Consequently, the Committee's major recommendation, contained in a preliminary report to the President in March 1954, was to adopt a "new bold stockpile policy." Since the stockpile objectives had already been completed, or nearly so, for most of the distressed minerals, industry relief required raising the objectives. Hence the Committee recommended the establishment of "mineral stockpile objectives which would authorize acquisition of materials beyond levels indicated by existing minimum objectives."[9]

President Eisenhower responded immediately on March 26, 1954, by authorizing the Office of Defense Mobilization to establish new "long-term" procurement goals for metals and minerals. Nonmineral materials on the stockpile list were excluded. The

[7] Senate Committee on Interior and Insular Affairs, *Stockpile Hearings,* 1953 and 1954, Part 7, p. 752.

[8] U.S. Congress, Senate, Committee on Armed Services, National Stockpile and Naval Petroleum Reserves Subcommittee, *Hearings, Inquiry into the Strategic and Critical Material Stockpile of the United States,* 87th Congress, 2nd session, 1962, Part 4, pp. 1091-94, 1357. [This major source will be referred to hereafter as Symington Hearings.] Senator Stuart F. Symington of Missouri chaired this Subcommittee which explored the stockpile program in great detail during 1962 and 1963.

[9] The report is printed in full in Symington Hearings, Part 4, pp. 1080-1085.

White House announced that the new program would involve additional acquisitions, over and above the existing "minimum" goals, of from 35 to 40 metals and minerals. Purchases were to be spread out over a considerable period of time (thus the "long-term" designation) and were to be confined to "newly mined metals and minerals of domestic origin."[10]

For political reasons, the new objectives could not be "picked out of the air." Some rationale was needed which would plausibly relate them to national security requirements. Two rationalizations were found. One lay in "reducing the risk" by adopting more pessimistic assumptions regarding probable wartime imports. In calculating the new objectives, the White House announcement said, it would be assumed that no supplies would be available during war from any foreign countries except those "to which wartime access can be had with the same degree of reliance as afforded by sources within our own country."[11] A later Presidential directive to the ODM defined access to mean "no wartime reliance on sources of minerals located outside of the United States, Canada, Mexico, and comparably accessible near-by areas as defined by the National Security Council." Even within such areas, "specific supply discounts" might be applied. Supply estimates were to reflect "possible destruction of key metal and mineral producing facilities in the United States and in strategically accessible sources" as a result of Soviet bombing attack. Finally, the President directed that the objectives be set high enough to reduce the need for large ocean shipments in wartime of "large-bulk" items and to make it unnecessary in wartime to introduce "conservation measures that will jeopardize essential war-supporting industries."[12] Fulfillment of the higher stockpile goals based on these new assumptions, the President said, would "mean that the risk of strategic and critical metals

[10] The White House, *Press Release*, March 26, 1954. Printed in Symington Hearings, Part 4, pp. 1087-1088.
[11] *Ibid.*
[12] Memo, President Eisenhower to Arthur S. Flemming, April 14, 1954. Printed in Symington Hearings, pp. 1115-1116.

and minerals becoming a bottleneck will be virtually eliminated."[13]

The other alleged national security contribution was the preservation of a "healthy" mining industry as an element of the "mobilization base." Purchases toward the long-term objectives were to take place at "advantageous prices" and at times when they would "help to reactivate productive capacity and in other ways to alleviate distressed conditions in connection with domestic mineral industries that are an important element of the nation's mobilization base." In addition, metals and minerals in the stockpile were to be refined and upgraded to the point where they would be more readily usable for war production, and the same principle was to be applied; that is, the processing was to be done during slack periods in the processing plants.

Minerals and metals toward the long-term objectives were to be obtained not only through open-market purchase, but also by transfers of material acquired under the Defense Production Act purchase and expansion programs and from the barter of surplus agricultural commodities.[14] Thus the new program would provide a convenient final resting place for the embarrassing metals surpluses which were flowing into government hands as the result of overexuberant expansion during the Korean War and would also serve as an auxiliary instrument for disposing of the equally embarrassing agricultural surpluses.

The announcement was received joyfully by congressional partisans of the mining industry. Senator Malone of Nevada praised the Administration for "at long last recognizing the importance of developing a healthy mining industry." He said the new plan was a complete reversal of the "New Deal-Acheson-Truman stockpile policies," with their "dependence" on foreign sources.[15]

Clearly it *was* a major shift in policy. It was not simply an

[13] The White House, *Press Release*, April 26, 1954.
[14] *Ibid.*
[15] *American Metal Market*, March 30, 1954, p. 6.

increase in stockpile objectives but a change in the whole philosophy of the program. Henceforth stockpile purchases were to be directed consciously toward two objectives: acquiring a pile of materials for wartime safety, and promoting the well-being of the mining industry. The latter objective was couched in terms of national security: a prosperous mining industry was an "important element in the mobilization base." However, even if one grants the premise that an industrial mobilization base has much significance in the nuclear age, its utility in terms of increased production capacity would be diminished by the means used to create it—namely, more stockpiling. If the stockpile were to be large enough to provide "absolute" materials security (and even this is dubious policy, considering that no other security program attempts to provide this much insurance), the desirability or necessity of supporting in addition a level of domestic mining activity beyond that which would result from a normal play of economic forces could well be questioned. There is no reason to doubt President Eisenhower's sincerity in believing that a larger mobilization base in minerals was essential to national security. Probably he had not studied the problem thoroughly, and the concept harmonized with his general notion that a sound economy and a strong industrial base were important components of an adequate defense posture. But those who formulated the new policy certainly had other objectives in mind; they were interested in supporting the mining industry as an end in itself, even though they may also have sincerely believed that the pursuit of this end would concurrently promote the nation's security.

The restriction of the long-term program to minerals, thus excluding other strategic materials, and the policy of purchasing only when the mining industry was distressed, suggested that values other than national security were involved. Also, the two metals which were most in need of aid and for which the program was mainly designed—lead and zinc—were among the least likely commodities to be denied to the United States in time of war, since most of the imports come from Canada and Mexico.

Parenthetically, the "New Look" in stockpiling stood in odd contrast to the "New Look" in the remainder of the Eisenhower Administration's national defense program. An important aspect of the latter was a reduction in defense expenditures—more security for less money, as it were. But in stockpiling, more, not less, money was to be spent than had been contemplated by the previous Administration.[16] The contrast is the more startling when it is noted that George Humphrey is reported to have been a prime mover in both new looks.

Although the ODM did not produce new objectives for lead and zinc until the late summer of 1954, and for other minerals until early 1955, new procurement programs for lead and zinc were authorized on June 7, 1954—at which time the existing goals for these two metals were already overfulfilled to the tune of some $20 million. Apparently the reasoning was that since the objectives were to be increased soon, there would be no harm in starting the buying. There is no doubt that the ODM was under terrific pressure from the Interior Department and the lead and zinc mining industries to "do something quick" after the President indicated he would reject the Tariff Commission's recommendation in May for an increase in import duties. Consequently, the General Services Administration, acting under ODM directives, bought 27,000 tons of lead and 50,000 tons of zinc, at a total cost of $19,648,058, before the new objectives were established.[17]

In directing these purchases, Flemming relied heavily on the Department of the Interior (specifically Wormser) for guidance as to the appropriate level of the mobilization base and the approximate prices required to maintain production at this level. In fact, he formally delegated this function to Wormser. On May 17

[16] Inauguration of the long-term program brought an increase in estimated expenditures for fiscal 1955 by $315 million over those previously projected and $250 million over the previous year. As pointed out below, the long-term objectives were valued, on June 30, 1955, at $10.4 billion, compared with minimum objectives of $7 billion.

[17] Symington Hearings, Part 4, pp. 1246-1247.

Wormser recommended that domestic mine production of lead be maintained at a minimum annual rate of 350,000 tons, as compared to estimated 1954 production of 300,000 tons, and that zinc production be maintained at a minimum of 550,000 tons per year, 100,000 tons over the estimated 1954 output. The prices necessary to maintain these levels, according to Wormser, would be 14 cents a pound for lead and 13 cents for zinc (market prices at the time were 13 cents for lead and 10¼ cents for zinc). Inasmuch as the two metals are usually mined together, he suggested as a "rough policy guide" a combined price of from 27 to 28 cents a pound for the two metals. He went on to recommend for zinc a stockpile purchase program of 5,000 tons a month for one year in order to "cut down excess industry stocks." For lead he recommended stockpile buying at the rate of 3,500 tons a month for a year, as a starter. Additional purchases should be made "only after a program for acquisition has been recommended by this Department." Finally, he recommended that some action be taken to limit imports so that the higher prices generated by stockpiling would not stimulate imports to the point where they would defeat the purpose of the program.[18] Wormser made similar recommendations on amounts and prices on subsequent occasions, and almost always, with the exception of the recommendation to limit imports, his instructions were followed by the ODM. In effect, Interior controlled the buying program for lead and zinc.

In late August President Eisenhower officially rejected the Tariff Commission's recommendation for an increase in lead-zinc duties and, apparently to mollify the mining-state congressmen who had pushed for such increases, announced that he was directing the ODM to increase its purchases of lead and zinc. He also stated, in letters to the Senate Finance Committee and the House Ways and Means Committee, that he was directing the Secretary of State "to seek recognition by the foreign countries

[18] *Ibid.*, pp. 1135-1136.

which are the principal suppliers of lead and zinc that this in-ceased stockpile buying is designed to help domestic produc-tion and that they will not themselves seek to take any unfair ad-vantages of it." In addition, he was directing the Secretary of Agriculture to acquire foreign lead and zinc from the proceeds of sales abroad of surplus agricultural commodities and to place the metal in a "supplemental stockpile." This measure, like the diplomatic action by the Secretary of State, was designed to minimize the increased flow of imports to the United States commercial market which might be stimulated by the stockpile's price-support operations.[19]

Meanwhile, the ODM was seized with the task of calculating new long-term objectives to legitimize the lead-zinc purchasing already started and the anticipated further acquisition of other minerals. Very early in its studies, it made the rather embarrass-ing discovery that application of the new formula for figuring long-term objectives would raise the goals for lead and zinc very little—not even enough to cover the additional purchases already made. The reason should have been obvious from the start: Unit-ed States imports of lead and zinc came chiefly from Canada and Mexico, and the new formula assumed that supplies from these two countries would be available in wartime. In short, the Cabi-net Minerals Policy Committee had sold the President a formula which would permit increased stockpiling of many minerals, but precisely *not* those particular minerals whose producers and con-gressional partisans had been the principal sources of the politi-cal pressure behind the idea of increased stockpiling. The only conceivable explanations for this rather ridiculous outcome are sloppy staff work by the Cabinet Committee or, more subtly, a belief that once the President had been convinced of the need to step up the stockpiling of lead and zinc, he could later be in-duced to approve a further change in the formula in favor of these two metals.

This is exactly what happened.

[19] *Ibid.*, pp. 1097-1098.

On June 24 E. H. Weaver, Assistant Director for Materials for the ODM, told Director Flemming that it would be "very difficult, under present assumptions, to develop estimates of long-term objectives for these two materials that will be larger than present minimum objectives. . . ." He proposed the additional criterion that the stockpile should contain the equivalent of "at least one year's normal U.S. use of any strategic and critical metal and mineral." This formula was completely arbitrary, of course, having no relation whatsoever to any objective calculation of probable supplies versus probable requirements in wartime. However, as Weaver pointed out, it *would* permit the buying of 450,000 more tons of lead and 310,000 more tons of zinc, besides covering the surpluses already acquired.

In his memo Weaver pointedly indicated his personal opposition to such manipulation—in fact, to the whole concept of the long-term program, particularly as applied to lead and zinc. He said, among other things, that the program was no permanent solution to the lead-zinc industry's problems; that if it raised prices, it would only attract additional imports which would displace domestic production; that if it did help domestic producers, it would help only the big ones, not the little ones; that the use of stockpile funds to buy "low-priority" items like lead and zinc would leave less for higher-priority materials; and that it would "tend to reverse the generally expressed intent of the administration to refrain from direct interference in commodity markets, especially through actions of a price-support type."[20] These views were shared by most ODM staff members.

Flemming then went to the President, explained the situation to him both orally and in writing, and requested authorization of the "one year's normal use" criterion as a general "safety factor." He based his case entirely on national security grounds:

The adoption of this rule will, in certain few instances where present procedures would result in smaller objectives, provide sufficient material to meet any unforeseeable contingencies such as destruction

[20] *Ibid.*, pp. 1145-1147.

of major ports, destruction or disruption of internal U.S. transportation, loss of key facilities through atomic attack, or development of
new requirements by the Department of Defense or the Atomic
Energy Commission.[21]

President Eisenhower discussed the matter with other advisers,
including the Joint Chiefs of Staff. The discussions precipitated a
minor debate, with the Joint Chiefs on one side and the ODM
(Flemming) and presumably Interior on the other. The JCS,
especially the chairman, Admiral Arthur W. Radford, were unan-
imously and vigorously opposed to the idea. The JCS had always
been rather unenthusiastic about stockpiling, even when it had
been under Department of Defense jurisdiction. They were especially cool toward the long-term program, which they regarded
as essentially a "political" program masquerading as a national
security measure and competing for appropriations with much
higher priority military programs. The old minimum objectives
were acceptable since they were logically tied to more or less
realistic strategic assumptions provided by the Joint Chiefs themselves. The long-term objectives were not and consequently were
intended mainly as a price-support operation to line the pockets
of the mining companies. The Joint Chiefs consistently maintained this general attitude in subsequent disputes about stockpiling.

Despite the opposition of his military advisers, the President
decided in favor of Flemming and authorized the new guideline
on July 15. The ODM then established a long-term objective for
zinc of 1,100,000 tons, effective August 3, 1954, and a long-term
objective for lead of 1,130,000 tons, on September 8.

The "one year's normal use" criterion theoretically applied to
all metals and minerals in the stockpile, not just lead and zinc.
The rule was to use this criterion only when it would yield a
higher objective than did the discounting of overseas imports,
which was the criterion in the President's original directive. In
practice, the rule applied only to lead and zinc, and, to a minor

[21] *Ibid.*, Part 9, p. 3854.

degree, antimony, these being materials for which distant imports represented only a small part of normal United States supply. For all the other items, the assumption of no wartime imports from distant sources was expected to result in stockpile goals higher than one year's consumption. It is clear, therefore, that the "one year's use" criterion was specifically designed to rationalize an increase in the lead and zinc objectives. It is ironic and instructive to realize that the stockpile "calculus" was manipulated solely to create some justification for increased purchasing of the two materials which were lowest in priority on the stockpile list—lowest in the sense that virtually all of the supply comes from domestic sources and the adjacent and easily accessible countries of Canada and Mexico. Paradoxically, the low security priority and the relatively high political influence of lead and zinc producers stemmed from the same cause: a greater proportion of these materials is produced in the United States than of most other materials.

Another civilian-military dispute arose over the long-term objectives for metals and minerals other than lead and zinc. The President's original directive had postulated "no wartime reliance on sources of minerals located outside of the United States, Canada, Mexico, and comparably accessible nearby areas as defined by the National Security Council." Pending NSC action, the ODM went ahead and calculated tentative long-term objectives on the assumption that "comparably accessible nearby areas" meant Central America and the Carribean area. When the issue finally reached the NSC agenda in December, the Joint Chiefs challenged the ODM assumptions, contending that the ambiguous phrase should be interpreted to mean all of South America. In substance, the JCS argued that the United States in wartime could count on receiving its normal volume of supplies from the entire Western Hemisphere. An ODM analysis showed that for some items adoption of the JCS position would reduce substantially the objectives already calculated by the ODM. For example, the bauxite objective would go from 15.4 million tons to

6.5, copper from 3.5 to 1.7 million tons, and tungsten from 94 to 63.6 million pounds.

Flemming supported his staff's interpretation on the ground that it was more in harmony with the over-all objectives of the long-term program—namely, to create a safety factor by minimizing the risk of losing access to foreign supplies and to provide maximum scope for domestic purchasing to build up the domestic mobilization base. Again the President supported Flemming.[22]

The establishment of higher long-term objectives did not supersede the previous objectives, but rather superimposed a new and differently conceived stockpile program on the old one. Each mineral or metal now had two objectives: the old one (now called the minimum objective) and the higher, long-term objective. Materials other than minerals and metals had only the minimum objective since the long-term buying program did not apply to them. The reason for maintaining two sets of goals for minerals and metals, according to the ODM, was that the minimum objectives represented stockpile requirements considered "essential to materials security," which therefore should be completed as quickly as possible. Acquisition toward the long-term objectives (which of course did not start for any mineral until the minimum goal had been achieved) was supposed to be less urgent. Hence, following the President's directive, purchases beyond the minimums were to be made over a considerable period of time and only when necessary to relieve distress in the mining industry.

In establishing and reviewing the minimum objectives, the basic framework of the factoring system as established in 1950 was used. As before, responsibilities for generating military, political, and economic assumptions as inputs to the factoring system were dispersed among several agencies—the JCS, the Departments of State, Commerce, Agriculture, and the Interior—and the ODM, with the advice of interagency commodity committees, had the job of pulling all the inputs together and formally establishing the objectives.

[22] *Ibid.*, pp. 3830-3833.

Setting the long-term objectives involved simply a recalculation for each metal and mineral, applying the new assumptions contained in the President's directive, notably the assumption of no distant overseas imports, and the additional requirement for stocks of lead and zinc for "one year's normal use."

Writing off all but the neighboring sources of supply affected each mineral in different degree. Obviously, the effect was greatest for items normally imported in substantial amounts from countries previously considered accessible in war. In this group were, for example, beryl (Brazil, India), copper (Chile, Union of South Africa), cobalt (Southern Rhodesia, Belgian Congo), quartz crystals (Brazil), and tungsten (Korea, Australia, Bolivia, Peru). For some items, the long-term objectives were more than double the minimums. The effect was least for materials from areas which had already been judged inaccessible in war (tin from Southeast Asia) and for those produced largely in North America and the Caribbean area. Ironically, lead and zinc fell in the latter group.

The ODM reported a money figure representing the total anticipated value of the completed long-term stockpile on June 30, 1955—$10.4 billion for about 50 metals and minerals valued at then current market prices. The minimum objectives for all 76 materials totaled $7 billion. Of the $3.4 billion difference, $1 billion worth of materials had already been acquired for the long-term objectives (mostly by cash purchases but some by transfer from the DPA inventory), leaving $2.4 billlion worth yet to be acquired.[23]

The initial long-term objectives for lead and zinc provided some leeway for additional purchases of these metals but not much. As the buying proceeded in subsequent years, the amounts in the inventory or on order kept pressing against, and sometimes exceeded, the established goals. Consequently, Flemming was under continual pressure to raise the goals, pressure which he transmitted to his staff in the form of repeated orders and re-

[23] Office of Defense Mobilization, *Stockpile Report to the Congress*, January-June 1955, p. 1.

quests to find some plausible justification for raising the objectives without violating the Presidential guidelines. The story was told in detail and with some bitterness by William N. Lawrence, Deputy Director, Mobilization Base Analysis Branch, Office of Emergency Planning (successor agency to the ODM), during hearings held by Senator Stuart Symington's Subcommittee of the Senate Armed Services Committee in 1962.

The manipulation was accomplished mainly by changing the base year which was assumed to represent one year's normal use. The first long-term objective for zinc, 1,100,000 tons, was based on United States consumption during 1953. By November 1956 the stockpile had 1,003,500 tons on hand and on order. An additional 100,500 tons was in stock or on order in the DPA inventory and the "supplemental stockpile." (The latter two stockpiles, which were not officially counted as part of the national or strategic stockpile, are discussed below.)

According to Lawrence, the staff received an order from Flemming to change the base year "to find a basis for continuing the procurement of zinc." They selected 1955, the year of the largest consumption of zinc in United States history. Flemming formalized and justified this selection in a staff memo directing that henceforth they should use "the last complete calendar year." This would enable the ODM "to take cognizance of changes that take place in the rate of consumption."[24] The effect of the shift in base years was to raise the zinc objective to 1,250,000 tons.

By May 1957 the inventory of zinc was again pressing against the objective, so the objective was again reviewed. A few weeks earlier Gordon Gray had replaced Flemming as ODM Director, and Gray ruled that Flemming's earlier order be set aside and the old objective reaffirmed. According to Lawrence, this was done because the use of the "last complete calendar year" would have lowered the objective, the consumption of zinc having dropped in 1956.[25] The official reason for the change was that 1955 rep-

[24] Symington Hearings, Part 4, p. 1182.
[25] Ibid., p. 1185.

resented more accurately than 1956 a year of normal use.[26] The objective for zinc was pushed up another 6,000 tons in March 1958, upon receipt of figures from Interior purporting to show that consumption for 1955 had been miscalculated by that amount.[27] Actually, Gray took these actions very reluctantly, for he was personally opposed to any further buying of zinc. He was forced to capitulate to strong pressures from Interior.

Similar manipulation occurred with lead. Here the initial objective was set not by using a single base year for calculating one year's normal use but by taking an average of the consumption figures for 1950 through 1953, which yielded an objective of 1,126,000 tons. Had the year 1953 been selected, as for zinc, the objective would have been 11,000 tons lower. Again, the averaging method was used under directions from Flemming to find a basis for buying the maximum amount of lead.

The objective for lead was increased to 1,154,000 tons on November 8, 1956. This time the averaging method was dropped, and the last calendar year, that is, 1955, was adopted as the base year for zinc. Again, according to Lawrence, this was done because consumption of lead in 1955 was the highest ever, therefore resulting in the maximum possible stockpile objective. On May 3, 1957, the lead objective was reaffirmed at 1,154,000 tons, using 1955, not 1956, as the base year because lead production had declined in 1956.[28]

Flemming's staff repeatedly protested against these manipulations of lead-zinc objectives but were told by the Director that he had no choice since he was under orders from "higher authority" to buy as much lead and zinc as possible.[29]

From the start of the long-term lead-zinc buying program in 1954 until its termination in 1958 (when the objectives were filled) the stockpile acquired 293,665 tons of lead and 457,718

[26] Ibid., p. 1188.
[27] Ibid., p. 1189.
[28] Ibid., pp. 1212 ff.
[29] Ibid., p. 1220.

tons of zinc at a total cost of $204,040,395. It absorbed 42 per cent of domestic lead production and 45 per cent of domestic zinc production during the last seven months of 1954 and percentages ranging from 14 to 22 per cent in subsequent years. The program was successful in raising prices for a time. Prices began to move upward as soon as the buying program was announced and reached the combined price of 28 cents a pound in September 1955. Stockpile buying was not curtailed at this point, as might have been expected under Wormser's ground rules. The combined price reached 29.6 cents per pound in January 1956 and was supported at approximately this level until April 1957. Then, even though stockpile buying continued, prices began to fall until by June 1957 they were back to where they had been when the program started. The chief reason was that the artificially high prices stimulated by stockpile buying caused foreign imports to flood the market. Wormser and Budget Director Dodge had warned at the very beginning that this would happen, and consequently President Eisenhower, in lieu of tariff increases or import quotas, had instructed Secretary of State Dulles to persuade foreign producing countries to limit voluntarily their exports to the United States. Whatever efforts were made in this connection were futile; in effect, the United States found itself buying up world surpluses rather than building up a domestic mobilization base. Prices continued to fall, and by the end of the buying program in 1958 they had dropped well below the 1954 level.

In terms of reaching and maintaining the levels of production which Wormser had judged to be required for a mobilization base, the program was a failure. Domestic lead production barely reached the 350,000-ton target in 1956 and dropped sharply thereafter. Zinc production during the period never did reach the goal of 550,000 tons, and by 1958 both industries were operating at substantially below the levels antedating the government's purchase program.

There is no doubt, however, that lead and zinc producers did benefit from the higher prices and somewhat higher production during the period. The principal beneficiaries were a few large companies, notably Wormser's own company, the St. Joseph Lead Company, which received about $54 million of the business, and to which Wormser returned after his governmental service. It had been the fond hope of most of the congressional partisans of lead and zinc that the program would put in business and keep in business the hundreds of small mining companies which could operate only at premium prices. It may be that some of the benefits did "trickle down," as Secretary Wormser put it, to some of the smaller producers, but by the time the program stopped, in 1958, most of those who had started operating during the 1954-1957 boom were again out of business.[30]

Although the manipulation of stockpile goal calculations occurred most flagrantly for lead and zinc, it was done for some other materials as well. For example, application of the import discount in the President's long-term guidelines did not substantially increase the cadmium objective (since much of the supply is domestic). The stockpilers then introduced a new discount factor for concentration of production of this material in the United States. That is, they wrote off one year's production from one large smelter in Denver, ostensibly to hedge against destruction of this plant by sabotage, thereby raising the objective substantially. Later on, they discounted three other plants for concentration, further increasing the goal.[31]

Withdrawals and Diversions

The long-term stockpile program could be considered a device for stabilizing metals and minerals markets "on the low side"— that is, for encouraging and maintaining domestic production by

[30] U.S. Congress, Senate, Committee on Armed Services, National Stockpile and Naval Petroleum Reserves Subcommittee, "Inquiry into the Strategic and Critical Material Stockpiles of the United States," *Draft Report* (committee print) 88th Congress, 1st session, pp. 36-45. [Referred to hereafter as Symington Subcommittee, *Draft Report*.]

[31] Symington Hearings, Part 3, pp. 605-607.

extra stockpile purchasing designed to support prices. Other operations tended to stabilize markets "on the high side"—that is, to deflate rising prices and relieve shortages. The latter took the form of the sale to industry of materials in government inventories and the cancellation or deferral of scheduled stockpile deliveries. Both types of operation, however, were rationalized and publicly described as national defense measures. The first type was stimulated by pressures from producing industries and their governmental supporters; the second by pressures from consuming industries and their spokesmen in government.

Stabilization on the high side occurred during the Eisenhower Administration for copper, aluminum, and nickel—most prominently copper. When increased industrial activity and work stoppages in copper production caused a severe shortage in the last quarter of 1954, copper consumers demanded and got relief. Between October 16 and December 31, 1954, 19,007 tons of copper were sold from DPA stocks, delivery under stockpile contracts was postponed to make available 17,863 tons to industrial consumers, and DPA deliveries were deferred to provide 1,877 tons more. An additional 2,600 tons was diverted from stockpile delivery to Canadian industry. The practice continued during 1955 and the first half of 1956 and then stopped after copper prices had declined and shortages were relieved. All told, during this period, 41,874 tons of copper with a market value of $29,086,616 was diverted from stockpile delivery to industry, and more than 20,000 tons was sold from the DPA inventory.[32] Virtually no deliveries to the stockpile occurred during this period. This was at a time when the long-term stockpile objective for copper was 3.5 million tons, the minimum objective was 1.6 million tons, and the amount on hand in the strategic stockpile was 860,691 tons. In other words, the minimum objective was only slightly more than

[32] Office of Defense Mobilization, *Stockpile Report to the Congress,* January-June 1955, pp. 5-6; Symington Hearings, Part 2, pp. 503, 578, and facing p. 285.

half completed, and the long-term objective was only about one-fourth completed.[33]

In aluminum, faced with "expanded demand, fired by heightened economic activity and a desire to rebuild business inventories," the ODM decided to reduce scheduled acquisitions in 1955, even though the minimum objective was less than half completed. Stockpile procurement schedules were reduced by 175,000 tons during that year.[34]

Early in 1955 many users of nickel encountered "supply difficulties." At the urging of the Department of Commerce, the ODM made available more than 11 million pounds during that year by reducing deliveries under stockpile contracts.[35]

The Department of Commerce, as the recognized governmental spokesman for the materials-consuming industries, took the initiative in recommending all these actions. In almost every instance, the Commerce recommendation was followed, after discussion in the Defense Mobilization Board.

The domestic market price of copper rose from 30 cents a pound in October 1954 to a high of 45 cents in the fall of 1955. Contract prices for the shipments diverted from stockpile delivery ranged from 27 to 32 cents a pound. The diverted materials were of course sold at the market price, which meant that the suppliers gained substantial "windfall profits" over what they would have received from their stockpile contracts. The total amount of such profits, computed on an average-price basis for the period, came to $2,993,302,[36] an amount the government would have realized had it taken delivery of the materials and resold them to industrial consumers.

Of course, the ODM could not have taken delivery of copper destined for the strategic stockpile and then resold them; this

[33] Symington Hearings, Part 2, pp. 402, 403, 415.
[34] Office of Defense Mobilization, *Stockpile Report to the Congress,* January-June 1955, pp. 5-6.
[35] *Ibid.,* pp. 8-9.
[36] Symington Hearings, Part 2, table facing p. 285.

was forbidden by the restrictive disposal provisions of the Stock-piling Act. About 70 per cent of the materials diverted had been ordered under strategic-stockpile contracts. But there was no re-striction on disposal of DPA stocks. Flemming, Director of the ODM at the time, later was subjected to severe criticism by the Symington subcommittee for his failure to accept and then resell these deliveries for the government account, thus allowing the government rather than the copper suppliers to reap the profit. He was further criticized, with respect to the deferral of contract-ed deliveries to the strategic stockpile, for failing to negotiate deals with the suppliers which would have allowed the govern-ment to share in the windfall profits.

Flemming's specific actions with respect to copper between 1954 and 1956 were of four types: sale of materials already in the DPA inventory, outright cancellation of contracts for delivery to that inventory, deferral of deliveries to DPA stocks, and deferral of deliveries to the strategic stockpile. In all deferrals, contrac-tors were required to make good on their contracts at a specific later date, usually at the original contract price.

Flemming defended these actions in testimony before the Symington subcommittee in the spring of 1962. His defense re-volved around three issues: whether stockpiling should be used to manipulate commodity markets, what kinds of actions consti-tuted manipulation, and whether the government should attempt (or even allow itself) to make a profit.

Flemming said his actions were guided by three precepts: to make steady progress toward achievement of the stockpile goals, to "avoid weakening the economy," and to avoid using the stock-pile program to "manipulate metals and materials markets." He believed the diversion policies were made necessary by the sec-ond principle, yet did not constitute "market manipulation." He repeatedly insisted that his decisions had been based chiefly on national defense grounds, meaning apparently that the copper shortage was hindering the fulfillment of defense contracts.[37]

[37] *Ibid.*, pp. 391, 415, 421, 438, 442.

This particular rationale was pretty much deflated when it was brought out at the hearing that defense contractors had not been given any preference when the Secretary of Commerce allocated the diverted shipments to industrial users.[38]

Flemming declared that in fact it would have been illegal *not* to have diverted the strategic-stockpile deliveries because it was clear that the amounts to be delivered were not "in excess of current industrial demand." He correctly pointed out that it would have been unlawful to take the copper into the strategic stockpile and then sell it, because of the law's disposal restrictions. He also stated rather fervently that he favored retention of these restrictions to insure that "no one could play with the stockpile" to manipulate the market.[39] Yet the fact that Flemming was quite willing to sell the DPA inventory and cancel and defer contracts for essentially a market-stabilization purpose tends to indicate that his stated conviction on this point represented something less than an inviolable principle.

The outright cancellations of DPA contracts (which represented a rather small percentage of the total diversions) took place in the spring of 1955. When the General Accounting Office heard of this action, it protested to the ODM that since the market price was higher than the contract price, the suppliers would gain windfall profits amounting to about $400,000 which might otherwise be realized by the government.[40] Flemming then changed his mind and directed that further diversions should take the form of postponement of deliveries rather than cancellation. At the time, he justified the reversal on the GAO's grounds, saying he realized that the cancellation order had been a "mistake" because of "possible windfalls to the suppliers." However, at the Symington hearings he said the mistake consisted of giving up the government's claim to equivalent future deliveries to the stockpile.[41] Both reasons were apparently specious. The shift to

[38] *Ibid.*, p. 444.
[39] *Ibid.*, p. 389.
[40] *Ibid.*, p. 473.
[41] *Ibid.*, pp. 257, 393.

deferral did not eliminate the windfall profits to suppliers (which Flemming indicated did not concern him anyway) because the suppliers sold the material to industrial buyers immediately at high prices and delivered equivalent amounts to the stockpile later, when market prices were much lower, as could have been foreseen. Nor is it easy to imagine that Flemming had not realized earlier that the cancellations would eliminate the government's claim for eventual stockpile delivery. It seems rather clear that Flemming changed his mind simply because of the pressure exerted by the GAO, pressure made potent by the implicit threat of public disclosure.

As to why the ODM did not take delivery on the DPA contracts and then sell the material on the market for its own profit, Flemming explained that this would have meant "governmental trading" or market manipulation, which he felt the government should not do. The idea of market manipulation seemed to be tied, in Flemming's mind, to the immorality or unwisdom of the government's taking a profit on its operations. That is, it was not manipulation to postpone stockpile deliveries to relieve industrial shortages (and incidentally reduce prices), but it *was* manipulation for the government to buy and sell at a profit.

One company, the International Nickel Company, even offered to "buy out" its stockpile commitments in the spring of 1956 by paying the government the difference between the contract purchase price and the higher market price. Flemming refused, on the ground that this action would delay reaching the stockpile objective. His refusal cost the government about $2.1 million. Instead he insisted that the company postpone delivery to the stockpile and reap the profit in immediate sales to industry.[42]

In sum, Flemming chose deferral of deliveries rather than government acquisition and resale (or allowing suppliers to buy out their stockpile contracts) on the basis of two principles: the government should not deliberately attempt to profit by its stockpile operations, and deferrals would preserve the government's claim

[42] Symington Subcommittee, *Draft Report*, p. 51.

to eventual deliveries of the contract amounts to the stockpile. Both principles were an attempt to reconcile the real motive and effect of the actual decisions with the alleged national security purpose of stockpiling. All of Flemming's decisions were, despite his denials, directed toward manipulating the market by relieving shortages and incidentally (or consequently) reducing prices. But they had to be carried out and defended in such a way as to minimize overt conflict with the national security ideology. Postponing stockpile deliveries was at least not flagrantly inconsistent with this ideology, but making a profit certainly was. Flemming was in a difficult position. He was subject to strong pressures from both within and outside the government to help the copper-consuming industry; yet he was supposed to be running a national defense program. That he did capitulate to the pressures is a fact. That he was virtually forced to find a rationale for his behavior in the symbolism of national security is also a fact. Whether the decisions themselves were "improper" or "immoral" is a difficult question which the reader must answer for himself.

Incidentally, there is no evidence whatsoever of any collusion between Flemming, or any member of his staff, and the copper suppliers who benefited financially from the diversions program. The staff, as well as the purchasing agents in the GSA, were for the most part either opposed to or very lukewarm toward the actions that were taken—which perhaps only goes to show that the integrity of the politically insulated expert is much easier to come by than that of the politically responsible official.

DPA Stockpile and Domestic Purchase Programs

As described in the preceding chapter, the Defense Production Act of 1950 had provided for government purchase of minerals and metals in support of efforts to expand domestic production and enlarge the mobilization base. Large quantities of material flowed into government hands during the early Eisenhower years as a consequence of expansion contracts negotiated by the pre-

vious Administration, although some new contracts were also
made during the Eisenhower Administration. As it turned out,
the contracting agents had done their job rather too well: expansion was carried so far that in many cases the market could not
absorb the increased production, prices fell, and the producers
unloaded the material on the government under their contractual
right to "put" the material to the government if the price fell
below a certain level. The material thus accumulated was administratively held in a stockpile separate from the strategic stockpile although often materials for both stockpiles were stored at
the same locations, and the same agencies—the ODM and the
GSA—were responsible for both. Some material from the DPA
inventory was transferred to the account of the strategic stockpile when the latter's objectives could accommodate it.

In addition to specific expansion contracts with particular producers, another program known as the "domestic purchase program" was established pursuant to the Defense Production Act.
Under this program, the GSA simply announced that it stood
ready to buy from all comers certain amounts at specified prices
at certain locations. Large amounts of asbestos, beryl, chromite,
columbium, fluorspar, manganese, mercury, mica, and tungsten
were purchased between 1951 and 1962, often at prices several
times higher than the market price—the ostensible purpose being,
as usual, to expand the domestic mobilization base. As of December 31, 1962, the government had spent $435,620,876 on this pro-
gram, representing 12 per cent of all purchases under the Defense Production Act. Because of the premium prices paid, the
market value of this material was, and is, only a small fraction of
its cost. Also, since much of it was of low quality, it did not qualify for the strategic stockpile and was therefore surplus from the
moment it was acquired. The purpose of the program—to expand
domestic production—was not achieved, since by 1962, when the
program finally ended, the high-cost producers who had been
taking advantage of the government's generosity had quit operating. For example, at the height of the tungsten buying program,

there were 715 tungsten mines operating in the United States. When the buying program stopped, all but 3 closed down.

These programs were repeatedly extended during the Eisenhower Administration either by act of Congress or by the ODM. The fact that this was done when it was clear that no permanent expansion of the mobilization base would result and when the stockpile objectives were rapidly being completed seems to indicate that political pressures were the determining factor.

A good example is the case of chromite. A GSA depot to purchase this material was set up at Grants Pass, Oregon, in 1951. In 1955 ODM Director Flemming considered extending the program. His staff recommended terminating the purchases since the minimum stockpile objective for chromite had been attained and the price being paid was more than double the world price. Wormser in Interior, erstwhile booster of lead and zinc stockpiling, thought otherwise about chromite and advised termination on the ground that the program would not establish a permanent mobilization base. Flemming, dissatisfied, asked Wormser to reconsider. Wormser did so, and after reciting all the reasons he had previously advanced for ending the program, ultimately reversed himself and recommended extension. Wormser later said he had changed his opinion because of pressure from Western congressmen.

In June 1956 Douglas McKay, former Secretary of the Interior and then a candidate for the United States Senate from Oregon, wrote Flemming requesting that the chromite buying program be extended. Flemming wired McKay's campaign headquarters a week later that he would do so since the Department of the Interior had advised that "continuation of the program . . . may serve to develop a significant mobilization base."

All told, the government paid $18,588,036 for Oregon chromite at prices ranging from 2 to 2½ times the market price. When the government purchases stopped, the producers went out of business; Wormser was right the first time.[43]

[43] *Ibid.*, pp. 64-65.

By December 31, 1962, a total of $3,549,391,852 had been spent for acquisitions of material under expansion contracts and domestic purchase programs. A large amount of this material had been transferred to the strategic stockpile; the amount remaining in the DPA inventory on that date was acquired at a cost of $1,478,766,800.[44]

Supplemental Stockpile and Barter Program

The stockpiling picture was further complicated when Congress established a "supplemental stockpile" by the Agricultural Trade Development and Assistance Act of 1954 (Public Law 480). This new stockpile, to be administered by the Secretary of Agriculture, was to be a repository for strategic and critical material purchased with foreign currencies acquired by the sale of surplus agricultural commodities.[45] The Act also expanded and reemphasized the Commodity Credit Corporation's authority to barter agricultural surpluses for strategic materials of foreign origin. Later legislation provided for the transfer of these barter acquisitions to either the supplemental stockpile or the strategic stockpile.

The purpose of this legislation was not primarily to acquire additional materials for their national defense value but to facilitate the disposal of agricultural surpluses in foreign markets. The Department of Agriculture would receive something of value in exchange for the surpluses, materials which would be much less perishable and less bulky, hence much less costly to store, than agricultural goods. For example, storage cost for a ton of wheat is about $5 a year, as against about one fifth of a cent for a ton of ore. Framers of the legislation also had in mind that the United States was a have-not nation with respect to many minerals, and for those it did produce, its own reserves were being depleted year by year. Unlike agricultural goods, these materials

[44] *Ibid.*, p. 20.
[45] Such purchasing was one of eight possible uses of the funds accumulated.

were "nonrenewable." Hence the supplemental stockpile would be a "permanent national asset" whose value and utility would increase with time. This was not precisely a national security utility in the narrower military sense on which the national strategic stockpile was rationalized; yet it is obvious that if the latter had national security value, the same materials in the supplemental stockpile would have such value as well, pound for pound and ton for ton. On the other hand, it could be argued (and was, by skeptics in the ODM and the Department of Defense) that the strategic-stockpile objectives would generously meet all conceivable national security requirements, so the additional amounts in the supplemental stockpile would be simply redundant. The ODM ranked the supplemental stockpile as "third in strategic importance," behind its own "minimum" and "long-term" programs.[46]

The Department of the Interior and the mining interests supported the supplemental program, at first mildly and then enthusiastically after an amendment made the new stockpile subject to the same stringent disposal restrictions as was the strategic stockpile. The obvious reason was that the supplemental stockpile would sop up foreign surpluses which might otherwise be imported commercially at the expense of domestic producers and would generally help to support world minerals prices. Furthermore, many large domestic producers with foreign mining subsidiaries could expect to benefit directly from barter and foreign-currency transactions. It will be recalled that President Eisenhower, in announcing the long-term lead and zinc domestic procurement program, had specifically directed that the supplemental stockpile would be used to help limit commercial imports of these two metals.

For various reasons not relevant here, only small amounts of strategic materials were bought with foreign-currency "counterpart funds"; the acquisitions by the Department of Agriculture

---

[46] Office of Defense Mobilization, *Stockpile Report to the Congress,* July-December 1954, p. 6.

therefore have been almost entirely by the barter method. The Department had been authorized to barter for strategic materials as early as 1949, but until 1954 these operations were on a very minor scale. They were stepped up in 1954 after the additional authority and encouragement given by Public Law 480. Since Congress did not authorize the transfer of barter materials to the supplemental stockpile until 1956, barter procurement between 1954 and 1956 was entirely for the strategic stockpile. About $75 million worth of strategic materials was acquired during the last six months of 1954, an amount nearly as large as the total for 1950 through June 1954, and acquisitions increased substantially in subsequent years.

Between 1954 and 1958, Agriculture received guidance from the ODM in the form of two sets of yearly quotas: one for barter procurement for the strategic stockpile, and the other for the supplemental stockpile. The ODM restricted its barter list to materials primarily of foreign origin, and to materials whose long-term objectives were "large enough to permit barter procurement without impairing the domestic mobilization base." No materials were to be acquired by barter which were available from domestic production. Consequently only 20 materials were authorized for barter acquisition during fiscal 1955.[47] Some 30 materials, and in considerably larger amounts, were "suggested" for the supplemental stockpile.

After 1956, when Congress authorized the transfer of bartered materials to the supplemental stockpile, guidance from the ODM was less relevant, since if the strategic stockpile would not take materials acquired by barter, they could always be put in the supplemental, which had no formal objectives or limits on quantities to be acquired. Apparently as a result of this development, Gordon Gray, ODM Director, stated in the spring of 1957 that his agency would no longer provide guidance for the barter program. Subsequently, an interagency committee, the Supplemen-

---

[47] Symington Hearings, Part 4, p. 1335.

tal Stockpile Advisory Committee for Barter, on which the ODM
was represented, established the lists and amounts of strategic
materials to be acquired by barter.

Since 1956 by far the larger portion of barter acquisitions has
gone into the supplemental stockpile, although the strategic
stockpilers may take whatever they need to meet unfilled objectives, reimbursing the CCC out of their own funds. In fact, since
1958, when the stockpile program was cut back sharply, most of
the new acquisitions for the strategic stockpile have been from
CCC stocks.

By the end of 1961, materials acquired by barter and transferred to the strategic stockpile were valued at $223,243,000. The
total value of the supplemental stockpile, composed of some 45
materials, came to $1,103,506,000, of which $961,920,000 had
been acquired by barter and the rest by purchases with foreign
currencies acquired by sales of agricultural goods.[48]

In administering the barter program, the Agriculture Department is required by law to avoid displacing commercial dollar
exports of agricultural goods and to avoid undue disruption of
world prices of these commodities. The effect of these restrictions
has been generally to limit barter transactions to underdeveloped
countries with low import purchasing power. During the Eisenhower Administration, Agriculture was not restricted as to the
amounts of strategic materials it could acquire for the supplemental stockpile; the chief criterion for procurement was whether
a profitable deal could be made, not some ultimate objective as
with the strategic stockpile. The objectives for the strategic
stockpile, the extent of fulfillment of these objectives, and the
amounts of materials in the DPA inventory were all considered
irrelevant to the administration of the supplemental stockpile.[49]
Agriculture continued acquiring materials by barter for the supplemental stockpile long after much of the material in the strate-

[48] *Ibid.*, Part 1, pp. 144-145.
[49] *Ibid.*, pp. 141-142.

gic stockpile had been declared surplus by a change in strategic assumptions in 1958.[50]

On the other hand, Agriculture has recognized collateral objectives in addition to that of simply exchanging agricultural goods for materials less costly to store. It has on occasion made special efforts to acquire by barter certain materials for the strategic stockpile. It has sometimes used the barter program to support foreign-aid programs in the underdeveloped countries, at the request of the Department of State. In some instances, it has bartered for specific materials in order to support the market price for the benefit of domestic producers, at the request of the ODM and the Department of the Interior.[51] For example, beginning in 1956 and up to the end of 1961, the Department bartered for more than $166 million worth of lead and zinc as part of the government's program for reducing imports and supporting domestic production.[52]

As a further aspect of its contribution to the domestic mobilization base, the supplemental stockpile was also used as a final depository for materials acquired by the Department of the Interior under the special domestic purchase programs for certain minerals, described earlier.

The 1954 Act and the stepped-up barter activity reflected mutual support between the agricultural price-support program and the stockpile program. This was in part a natural result of the gradual transformation of the stockpile program into a price-support operation, plus the increasing political urgency of disposing of domestic farm surpluses. There had been for some time a certain amount of "back-scratching" between farm-district and mining-district congressmen. The mutual advantage of exchanging farm surpluses for mineral surpluses, with the latter securely locked up and labeled "not to be opened until wartime" had become more and more apparent to both groups. The Department of

---

[50] To be discussed in the next section.
[51] Symington Subcommittee, *Draft Report*, p. 39.
[52] Symington Hearings, Part 4, pp. 1264-1265.

Agriculture gained financially (despite the incongruity of its becoming a stockpiler of metals and minerals). The national security ostensibly benefited, and both the farm groups and the mining interests approved.

Policy Changes, 1958

From the very beginning of postwar stockpiling in 1944, it had been assumed, for purposes of computing stockpile objectives, that a future war would last five years and that the stockpile would have to be large enough to cover all material shortages for such a period. The military officers in the Munitions Board who originally had established this guideline had simply assumed that a future war would be much like World War II and then added another year or so, just for insurance. It was, of course, to be a conventional war. For these men, this was a "quick and dirty" assumption, which naturally would be subject to change in future years. Yet this assumption stuck until the incredibly late year of 1958—through all the kaleidoscopic changes in technology, weapons, and military doctrine, including the development of nuclear and thermonuclear weapons by ourselves and then the U.S.S.R., and the adoption of a military strategy centered around nuclear deterrence and "massive retaliation" during the early years of the Eisenhower Administration.

There is no evidence that the Joint Chiefs of Staff questioned the five-year assumption prior to 1954. Undoubtedly the reason was that the Chiefs were at odds among themselves on this question. The Army (mildly supported by the Navy) assumed that World War III would be much like World War II and therefore based its requirements projections on the contingency of a long conventional war, with perhaps a marginal assist from nuclear airpower. The Air Force, on the other hand, tended to assume a very short, highly destructive nuclear war, which would leave neither the time nor the functioning industrial capacity for any significant output of weapons during the war.

The adoption of the "New Look" strategy in 1953 and 1954, with its emphasis on nuclear weapons and massive retaliation and its deemphasis of conventional forces, forced some compromise between these sharply opposing views. The Army was directed by the President to cease planning for a long, large-scale conventional war, to visualize its mission more in terms of a shorter, limited war, and to adjust its requirements figures accordingly. Policy papers from the National Security Council stated, albeit somewhat vaguely, that any future war of greater intensity than the Korean War very probably would become nuclear and all-out, in which case large-scale industrial mobilization would be both irrelevant and impossible. The New Look decisions, however, did not make a clean choice between the Army and Air Force images of a future war. They did force a compromise, but one which was much more political than logical. The Joint Chiefs apparently agreed that for procurement and mobilization planning purposes, the services should assume that future wars would be no longer than three years. This was a "bargained" rather than a "calculated" assumption, since if the Air Force was correct, three years was obviously much too long, and if the Army was correct, three years might be too short. While the assumption reflected relative bargaining strengths in the Joint Chiefs of Staff (the Army and Navy vs. the Air Force), it also was symptomatic of the rather "schizophrenic" thinking of the Eisenhower Administration concerning military and mobilization policy. While emphasizing massive retaliation with nuclear weapons in its declaratory policy, consistently reducing the *active* conventional armed forces and generally favoring the Air Force image of a short war, at the same time, Administration leaders were often heard extolling the importance of a strong industrial mobilization base which apparently was to swing into action upon the outbreak of war and begin producing huge amounts of conventional military equipment. It is true that the original New Look did include some narrowing of the mobilization base by reducing the number of defense contractors and by closing some standby plants, and this trend was to continue. But the Administration never really succeeded in reconciling its intellectual legacy from World War II with its exploitation of nuclear technology to reduce the defense budget and with the probable nature of the war which it was preparing and apparently intending to fight if deterrence of a major challenge should fail. Even critics of the Administration's policies betrayed a similar failure to think through to some logical amalgamation of the old and the new. General Maxwell Taylor, for example, the Army Chief of Staff from 1955 to 1959, who was repeatedly at odds with his superiors on military policy, could recommend to the JCS in 1956 "a war-production, mobilization and training base to support an atomic general war."[53]

At any rate, the officially approved JCS planning assumption for the length of a future war was now two years less than the five-year assumption guiding the stockpile program. The JCS pointed out this fact to the National Security Council early in 1954. Their motive, of course, was more than one of simply achieving consistency between military and stockpile planning. The economy drive in the early years of the Eisenhower Administration introduced considerable budgetary stringency and sharpened the competition for available funds. The stockpile became more obviously and sharply a competitor with military end-item procurement. The competition was aggravated by the adoption of the long-term stockpile program, which indicated more spending for stockpiling, in curious contradiction to the Administration's over-all drive to reduce military spending. The JCS recommendation to reduce the planning period to three years for stockpiling was supported vigorously by Joseph Dodge, Director of the Bureau of the Budget, and also by Charles E. Wilson, Secretary of Defense, and George M. Humphrey, Secretary of the Treasury.[54] Humphrey's position was rather surprising in view of

[53] General Maxwell D. Taylor, *The Uncertain Trumpet* (New York: Harper, 1959), p. 34.
[54] Symington Hearings, Part 9, pp. 3836-3843.

his membership on the Cabinet Committee on Minerals Policy and his reported role as a prime mover in the adoption of higher, long-term stockpile goals.

Against this formidable opposition, ODM Director Flemming stood firmly for the five-year concept. This position was also somewhat surprising, in view of the fact that the "duration of a probable war" was one of the points on which the ODM was supposed to accept "guidance" from the Department of Defense, according to procedures established by Flemming's own agency.[55] At any rate, the President decided in favor of Flemming. In subsequent testimony before the Symington subcommittee, Flemming credited this result not to his own persuasiveness but to the military expertise of the President. He felt that President Eisenhower was "not so much taking my advice as he was drawing on his own experience in the military area . . . on matters to which he had devoted his entire life."[56] Certainly, if the President had decided otherwise, he would have contradicted his earlier approval of the long-term program, which substantially raised most stockpile goals.

It seems clear, however, that the President sincerely believed in the need for a large stockpile and did not need much convincing from Flemming. In September 1963 Eisenhower wrote to Senator Clifford P. Case of New Jersey:

The Nation's investment in these stockpiles is comparable to the investment made in any insurance policy. If an emergency does not arise, there are always those who can consider the investment a waste. If, however, the investment had not been made and the emergency did arise, these same persons would bemoan, and properly so, the lack of foresight on the part of those charged with the security of the United States. I firmly rejected the policy of too-little, too-late stockpiling. As a result, when my administration left office in 1961, the Nation was strongly situated in this regard to deal with the forces of international communism.[57]

[55] *Ibid.*, p. 3787.
[56] *Ibid.*, p. 3839.
[57] Symington Subcommittee, *Draft Report,* p. 121.

The Department of Defense returned to the charge in the fall of 1955. The first formal move was made by T. P. Pike, Assistant Secretary of Defense for Supply and Logistics, in a letter to Flemming. The following excerpt is worth quoting.

The 5-year stockpile concept goes back for many years, and it is our present feeling that it represents a degree of security, in its field, far in excess of the degree reached in other fields of mobilization preparedness. This inconsistency becomes particularly noticeable under conditions of tight budgeting for all Government activities and there is a strong possibility that funds being presently obligated and spent for stockpiling might better be channeled to other security programs with the result that our overall security position might be improved through better balance. This apparent imbalance becomes more noticeable when we consider the additional funds required to reach the long-range stockpile objectives as differentiated from the minimum objectives.

It is fully realized that the 5-year war planning concept of stockpiling was reaffirmed by the National Security Council as recently as April, 1954; nevertheless, we feel that the present emphasis on economy in Government operations dictates a review of this question. As you are aware, the Joint Chiefs of Staff have established military mobilization programs covering only three years and the mobilization materials requirements which are furnished your office by the Department of Defense cover only three years. It is necessary for your office to extend these requirements for an additional two years in order to establish stockpile goals.

Pike enclosed a table which compared the existing minimum objectives for all 76 stockpiled materials against hypothetical objectives computed on a three-year basis and which clearly showed that inventories of most materials were already well over the three-year goals.[58]

The Pike letter precipitated a meeting of the Defense Mobilization Board on August 17, 1955, at which no less than 38 persons were present, including, besides Flemming: Secretary Humphrey; James P. Mitchell, Secretary of Labor; Donald A. Quarles, Secretary of the Air Force; and Under and Assistant Secre-

[58] Symington Hearings, Part 9, p. 3820.

taries (including Pike) representing the Departments of Defense, State, the Interior, Agriculture, and Commerce. At the meeting all the Board members supported the three-year assumption against Flemming, who held out for five years. It was agreed that Flemming would prepare a document setting forth the opposing views for consideration by the NSC.

Flemming did have one man in his corner, Felix Wormser, Assistant Secretary of the Interior for Mineral Resources, who, although he attended the August 17 meeting, was not a member of the DMB. Writing to Flemming on August 23, Wormser urged "a bit of caution" in presenting the matter to the NSC, specifically to "suspend any move to acquaint the NSC with our DMB conclusions until we have studied and produced acceptable alternate proposals." The shift to three years, he said, would be considered "a breach of faith by the mining industry" and would result in "unpleasant and, I may say, well deserved political difficulties," unless alternatives were available to "sustain our mobilization base and to foster a healthy mining industry. . . ."[59] In taking this position, Wormser, of course, was undercutting his own superior, Clarence Davis, Under Secretary of the Interior, who, as a member of the DMB, had voted for the three-year concept.

Flemming incorporated excerpts from the Wormser letter in his presentation to the National Security Council. The result was the same as in 1954: against the advice of the Departments of Defense, State, and the Treasury, the military Chiefs, and the Bureau of the Budget, the President supported Flemming and directed that the five-year planning base be continued.[60]

Nevertheless, the issue was far from dead. It was kept open and eventually resolved in favor of the Defense Department's position by a series of developments in Soviet military technology and capability which triggered a sweeping review of United States defense policy known as the "New New Look." In 1955 and 1956 the Soviets demonstrated that they had developed a

[59] *Ibid.*, p. 3849.
[60] *Ibid.*, p. 3848.

significant long-range bomber capability, and United States radar picked up evidence that the Soviet Union was testing long-range ballistic missiles. By 1956 intelligence reports indicated that the Soviets had accumulated a substantial stockpile of thermonuclear bombs and warheads. These developments reached a dramatic climax in the summer and fall of 1957, when the Soviet Union announced the successful firing of an intercontinental missile and launched the first spacecraft, Sputnik. All of these events added up to a fundamental change in the balance of military power: the full maturation of a "balance of terror" or "nuclear stalemate"; that is, a situation in which neither of the great powers could launch a nuclear strike against the other without suffering devastating retaliation.

In strict logic, the United States appraisal of the changed situation might have led to the conclusion that the policy of massive retaliation was bankrupt and that increases in conventional forces were now required to meet enemy challenges overseas which formerly had been deterred by the nuclear threat. This was not the conclusion of the New New Look, however. Very briefly, it did recognize that strategic nuclear power was now an effective deterrent only of major Soviet aggression against the United States itself or against areas of extremely vital interest, such as Western Europe. But because the Administration wished to hold down defense expenditures, the New New Look did not lead to an increase in conventional forces sufficient to deal with local attacks which formerly had been covered by the strategic nuclear umbrella. Attacks of this kind which could not be contained conventionally were to be deterred or met by an increased reliance on "tactical" nuclear weapons. The military budget for fiscal 1958 in fact still further reduced the conventional forces of the Army and Navy.

In the field of industrial-mobilization planning, the reappraisal sharply downgraded the wartime significance of industrial potential. It was assumed that any war with the Soviet Union either would be nuclear from the beginning or would inevitably

become nuclear if not terminated within six months at the outside. In a large-scale nuclear war, the United States "industrial
potential" would be largely destroyed. Local or limited conflicts
would be on such a small scale that they would not require any
significant additional output of weapons during the war.

In general, the new guideline was that future wars would have
to be fought primarily with equipment and manpower already
produced, trained, and deployed at the outbreak. The prospect of
a lengthy conventional war was rejected. Previous service schedules of "full mobilization requirements" of combat supplies and
equipment were slashed from 50 to 65 per cent.[61] And to the extent that supplies on hand at the outbreak fell short of these requirements, there would be only six months to make up the
difference from new production. Plans for production or mobilization of the nation's resources for more than six months after the
start of hostilities were dropped. New production during the six-
month period would come only from "hot" production lines, that
is, plants already producing military goods. There would be no
conversion from civilian to military production and no reliance
on standby plants and other elements of the mobilization base.

These new policies and assumptions were adopted at levels of
"high policy"—the National Security Council, the Department of
Defense, and the Joint Chiefs of Staff—and were not immediately
applied to the stockpile program. Nevertheless, it was obvious
that a stockpile of raw materials sufficient for a five-year war was
flagrantly inconsistent with them. The ODM saw the handwriting
on the wall as early as the summer of 1957. At that time it established a "procurement priority level" for all materials, which was
in effect a new set of objectives, lower than the previous minimums and based on a three-year war. New cash procurements
for the strategic stockpile were henceforth limited to those few
materials whose inventories had not yet reached this level, with
the exception of the most politically sensitive materials—lead and

[61] Samuel P. Huntington, *The Common Defense: Strategic Programs in
National Politics* (New York: Columbia University Press, 1961), p. 97.

zinc—for which additional purchases contributed to "maintenance of the domestic production component of the mobilization base." In a report isued in December 1957, the ODM said:

> it is expected that stockpile objectives, which must take account of the rapid progress in technological developments and the increased power of modern weapons, will be substantially reduced for a number of materials when next reviewed against materials requirements as calculated under new strategic concepts.[62]

By December 1957 all but 12 of the 75 materials on the stockpile list were in excess of their "procurement priority level."[63]

The proposal to shift formally to a three-year-war assumption for stockpile planning, along with other proposed policy changes, was submitted to the National Security Council for the third time in the spring of 1958, this time with the concurrence of the ODM. President Eisenhower, reversing his two earlier decisions, approved the change. The effect was to reduce all stockpile objectives by about 60 per cent across the board.[64] More than half of the long-term objectives dropped below the former minimum objectives, and the new minimums dropped approximately to the ODM's procurement priority levels. The reduction was 60 per cent rather than 40 for two reasons: One was that the two years which were lopped off had been assumed to be peak years of war production. In other words, the military plans for a three-year mobilization period had postulated a rising curve of requirements during the first two years of the war, reaching a peak in the third year. The ODM had simply added two more years of high-level production equivalent to the third year in the military plans. Eliminating these last two years thus had an effect on requirements more than proportionate to the assumed time change in the duration of the war. Second, the military stockpile requirements for the three years also were sharply reduced by a reduction in planned wartime force levels and by a decision to rely

[62] Office of Defense Mobilization, *Stockpile Report to the Congress,* January-June 1957, Preface.

[63] *Ibid.,* July-December 1957, pp. 4-5.

[64] Symington Hearings, Part 4, p. 1194.

more on "forces in being" and reserves of finished equipment
than on wartime production.

One can only speculate as to why the assumption of a three-
year war was adopted for stockpiling rather than, say, two years
or one year or even less. The strategic assumptions of the New
New Look went considerably further than had the original New
Look in embracing the short-war doctrine. If future wars were
either to be nuclear or so limited as not to require significant
wartime mobilization, why have a stockpile of raw materials at
all? Again, the answer is probably to be found in politics rather
than logic. To have abruptly written off the entire twelve-year
accumulation as unnecessary for national defense would have
provoked much criticism in Congress and the mining states as
well as creating a serious disposal problem. The NSC-JCS papers
which spelled out the new strategic doctrine (rather vaguely as
usual) had not changed the real convictions of those in the military services, particularly the Army, who still believed in the possibility of a long conventional war.[65] Thus, the concept of a moderately large stockpile still had considerable support within the
military services and, naturally, in the Department of the Interior
and the ODM. The President himself was rather partial to stockpiling, for reasons which are somewhat obscure. Certainly, a decision to abolish the stockpile entirely would have been embarrassing to an Administration which, only four years earlier, had
increased stockpile purchases in order to build up a mobilization
base.

Nevertheless, the 1958 decision, by a stroke of the President's

[65] Indeed the Army appears to have largely ignored the precepts of the
New New Look in its own planning. Soon after Robert S. McNamara assumed the post of Secretary of Defense in the Kennedy Administration in
1961, he reported as follows: "We found that the three military departments had been establishing their requirements independently of each
other. I think the results can fairly be described as chaotic: the Army
planning, for example, was based, largely, on a long war of attrition, while
the Air Force planning was based largely on a short war of nuclear bombardment. Consequently, the Army was stating a requirement for stocking
months of fighting supplies against the event of a sizable conventional conflict, while the Air Force stock requirements for such a war had to be
measured in days, and not very many days at that." Quoted in William W.
Kaufmann, *The McNamara Strategy* (New York: Harper, 1964), p. 30.

pen, automatically created large surpluses for many of the stock-piled materials. The amount of the surplus varied among the in-dividual materials, of course, according to how closely their ac-cumulations had approached the previous objectives. No public record is available as to the exact amount of the surpluses which resulted immediately. However, figures are available for the end of 1961, and since the objectives did not materially change, nor did much additional procurement or disposal take place during the intervening years, a sampling of these figures will provide some idea of the orders of magnitude involved. In zinc, for ex-ample, the new long-term or maximum objective was 178,000 tons, and the strategic stockpile had 1,256,000 tons on hand. Counting an additional 324,000 tons in the supplemental stock-pile, the surplus over the maximum objective was 1,402,000 tons, with a market value for the surplus of over $336 million. The lead objective was 286,000 tons, the strategic stockpile contained 1,050,000 tons, and other inventories carried 252,000 tons, for a total inventory of 1,302,000 tons, which was surplus in the amount of 1,016,000 tons. This excess tonnage was valued at about $208 million.

Incidentally, the reduction for lead and zinc was particularly sharp because the goals for these minerals, it will be recalled, had been given an extra boost in 1954 by application of the "one year's normal use" rule. The President's action not only shortened the assumed length of war but also eliminated the one-year rule.

As for other materials, aluminum, for example, became surplus in an amount valued at about $350 million; tin, $442 million; metallurgical grade chromite, $219 million; rubber, $213 million, and so on. All told, 57 of the 75 materials were held in amounts surplus to the long-term or maximum objective.[66] In terms of over-all dollar value, the strategic stockpile held surpluses valued at $1,743,976,800 on March 31, 1962, in a total inventory valued at $5,726,328,300. Out of total inventories in all the stockpiles (strategic, DPA, and supplemental) valued at $7,958,420,600, the amount of the surplus over the maximum strategic stockpile

---

[66] Symington Subcommittee, *Draft Report*, pp. 11-14.

goals came to $3,597,006,550.[67] In short, the amount of the surplus was close to half of the total amounts held.

It is worth repeating that these excesses were not acquired by the malfeasance of stockpilers buying beyond authorized objectives (as was sometimes later implied) but simply by an administrative decision which drastically reduced the previously authorized objectives. Whether the stockpile authorities (most notably the President) should have recognized earlier that their goals were too high in the light of developing technology and strategic concepts is another matter.

Following the NSC decision, the ODM made certain changes in stockpiling assumptions and policies, effective June 30, 1958. First was a change in nomenclature: the former minimum and long-term categories of stockpile objectives were renamed "basic" and "maximum," respectively. On June 30, 1958, only 10 materials were still short of the basic goals, and these plus 8 more were below the maximums. All the rest of the 75 materials were held in excess of the maximum goals and therefore were not subject to further procurement. For them, the looming policy problem was one of getting rid of the excesses, not further acquisition.

Ground rules for calculating the basic and maximum objectives were roughly the same as for the former categories, except for shortening the hypothetical future war. That is, the maximums assumed that no wartime supplies would be available from outside North America and the Caribbean area, whereas the basic goals did allow for some long-distance importing during war.

One may wonder why the ODM continued to cling to its confusing system of dual objectives—specifically, why it retained the maximum category at all when the whole rationale for accumulating these higher amounts had collapsed. There was no longer any room within the maximum objectives for giving further support to the domestic mining industry, and the type of war in

[67] *Ibid.*, p. 1409.

which overseas imports were likely to be denied the United States for a long period of time had been "assumed out" in the Administration's strategic planning. Part of the explanation undoubtedly lies in simple inertia: the President had created the maximum category, and his latest decision did not specifically order its removal. More important, however, was the fact that retaining the maximums minimized the surpluses. The surpluses were embarrassing to the ODM and to the Administration and raised serious administrative, legal, and political problems regarding their disposal. The maximum objectives had been sponsored initially by the mining industry and its governmental supporters as a device for raising prices by getting materials off the market and into the stockpile. After 1958 these objectives served the same interests as a means for keeping a maximum amount of material *in* the stockpile and off the market.

The ODM handled the disposal problem very gingerly in its new policy statement. Materials were to be retained "so long as they are needed to meet maximum stockpile objectives or any foreseeable increases in such objectives." Furthermore, "disposals of excesses shall be undertaken only if they do not cause serious economic disruption or adversely affect the international interests of the United States."[68]

Henceforth, stockpile planning would reflect the possibility of two distinct types of war, "limited" and "general" (that is, general nuclear war). Materials requirements and supplies, and tentative stockpile objectives, would be estimated for both contingencies, and the objective formally adopted for each material would be the higher of the two. Previous stockpile planning had given only cursory attention to the potentialities of nuclear weapons, chiefly in the selection and location of storage sites. Now, in 1958, thirteen years after the dawn of the nuclear age, the prospect of nuclear war was introduced for the first time into the for-

[68] Office of Defense Mobilization, *Stockpile Report to the Congress*, January-June 1958, p. 2.

mulation of stockpile goals. But it was to be a long time before this new assumption had any real effect on stockpiling policy. By the spring of 1965, almost seven years later, the stockpilers still had not developed stockpile objectives that took nuclear war into account. They blamed the delay before 1962 on their inability to extract suitable guidelines from the military; after 1962 they cited the complexity of the problem. At this writing they were working hard at it; their efforts and the issues involved are discussed in the next chapter.

Pending the determination of stockpile requirements for population survival and industrial recovery after a nuclear attack, the ODM adopted in December 1959 the so-called six-months rule—that the maximum objective for each material should be no less than the total of six months' normal consumption "in periods of active demand." Like the one-year rule, which had been dropped a year and a half earlier, this was just an arbitrary figure designed to raise some of the stockpile goals. The ODM's rationale was that this rule was necessary to hedge against the premature disposal of materials which might turn out to be needed in greater quantities for post-nuclear-attack recovery than for conventional war mobilization. Although it was expected that most stockpile objectives for nuclear war would be lower than for conventional war, the ODM could not be sure until its studies were completed. Whatever the validity and sincerity of this rationale, its immediate effect was to mitigate the politically sensitive disposal problem by legitimizing the holding of some materials previously declared surplus.[69]

The new policies adopted in 1958 also called for assuming "rapid mobilization in the event of an emergency." It had been assumed earlier that war production would rise gradually during the first two years of a war and reach a peak in the third year. Now it was assumed that the rise would be much sharper during the first year, particularly during the first six months.

Apparently the primary effect of this assumption was to give

[69] Symington Hearings, Part 1, p. 209.

increased emphasis to a policy of upgrading stockpiled materials from raw ores and metals to forms more suitable for immediate use in manufacturing. The object was to save processing time and facilities during war and "to meet the initial surge of demand and abnormal conditions of intensive mobilization" as well as to hedge against destruction of processing plants. A "minimum readiness inventory"—approximately a six-months requirement—of these upgraded materials was to be maintained. The rationale for this program lay, of course, in the above-mentioned high-policy assumption that the only significant wartime production of military goods would take place during the first six months and would have to be accelerated rapidly during this period. Of course, if this assumption had been applied fully and literally to stockpiling, there would have been no stockpile requirements at all beyond the needs of the first six months. That it was not is another tribute (as if another were needed) to the political potency of the mining industry. In addition, or alternatively, it is another instance of the failure to integrate stockpiling with military planning, or even with national policy decisions in the field of industrial mobilization.

It is worth noting, incidentally, that the upgrading policy provided employment for the metals-processing industries as the earlier long-term program had helped the miners. Moreover, this policy may have been designed partly to facilitate the ticklish problem of disposal since payment in kind, from materials in excess of objectives, could be used to pay for the processing.[70]

[70] *Ibid.*, p. 2.

```
      ┌─────────┐
      │   VII   │
      └─────────┘
```

Recent History and Current Problems

President John F. Kennedy opened his news conference on January 30, 1962, by saying he was "astonished" to find that the stockpiling program had accumulated $7.7 billion worth of materials, an amount nearly $3.4 billion greater than estimated wartime needs. He said that "this excessive storage of costly materials was a questionable burden on public funds, and in addition, a potential source of excessive and unconscionable profits." He disclosed that in the case of some materials the government "had acquired more than seven times the amount that could possibly be used." The President called for a thorough congressional investigation of the program together with a special Executive Branch review of stockpiling policies "in the light of changed strategy and improved technology."[1]

By prior agreement with Senator Stuart Symington, the President announced that the congressional investigation would be conducted by Senator Symington's National Stockpile and Naval Petroleum Reserves Subcommittee of the Senate Committee on Armed Services. For the President to take the unusual step of re-

[1] *The New York Times,* January 31, 1962, p. 1.

238

questing a congressional investigation seemed to indicate that he
sought the disclosure of past events and policies rather than anything that might reflect unfavorably on his own Administration.
At any rate, charges were heard then and later throughout the
investigation that it was motivated by partisan politics in an
election year. It was suggested that the Democrats needed something to neutralize the political effects of the Billy Sol Estes
swindle case in Texas, with its intimations of corruption in the
farm-surplus program.

The Symington Hearings

Senator Symington's hearings began on March 28, 1962, and
continued on and off through that year and until January 30,
1963. Significantly the hearings focused largely on stockpiling
policies and decisions of the Eisenhower Administration, although the Subcommittee did explore certain current and future
problems, such as disposal of surpluses and stockpiling for nuclear war. The history of the program before 1953 was hardly
touched.

The voluminous testimony taken at the hearings cannot be detailed here. It has been drawn upon heavily in the writing of the
previous chapter. We shall content ourselves with summarizing
and briefly commenting upon some of the criticisms leveled
against the stockpiling program during the hearings and in the
Subcommittee's "draft report." The report was made public by
Senator Symington under this designation because the Subcommittee by a tie vote failed to approve it formally.[2]

At certain points during the hearings and in the draft report,
Senator Symington and other Democratic members of the Subcommittee sought to show that the Eisenhower Administration

[2] The Democratic members, besides Symington, were Senators Strom
Thurmond of South Carolina, Clair Engle of California, and Howard W.
Cannon of Nevada. The Republican members were Senators J. Glenn Beall
of Maryland and Clifford P. Case of New Jersey. The tie vote occurred
when Senator Thurmond joined the Republicans in objecting to the report.

had violated at least the purpose, if not the letter, of the Stockpiling Act. This charge was made notably in connection with the establishment of long-term stockpile objectives and the special lead-zinc buying program. These devices were employed, it was said, "as a subsidy to mining interests and were unrelated to our national defense needs." Their primary object was to raise and maintain the prices of lead and zinc, and "this was not within the purposes of the Stockpiling Act."[3]

While these programs were certainly vulnerable to criticism on policy grounds, the implication of illegality was hardly justified. One of the express purposes of the Stockpiling Act is the "conservation and development" of domestic supply sources. The lead-zinc purchase program could be justified legally under this heading. Moreover, the "primary object" of the program, at least in the mind of President Eisenhower, if not in the minds of Arthur Flemming or Felix Wormser, was not to raise prices per se but to develop a "strong mobilization base" of domestic lead and zinc production, which was thought to be necessary for national defense. Price supporting was only instrumental to this end. Whether the end was justifiable in terms of national security is another matter.

Flemming was also accused of violating the President's directive to purchase for the long-term program only at "advantageous prices," when he used the lead-zinc purchase program to *raise* the prices of these materials to a particular level. The charge is unwarranted since clearly the intent of the President's order was to buy at low prices *in order to* raise them to the level necessary to maintain the volume of domestic production at mobilization-base requirements.

The Symington Subcommittee recommended that the practice of completely discounting overseas imports be discontinued—in effect, that the maximum stockpile objectives be discarded in favor of the much lower basic objectives as the criterion of wartime needs. The stockpiling authorities have not accepted this

[3] Symington Subcommittee, *Draft Report*, pp. 5-36.

suggestion, probably because lowering the objectives would greatly increase the surpluses and magnify the disposal problem.

In connection with lead and zinc, it is interesting to note that a good portion of the domestic production of these metals takes place in Senator Symington's home state of Missouri. There is no record of the Senator having opposed the lead and zinc purchase program when it was in operation from 1954 to 1958. In fact, in 1958 Symington cosponsored a bill to provide for the purchase of *more* lead and zinc, among other metals. In that year he also testified before a Senate subcommittee, urging continued stock-piling of lead and zinc to "relieve the market of some of the depressing effect of surpluses."[4] Of course, in 1962 Symington could criticize the lead-zinc stockpiling program without fear of adverse reaction from his mining constituents since it was clear by then that stockpiling could be of no further help to domestic mining. Ironically, in the summer of 1962, while his hearings were in progress, Senator Symington spoke in the Senate in support of a $2 million subsidy to small lead and zinc producers. When challenged by Republicans, he explained that there was no inconsistency between his current position and his retroactive assault on the Eisenhower stockpiling program because the bill in question did not provide for stockpiling; the government would simply pay out cash to the producers without taking any material in return.[5]

In its hearings and report, the Symington Subcommittee also took Flemming harshly to task for allowing some suppliers (mostly of copper) to make "windfall profits" when he canceled or delayed their scheduled deliveries to government stockpiles in order to ease industrial shortages. (The "profits" consisted of the difference between the stockpile contract price and the higher, prevailing market price.) The Subcommittee was not at all critical of the general practice of manipulating stockpile procurement

[4] Quoted by Republican Senator Prescott Bush of Connecticut in Symington Hearings, Part 4, p. 1276.
[5] *The New York Times,* June 13, 1962, p. 16.

for the purpose of price and supply stabilization (somewhat inconsistently with the tenor of its criticism of the *purchase* of lead and zinc to raise prices and domestic production of these materials). It took exception only to the fact that the profit went to the private suppliers instead of to the government. As indicated earlier, this author's judgment is that the criticism was somewhat less than fair. At least, there is much to be said in Flemming's defense. Except for the few contract cancellations, which were a very small fraction of the total amounts diverted to industry, all of the amounts were later delivered to the government at the original contract price. The government lost no money and little material. It had the legal right to make some money "on the side," but Flemming chose not to exercise this right. His principle that the government should not deliberately "speculate in commodities," as he put it, is certainly fully consistent with the prevailing conception of the proper role of the government in its relations with business. If some copper suppliers made more money by having their stockpile obligations delayed, they made no more than did nonstockpile suppliers who automatically benefited from the rising price trend. Flemming may be faulted more for his hypocrisy in claiming that he had not manipulated the market than for the alleged sin which the Subcommittee actually attributed to him. But is not *some* degree of hypocrisy virtually a necessary component of the political vocation?

The Subcommittee spent a good deal of its time exploring the details of specific procurement contracts and contract negotiations. Several instances of what appeared to be "excessive and unconscionable profits" were uncovered. Perhaps the most spectacular of these was a nickel contract with the Hanna Mining Company, a subsidiary of M. A. Hanna Company, a widespread holding company with many mining interests. The Subcommittee's almost microscopic investigation of this contract was no doubt stimulated by the fact that Hanna's Chairman of the Board was George M. Humphrey, former Secretary of the Treasury in the Eisenhower Administration.

During 1952, when the government's industrial mobilizers were very concerned about nickel shortages and anxious to build up a domestic mobilization base, Hanna Mining proposed the following rather complex deal. Under one contract, Hanna would open a new nickel-ore body at Riddle, Oregon, and sell the output to the government at the premium price of $6 a ton. Under a second contract, the government would sell the ore at the same price to the Hanna Smelting Company, a new company to be created specifically to smelt the ore at the minesite. The government would advance $22 million to build the smelter and provide working capital. After refining the ore, the smelter company would sell the nickel metal to the government at cost. Should the smelting process prove unfeasible, Hanna had the right to cancel the contract and the government would reimburse Hanna for its capital investment in the mine, take back the unusable smelter, and excuse Hanna from repayment of the $22 million. If the smelting process did work out and the contract was fulfilled, Hanna would then be allowed to buy the smelter from the government at 7½ per cent of cost. Apparently the reason for having two contracts—one with the mining company and one with the smelter—was so that all profits would accrue to the mining company, which, as an extractive enterprise, could qualify for a large tax depletion allowance.

In brief, under this arrangement, the government would expose itself to a possible loss of about $30 million (not counting the premium price to be paid for the nickel), and Hanna would take no risk at all. Hanna stood to gain a large profit from sale of the ore, plus a tested and proved smelting process, plus a smelter at nominal cost.

Government negotiators resisted these terms vigorously, but Hanna would not budge. Finally, Humphrey intervened personally in December 1952, informing the government that if the contracts were not signed before he was sworn in as Secretary of the Treasury on January 21, the deal would be off. The General Services Administration signed the contracts. As Jess Larson, former GSA Administrator, put it: "The overriding and crucial need for additional nickel production left me no alternative . . ."[6] Humphrey thus avoided a conflict-of-interest charge, but he did share in the profits from the contract since he retained his Hanna stockholdings during his government tenure.

So the operation went ahead as planned. The smelter was built by the government for $22,300,000, the smelting process proved feasible, and the contract was completed with the sale of just under $100 million worth of smelted nickel to the government. Then Hanna acquired the smelter at a cost of $1,722,000. According to the General Accounting Office, the mining company made a profit of just over $15 million before taxes—representing a 57.4 per cent profit on sales, 135 per cent profit on costs, and 457 per cent profit on capital investment—over a period of seven years. The mine and the smelter are still operating profitably for the commercial market. In November 1963 the Justice Department sued the Hanna Mining Company to recover more than $1.8 million in alleged overcharges.[7]

It would be tedious to go into the other cases which the Subcommittee examined. Suffice to say that Senator Symington and his colleagues did uncover enough evidence to justify the President's suspicion of "excessive and unconscionable profits." With the possible exception of the Hanna case, they did not produce convincing evidence of outright illegal action or blatant corruption in a financial sense. Yet, moral corruption and political favoritism there certainly was.

Among the specific recommendations made by the Subcommittee for reforming the stockpile program were the following:

1. Consolidation of all inventories of strategic materials into a single stockpile.

2. Preparation of long-range disposal plans "with appropriate publicity and consultation with suppliers."

3. Abolition of the Interdepartmental Materials Advisory Com-

[6] Symington Subcommittee, *Draft Report*, p. 76.
[7] *The New York Times*, November 8, 1963, p. 10.

mittee to prevent conflicting interests of various agencies from inhibiting the efficient administration of the stockpile.

4. Reduction of the assumed length of a future war below the present assumption of three years, which, the Subcommittee said, "is an anachronism if not an absurdity."

5. Early determination of the feasibility of stockpiling products needed for post-nuclear-attack survival and industrial recovery.

Executive Stockpile Committee

Immediately after his press conference statement the President appointed an Executive Stockpile Committee to review the stockpiling program. The Committee was composed of the Secretaries of Defense, State, the Interior, Commerce, and Labor, the Director of the Central Intelligence Agency, the Administrator of the General Services Administration, and the Director of the Office of Emergency Planning. The latter, Edward A. McDermott, served as chairman. Following successive reorganizations, the OEP was at that time, and still is, the agency in direct charge of the stockpiling program.

The Committee submitted its first formal report on March 19, 1962. Among its recommendations were the following:

1. The objectives of the stockpile should continue to reflect the requirements of limited war, but a study should be initiated to determine possible requirements for a reconstruction period following a general nuclear war.

2. The two sets of objectives for the strategic stockpile should be eliminated and replaced by a single objective for each material.

3. The new objectives should reflect the possibility of "multiple consecutive small wars" and "the possibility that in a mobilization situation short of war, sources of raw materials may be denied to us."

4. The assumption of a three-year war should be retained

pending "a thorough study of the various factors which would
determine the length of the period."

5. A study should be made to determine whether the stockpile
should include a reserve for allied war production.

6. The Office of Emergency Planning, in cooperation with
other interested agencies, should prepare a long-range disposal
program for excess materials.

7. Pending the determination of new objectives, the current
maximum objectives should be used as the criterion for determining excesses subject to disposal.[8]

The Committee's report was most noteworthy for its conserva-
tism—that is, its implied support for the current maximum objectives, or at least fairly high objectives, and its suggestion of possible grounds for keeping them high, as in 3, 4, and 5 above. Otherwise, the report called for action on the three most important
current stockpiling problems: surplus disposal, revision of the objectives to reflect accurately the requirements of conventional
war, and stockpiling to insure and facilitate recovery from a general nuclear war.

Disposal of Surpluses

The acquisition phase of stockpiling has long since passed; in
fact, it ended in 1958 when the adoption of new strategic assumptions automatically created vast surpluses for all but a few
materials. The chief policy problem now and for the future is the
disposition of these surpluses. Very little progress in disposal was
made between 1958 and 1964 because of legal restrictions, cum-
bersome administrative procedures, and strong resistance from
domestic and foreign interests (and their governmental friends)
which stand to lose by the price reductions which could result
from the large-scale release of stockpiled materials. However, the
OEP tackled the problem more energetically late in 1963 and

[8] Symington Hearings, Part 9, pp. 3088-3090.

during 1964, and with more success. By January 1965 it had made plans for the long-range (that is, slow and gradual) disposal of excess amounts of some 55 materials in the strategic stockpile, authorized the disposition of 12 materials in the DPA inventory, and received congressional consent, during the 1964 session, to dispose of the surpluses of 17 stockpiled materials. Disposal is now (January 1965) going forward at an annual rate of $300 million. There is still a long way to go, however, and it seems clear that successful handling of the disposal problem will require careful planning and the courage to resist the producing interests which are strongly entrenched in Congress, the Department of the Interior, and the Department of State, and may also require new legislation.

As of June 30, 1964, the total of all materials in all four stockpiles—the national or strategic stockpile, the DPA inventory, the supplemental stockpile, and the Commodity Credit Corporation's barter holdings—was valued at $8,514,476,000 in acquisition cost or $7,784,940,600 in current market value. Of this amount, $5,108,113,200 at cost prices (or $4,340,905,700 at current prices) was in excess of the objectives.[9] In percentage terms about 60 per cent of the stockpile was surplus and subject to disposal. Surpluses were held in 61 of the 76 materials, although more than 80 per cent of the total excess was concentrated in 12 materials— aluminum, chromite, cobalt, copper, lead, manganese, molybdenum, nickel, rubber, tin, tungsten, and zinc.[10]

The possible surpluses loom much larger when one remembers that the stockpile objectives are still based on the assumption of a three-year conventional war at full industrial mobilization and on the extremely pessimistic assumption of no wartime imports. If these assumptions were relaxed, as they might well be, larger

[9] This figure includes relatively small amounts (if $246 million can be considered "small") of materials which did not meet official stockpile quality standards and materials which had been entirely eliminated from the stockpile list because of technological change. Office of Emergency Planning, *Stockpile Report to the Congress*, January-June 1964, p. 4.

[10] *Ibid.*, p. 5.

amounts would become surplus. On the other hand, the political pressures militating against surplus disposal are also likely to inhibit any new assumptions which would lower the estimated stockpile requirements.

Storage costs applicable to the surplus inventories amount to more than $4 million annually.[11] If the interest cost on the investment is figured at 4 per cent of the current value of the surpluses, the total cost of holding these surpluses is a little over $175 million a year. The storage and administrative budget for *all* of the strategic and DPA stockpiles is approximately $11 million a year, but again if the interest cost is included, the aggregate annual cost of maintaining the stockpiles is about $300 million. (The interest cost might be described as the amount by which the government could reduce its current expenses by selling stockpiled materials and retiring an equivalent value of government bonds.)

Under the Stockpiling Act, materials can be freely sold from the strategic stockpile only for purposes of rotation—that is, to replace deteriorated materials, such as rubber and other nonmineral items. The Act specifies three other occasions for disposal: obsolescence because a substitute has been developed or because the material "has no further usefulness in time of war"; a revised determination for other reasons; and a national emergency as declared by the President. In the event of obsolescence or a revised determination, a detailed description of the proposed disposal plan must be published in the Federal Register, and sales cannot start until six months after publication. In addition, disposals on account of a revised determination must receive the specific approval of Congress for each material. The same set of rules applies to disposals from the supplemental stockpile. Materials in the DPA inventory can be sold freely, except that in practice, the OEP has sometimes deferred to objections by other agencies.

Disposals have been severely hampered by the practice of the OEP and its predecessors of obtaining the concurrence of other

[11] Symington Hearings, Part 9, p. 3093.

interested agencies for any disposal plan—in effect, granting a veto power to these agencies. The case of rubber provides an interesting example of how this process worked.

Throughout the early 1950's, John L. Collyer, former president of the B. F. Goodrich Company and widely recognized as the leading spokesman for the rubber-manufacturing industries, made repeated efforts to persuade the ODM to reduce sharply its stockpile objective for natural rubber and sell the surplus that would be created thereby. He argued that because of progress in the development of new types of synthetic rubber, the United States had become self-sufficient in this material. We may speculate that he was also interested in reducing the price of natural rubber by stockpile disposals. His representations were finally acted upon in February 1956, when the Interdepartmental Materials Advisory Committee recommended a reduction in the goal which would have created a surplus worth about $150 million. Disposal of this amount would have reduced storage and maintenance costs by $6 million annually. However, the Department of State strongly objected, largely on the ground that disposal would seriously depreciate the world price of rubber, to the particular detriment of such Southeast Asian countries as Indonesia, Malaya, Burma, and Thailand. For good measure, the State Department threw in two other arguments for keeping a large stockpile of natural rubber: "to take care of additional domestic contingencies," and to provide supplies of natural rubber to wartime allies of the United States.[12] ODM Director Flemming decided not to cut the objective because of these foreign-policy considerations advanced by the Department of State.[13]

Later, Treasury Secretary George M. Humphrey brought to bear his considerable persuasive powers in favor of rubber disposal. Generally, Humphrey was opposed to any disposal of surpluses, but in this case he thought differently, possibly because it would be foreign rather than domestic producers who would be

[12] *Ibid.*, pp. 3633 ff.
[13] *Ibid.*

adversely affected. And, of course, disposal of rubber would mean income for the Treasury.[14] Whether or not as a consequence of Humphrey's pressure, the State Department modified its objections in 1958, and in 1959 a substantial disposal program got under way. It is perhaps significant that by far the largest disposals which have taken place are of natural rubber and tin, two materials which are not produced at all in the United States.

The primary inhibition against disposal seems to be the fear of depressing prices and thus hurting domestic producers. The General Services Administration repeatedly proposed the sale of various materials, only to be turned down by either the OEP or the Department of the Interior because of market weakness. The latter agency, as the recognized governmental protector of the interests of domestic minerals producers, has been the principal bottleneck to disposals. Prior to 1962, it wielded an absolute veto over disposal plans. Although it did approve some sales, it blocked proposals to dispose of fluorspar, palladium, tungsten, and nickel, among others. One Interior man revealed that the Department decided to veto all disposal plans in the fall of 1960 "because of the upcoming elections."[15]

The OEP and its predecessors have also been extremely sensitive to the political risks involved in placing government stockpiles on the market. At one point in 1957, ODM Director Flemming decided, with the specific approval of President Eisenhower, that *no* materials on the stockpile list would be sold. This rule was relaxed in 1958, but even then the policy was to retain not only all materials within the maximum objectives but also amounts which might be needed to meet "foreseeable increases" in such objectives. And disposals were to be undertaken "only if they do not cause serious economic disruption or adversely affect the international interests of the United States."

President Kennedy took a major step forward in April 1962, when he canceled the veto power previously granted by the OEP

[14] *Ibid.*, Part 2, p. 353.
[15] *Ibid.*, Part 4, p. 1316.

to the Department of the Interior and certain other agencies. Henceforth, the OEP would only have to "consult" with other departments concerning disposal plans; if the Department of State or the Interior indicated an objection within thirty days, the dispute would be referred to the President for decision.[16]

Considerably better progress has been made since then, although not enough to make a very significant dent in the massive surpluses. Disposals have been carried out by several methods, including cash sale, sales to other government agencies, and payment in kind to processors for upgrading stockpiled materials. The Department of Defense has taken some materials for use in the current manufacture of military items. For example, it took over 650 tons of surplus goose and duck feathers to stuff sleeping bags. It agreed to use surplus natural rubber for military truck tires. Manufacturers of all other government tires are required to buy certain amounts of natural rubber from the stockpile. A considerable amount of lead was bought by the Navy for ballast in submarines. Some copper was sold to the Mint for minting into pennies. Some small amounts of rubber and other materials have been purchased for export under the foreign-aid program.

In January 1963 the Executive Stockpile Committee produced a report on disposal which seems to represent the government's current thinking on the problem. The report was particularly notable for its general aura of caution and sensitivity to the political implications of disposal. The Committee emphasized that a disposal program must be long range and should give adequate consideration to potential "adverse effects on domestic and world markets and the economies of various nations." It recommended that the then current maximum objectives should be the criteria for the calculation of excesses (thus putting itself at odds with Symington) and even suggested that some materials beyond these objectives might be retained to meet peacetime shortages "because of the unanticipated consequences of economic or political activities in foreign countries . . ."

[16] *Ibid.*, Part 1, pp. 211-212.

While noting that preference should be given to cash sales as a method of disposal, it suggested various other methods by which excesses could be reduced, presumably with less adverse effect on prices. These included direct government use, requiring defense contractors to purchase from the stockpile, and the barter of materials as payment for government procurement.

In formulating disposal plans, there should be "greater coordination within government" and "effective consultation with industry." This cooperation would mean maximum representation and influence for the interests affected and would probably not be conducive to speedy disposal.

Finally, the Committee recommended certain legislative amendments to existing stockpiling laws—in particular, eliminating the requirement for congressional approval of sales and reducing the "waiting period" from six months to sixty days.[17]

Stockpiling for Conventional War

The Executive Stockpile Committee recommended that a single quantitative objective be established for each material for the contingency of limited or conventional war, in place of the rather confusing practice of having two objectives—a basic and a maximum. It recommended further that the OEP undertake a study of stockpile needs for general nuclear war and the reconstruction period thereafter.

The OEP then undertook two separate reviews of the stockpile goals: one in the context of conventional war assumptions, the other assuming a nuclear attack on the United States. It made much faster progress on the first task, probably because it was far and away the simpler. By April 1964, with the assistance of its interagency advisory committee, the OEP had established new single objectives for a conventional war emergency for all 79 materials in the stockpile. The new objectives were based on the assumption of a three-year war involving substantial industrial mo-

---

[17] Executive Stockpile Committee, "Disposing of Excess Stockpile Materials," *Report to the President,* January 16, 1963.

bilization and on the assumption that no supplies would be imported during the war except from Canada, Mexico, and a few other "comparably accessible" countries in the Caribbean area. The latter assumption, it will be recalled, was the same as had guided the estimates of wartime supplies in establishing the previous maximum or long-term objectives. In short, the stockpilers did not, as might have been expected, attempt to strike a compromise between the two sets of supply assumptions used previously, but merely recalculated the maximum goals and threw out the basic figures and the more liberal supply assumptions on which they had been based. They did, however, drop the old six-months rule—that the maximum objectives had to be at least high enough to provide for the *total* normal requirements of United States industry during a six-month period.

The over-all result of the review was to increase 35 of the goals, decrease 32, and leave 6 unchanged; 3 new materials were added to the list, and 3 were removed.

Some of the increases were substantial: for example, Jamaican-type bauxite, nearly doubled; iodine, nearly doubled; cobalt, more than doubled; and certain types of platinum, trebled or quadrupled. Quinine was restored to the list and given an objective of 4,130,000 ounces, which happened to be exactly the amount already in the stockpile and previously considered surplus. Some of the reductions were also large: the lead and zinc objectives, for example, were reduced to 0, and those for aluminum, nickel, rubber, and goose and duck feathers were cut markedly. (But 3 million pounds of feathers were still considered essential for the national defense.) The OEP has not explained the reasons for these changes; presumably they reflect a variety of factors which influenced the estimates of wartime supplies and requirements, probably including some of those suggested by the Executive Stockpile Committee. The over-all effect was to reduce the valuation of the strategic stockpile objectives from $3.7 billion to $3.5 billion, and of course the amount of the surplus was increased by an equivalent sum.

In addition to establishing new objectives for raw materials, the OEP also reviewed 28 "subobjectives" for upgraded (that is, processed) forms of some metals, such as ferro chromium, columbium carbide powder, and oxygen-free copper. Of these, 13 objectives were increased, 7 were decreased, 5 remained unchanged, and 3 new items were added. As noted earlier, such forms are being stockpiled to meet the "initial surge of demand" immediately after the outbreak of war and thus reduce the burden on processing facilities.

Stockpiling for Nuclear War

Until recently, stockpiling policy reflected the possibility of general nuclear war only in a very limited and haphazard fashion. The types and quantities of materials to be stockpiled have been determined almost entirely in the context of conventional war. From time to time, official statements have referred to the vulnerability of producing, processing, and consuming industries to nuclear attack. For example, President Eisenhower's announcement of the long-term program in 1954 said: "It will be assumed that in the event of an emergency some supplies from domestic sources may not be available in view of the fact that the Soviets now have the capability of attack on the United States." Such statements and assumptions never were applied systematically in the calculation of stockpile objectives, although they may have affected the size of supply discounts for excessive concentration of supply sources. The new policies adopted in 1958 made the distinction between limited war and general war for the first time and called for the calculation of stockpile needs for both contingencies. However, at least until 1962, there was no serious attempt to determine stockpile requirements for nuclear war. Apparently the main reason for the delay was the stockpilers' failure to obtain the guidance they sought from the Department of Defense.

Oddly enough, the only aspect of the stockpile program in which nuclear war considerations were applied earlier was in storage policy. As early as the spring of 1955, the ODM started moving stockpiles away from "known target areas" even though it recognized that there was only "moderate risk of major damage to the stockpile in the event of nuclear attack."[18] Principal considerations were the risks of fall-out contamination, losses by fire, and blast damage. The ODM gave increasing attention to these matters in subsequent years, using complex computer studies and simulations of the postattack environment, and took further measures to disperse and "harden" the stockpiles against nuclear damage.[19] All this activity seems odd since there would appear to be nothing so invulnerable to nuclear damage as a pile of lead, zinc, or copper ingots (although, of course, the stockpile does contain more destructible materials), and it is especially striking in view of the conventional-war orientation of all the rest of stockpiling policy.

The OEP began a study of nuclear-war stockpile requirements soon after this course of action had been recommended by the Executive Stockpile Committee in March 1962 and strongly urged also by Senator Symington and his Subcommittee. It soon found that it had a very complex problem on its hands, involving no less than a complete audit of the economy, modified by various assumptions concerning the nature and targeting of several possible types of nuclear attack. At this writing (January 1965) the study is still under way and is not expected to be completed for many months. It is an interagency effort, with inputs from the National Security Council, Department of Defense, Department of Commerce, and other agencies, coordinated by a small staff in the OEP.

In bare outline, the study is proceeding somewhat as follows:[20] The first task is to take an inventory of all the preattack facilities for producing selected finished goods, components, and materials

[18] Office of Defense Mobilization, *Stockpile Report to the Congress*, January-June 1956, p. 9.

[19] *Ibid.*, July-December 1961, p. 8.

[20] This description of the nuclear war stockpiling study is based chiefly on interviews with officials in the OEP and the Department of Defense.

which are considered essential for either population survival or industrial reconstruction after a nuclear attack. The exact capacity, location, and "input" requirements for each facility are noted. Among the basic industries being analyzed are steel, electric power, fuel refining, food processing, construction, and agricultural supplies. The audit will also include a survey of the national transportation network, for an important task in the postattack period will be to move goods, materials, and workers from surplus to deficit locations.

The next task in the study is to discount production capacity, inventories, labor force, and demand by percentages representing the estimated damage from enemy attack. These percentages are derived from a computer study called NAHICUS (Nuclear Attack Hazard in Continental United States). An important element in the NAHICUS model is an assumption of six possible attack patterns, provided by the Department of Defense, each with a probability estimate. The patterns include a strictly counterforce enemy attack, a purely countercity attack, and four intermediate mixes of counterforce and countercity. In addition, there are hypothetical estimates of the weight or intensity of attack under each pattern. When these data, along with the economic and geographical data developed in the first phase, are put through the computer, the result is a percentage figure representing the amount of the production facilities in each industrial sector which can be expected with reasonable certainty to survive the attack. When the percentages are applied to the preattack capacity figures, the result is an estimate of the postattack production capability for each industry.

The next step is to estimate postattack demand or requirements in four segments: civilian consumption, government demand, foreign demand, and capital investment. Civilian demand reflects estimates of surviving population together with estimates of minimum survival needs. It is assumed that the federal government will be in control of the economy and will be able to enforce rationing and allocation. The estimate of government demand reflects an assumption that military hostilities will continue after the nuclear exchange. It is not explained just what form these hostilities will take, but the indication is that the OEP has in mind a "broken-backed" conventional war after both sides have exhausted their nuclear capabilities. Thus, under these assumptions, civilian survival and industrial recovery will have to compete with the military forces for shares of the available resources.

The OEP further estimates a minimum export demand to friendly countries, based in part on assumptions concerning the damage likely to be suffered by these countries during the nuclear exchange. Exports to meet these demands are planned to begin three months after the end of the nuclear attack. Imports are expected to make some contribution to alleviating shortages in the United States.

Demand for capital investment reflects plans for the rehabilitation and reconstruction of the economy. In the first three months, only the lightly damaged and most essential facilities will be repaired. Provision is made for moving gradually in succeeding quarters toward a balanced and fully reconstructed economy.

The next step is to compare total requirements against estimated supplies, by industry and by time periods. The final step is to take or plan remedial measures to overcome supply deficits. One of these measures is stockpiling, but the OEP is giving equally thorough attention to possible alternatives, such as moving goods from surplus to deficit areas, using alternative production processes, using substitute goods and materials, and operating surviving facilities on a multi-shift basis. After considering all of the possible alternative measures, the OEP expects to come up with a set of stockpile objectives for nuclear war sufficient to meet all essential needs, ranging from immediate survival and subsistence of survivors to the requirements of industrial reconstruction during the first year following the nuclear attack.

The study just described tends to emphasize the problem of industrial recovery, but it interacts closely with the more urgent problem of keeping the surviving population alive in the immediate aftermath of the war. The OEP is responsible for developing and coordinating an over-all interagency program for the stockpiling of items considered essential for survival in the immediate postattack period. The agency has prepared a long list of such items in seven major groups: health supplies, food, body protection and household operations, electric power and fuel, sanitation and water supply, emergency housing and construction materials and equipment, and general use items. No decision has yet been taken as to which and how much of these supplies will be stockpiled. Presumably, such stockpiles will be in addition to small civil-defense stockpiles, which have been acquired or are being planned by other agencies.

The Office of Civil Defense in the Department of Defense, as of October 1964, owned a stockpile of food, medical supplies, radiological instruments, and other civil-defense items worth approximately $11.9 million. These supplies are mostly stored in warehouses at various strategic points throughout the nation. The OCD has undertaken a program for stocking existing fall-out shelters with such supplies. The water and food stocks in the shelters are to be sufficient for 70 million persons for a minimum period of two weeks, by which time radiation levels will have declined enough so that people can emerge from the shelters. The OCD also has a stockpile of emergency water-supply and purification units and is collecting data on all urban water-supply systems to determine their vulnerability to attack and the requirements for a stockpile of spare parts.

The Department of Agriculture has developed plans for a food stockpile to supplement the civil-defense shelter provisions. This will include ready-to-use foods, stored near population centers, sufficient to feed 100 million persons for fifteen days. Some of the wheat from the Department's surplus holdings is to be relocated near processing facilities in likely food-deficit areas—enough to provide the same number of persons with three quarters of a pound of wheat products per day for thirty days. Large amounts of feed grains are to be moved to rural areas which are likely to be short of livestock feed after a nuclear attack.

The Agriculture program is designed to hedge against the possibility of transportation disruption rather than food shortages as such. Most studies indicate that the nation as a whole will have enough edible food for the surviving population for at least one to two years without any new output from agriculture or food-processing plants, provided that transportation is available to move food from surplus to deficit areas. The Department of Agriculture estimates that the average home contains enough food to sustain its occupants for nearly two weeks, that retail stores hold a sufficient supply for another two weeks, and that wholesalers have enough for two or three weeks more. The Agriculture stockpile is designed to buy another two to six weeks of time for localities which, because of transportation blockage or other reasons, are unable to get immediate shipments from surplus areas. To date, however, the Department has been unable to obtain the funds necessary to carry out its plans.

The Department of Health, Education, and Welfare, in close collaboration with the Office of Civil Defense, administers a "back-up" stockpile of medical supplies valued at $200,878,138. It has received appropriations to continue acquiring such supplies.

Presumably the OEP study may point to additional stockpile requirements, both for population survival and for eventual industrial rehabilitation and recovery. The study has not yet progressed far enough to yield specific results. However, nongovernmental experts who testified before the Symington Subcommittee —notably Stephen Enke of the Institute of Defense Analyses and Herman Kahn of the Hudson Institute—felt that the most appropriate stockpile for nuclear-war conditions would be quite different from the present stockpile of industrial raw materials. When asked what he thought of the existing stockpile of raw materials, Kahn said simply, "I would sell most of it." He and Enke stressed the much higher priority of finished consumer goods such as processed foods, tents, blankets, stoves, hardware, and

winter clothing; heavy mobile equipment to remove debris; basic
construction materials and equipment such as steel beams, pipe,
lumber, cement, and bulldozers; critical components, such as
gauges and electric motors, needed to rebuild certain essential
facilities; machine tools; and petroleum products.[21]

The OEP staff members tend to be critical of the Kahn-Enke
view, which they consider to be too "off-the-cuff" and too extreme in its almost total rejection of the utility of industrial raw
or semiprocessed materials. They recognize that their completed
study may show a need for the types of things which Kahn and
Enke emphasized; in fact, they agree that assuring the necessary
supply of survival items must take first priority. But they also
feel that raw materials will be an important part of a nuclear-war
stockpile. They believe that although post-nuclear-attack requirements are likely to be lower than conventional-war requirements
for most of the materials currently in the stockpile, some of the
objectives may be increased and some additional raw materials
may be added to the stockpile list as a result of the nuclear-war
study. They also foresee some need for stockpiling materials in
semiprocessed forms, such as slabs, rods, sheets, and wire.[22]

The nonexpert in economics (such as this author) can hardly
presume to pass definitive judgment on this very complex matter.
The following remarks are bound to be superficial; yet they may
contribute something toward a general understanding of the
problem.

As Sidney Winter has pointed out, the problem of post-nuclear-attack recovery can be seen as a race between the restarting of the economy and the depletion of consumer inventories in the meantime.[23] The race could be lost if the damage

[21] Symington Hearings, Part 9, pp. 3148-3179.
[22] Interviews with OEP staff members.
[23] Sidney G. Winter, Jr., *Economic Viability after Thermonuclear War:
The Limits of Feasible Production* (RAND Memorandum, RM-3436-PR,
September 1963). The following discussion relies heavily on Winter's analysis, which does not, however, deal specifically with stockpiling as an aid
to postattack recovery. It also draws on testimony by Stephen Enke and
Herman Kahn before the Symington Subcommittee.

were so severe that the economy could not be reactivated until two years or more after the attack or if transportation facilities were so badly destroyed that many localities would run out of subsistence goods before new supplies could be brought in. Under the worst possible assumptions about the nature of the attack, winning the race might require the stockpiling of an entire "core" economy of basic industries underground. The cost of such a program would be so high that it must be ruled out for political if not economic reasons. At the other extreme, assuming more moderate damage, stockpiling could be directed toward stretching out and easing the survival period by building inventories of basic consumer goods and toward reconstruction of only those industries and supporting facilities which are absolutely essential for achieving a subsistence level of new consumer-goods production before the inventories run out. For cost and political reasons, stockpiling and other remedial measures probably should be focused on this lower end of the spectrum.

Fortunately, as already mentioned, food supplies do not seem to be a serious problem in an absolute sense. There would be enough to feed the survivors for two years or more if transportation were available. Studies have shown that transportation, under plausible assumptions, would not be seriously disrupted, although there are important potential vulnerabilities, such as the Sault locks, the bridges over the Mississippi River, and mountain tunnels. In view of the cruciality of transportation, perhaps construction materials and equipment should be stockpiled near these critical points. A more important vulnerability may be the availability of fuel. This problem indicates a possible requirement for stockpiling diesel oil, gasoline, and other petroleum products, and also possibly materials, components, and equipment for rebuilding refineries, which, incidentally, are rather dangerously concentrated.

The crucial industry for replenishing food supplies of course is agriculture. A nuclear attack is likely to affect agriculture in two different ways: destruction of resources needed to work the farms, such as farm manpower, petroleum supplies and refineries, and fertilizer plants; and contamination of the soil itself. Studies have shown that the latter would not be a serious problem for the nation as a whole, although there would undoubtedly be local areas in the path of heavy fall-out where the land would not be tillable for a long time. As in transportation, the most critical factor in agricultural production is likely to be the availability of petroleum products. American agriculture is highly mechanized; output could diminish radically if farm and local supplies of gasoline and lubricants ran out before the refineries and the transportation network were rebuilt. It is possible that commercial stocks of gasoline and oil which normally would be used for pleasure purposes (more than half of United States consumption) might be diverted to agriculture and other essential needs, assuming adequate government controls. But the latter assumption seems dubious. Hence, widely dispersed stocks of petroleum products, as well as materials, parts, and equipment for the rebuilding of refineries, would seem to have the highest priority in any stockpiling program for the rehabilitation of agriculture. Second-priority objectives probably would be the reconstruction of farm machinery and equipment production, fertilizer plants, and food-processing plants. And, of course, patching up transportation nets to allow the movement of farm produce to urban areas would be crucial.

Almost as urgent as food supplies and transportation would be the assurance of uncontaminated water supplies for the survivors. As noted above, the Office of Civil Defense had made a start by stocking water-purification equipment, but as of February 1963 only 45 units were stored at only 20 locations.[24] There is clearly a need for stocking more of these units and also for stockpiling essential parts and equipment for the prompt repair of urban water-supply systems.

Next in order of priority would probably be the stockpiling of what Stephen Enke has called "emergency camping equipment"

[24] Symington Hearings, Part 9, p. 3868.

—tents, bedding, stoves, winter clothing, fuel, and so on. Since people could not be expected to live for many months in a tent, there may also be a need for stocks of materials and equipment for the construction of temporary dwellings such as barracks.

The resumption of electric-power generation and transmission would very likely be a prerequisite for restarting the industrial economy on any significant scale. This would underline the importance of stockpiling not only construction materials and equipment but also fairly complex components such as generators and electric motors as well as simpler items such as copper wire.

It goes almost without saying that heavy equipment for the removal of debris would be a critical item. Such equipment would be especially valuable for the minimum rehabilitation of ports and for clearing a path between a port and the nearest railhead or highway.

The appropriate nature of the stockpiling program and other remedial measures are heavily dependent on the assumptions that are made concerning the postattack environment. One of the OEP's assumptions—that the federal government, cooperating with state and local governments, will have control over the postattack economy—is particularly crucial, and perhaps questionable. Rationing, allocations, and price control were difficult enough in the "normal" environment of World War II; the difficulties might be multiplied by several orders of magnitude in the chaotic conditions following a nuclear attack. Could federal control be asserted if Washington were destroyed? Even if it were not, would the government be able to take a quick and reasonably accurate inventory of the surviving assets and needs in different localities throughout the nation? Would it have the administrative resources and enforcement power necessary to carry out a large-scale movement of consumer goods, industrial assets, and labor forces from surplus to deficit regions? One can well imagine the political and enforcement problems which might arise if the government attempted to remove consumer goods, such as food, from a particular region for distribution elsewhere.

In general, *if* government control can be assumed, paper plans for the redistribution of surviving resources can substitute for stockpiling to a great extent. If not, the utility of local, dispersed stockpiles rises sharply. The assumption of government control does have the advantage of minimizing the calculated stockpile requirements, thus bringing them closer to the range of preattack political feasibility. But the assumption could be wrong. At the very least, this assumption carries the corollary implication of the need for the prompt repair of the nation's communication systems (perhaps with appropriate stockpiled items) and for the "stockpiling" of administrators highly trained to deal with post-attack survival and recovery problems.

The nature of the postattack environment depends heavily on the targeting and weight of the enemy attack. One wonders whether the NAHICUS model gives adequate consideration to the possibility that the enemy might deliberately destroy the most critical bottleneck points in the economy. If he is interested in maximizing our postattack recovery difficulties, such targets might well be of more interest to him than population concentrations or highly invulnerable military installations. For example, destruction of the twenty largest petroleum refineries might reduce postattack output below the minimum amount needed for population survival and industrial recovery. About fifty nuclear weapons directed at ports would eliminate the nation's port capacity and prevent any significant aid from imports. The huge hydroelectric dams in the West are important bottlenecks in the industrial system of that region. Specific vulnerabilities in the transportation system have already been mentioned. The steel industry is highly concentrated. An assumption of deliberate enemy destruction of such critical points might significantly increase stockpiling requirements.

Questions can also be raised about the OEP's assumption of a continuing broken-backed war after the nuclear exchange. While certainly possible, such a war is not considered likely by most professional strategists. If armies do continue to struggle for control over Europe and Asia, the United States' contribution to this struggle is likely to come from forces and equipment already in being; the economy can hardly be expected to produce tanks, planes, and guns in the aftermath of a massive nuclear exchange. To assume that it would introduces further complexity into a problem already fearfully complex. It seems plausible to assume that the tremendous nuclear superiority of the United States would be sufficient to eliminate the possibility of successful conventional action by enemy armies. Thus, there would be little or no need for continuing conventional defensive operations. Admittedly, if the war should continue on a nonnuclear level, the forces involved would require continuing supplies of consumables, such as food, clothing, petroleum, ammunition, and spare parts. It *may* be feasible to produce some of these items after a nuclear exchange or to stockpile them in advance. But if this requirement is added to the requirements for civilian survival and recovery, it is likely to raise projected stockpile objectives higher than Congress or the country would be willing to provide for in peacetime. One suspects that this assumption may be another manifestation of the "intellectual lag" about strategy which has distorted stockpile policy throughout its postwar history.

It is very difficult to believe that a stockpile of industrial raw materials would be of much immediate value for survival and recovery after a nuclear attack. Many of the processing plants which would use these materials might be destroyed or inoperable. Eventually, of course, after reconstruction of manufacturing and processing facilities, raw materials would be needed. But prewar commercial inventories of these materials are likely to escape heavy damage, and the extractive industries themselves, being rather well-dispersed from population centers, probably would survive any but the severest attack. The stockpile of raw materials for conventional war, under current assumptions, should be more than sufficient to fill any further needs for industrial reconstruction after a nuclear exchange.

To summarize the implications: A nuclear-war stockpile should be viewed mainly as a complement to the civil-defense program. That is, it should be directed primarily toward the immediate, urgent, and limited objective of assuring the survival of people, only secondarily to the problem of over-all industrial recovery, and not at all to assuring the continuation of military operations. This appraisal indicates priority for the stockpiling of essential consumer goods, basic construction materials, and heavy equipment for both construction and clean-up—all well-dispersed to smaller towns and cities and on the periphery of major cities. Stockpiling for industrial recovery should be limited to speeding the rebuilding of those facilities which are critical to the production and distribution of essential consumer goods (for example, food processing, drugs and medical supplies, transportation, petroleum refineries, and water-supply systems) and also perhaps of those bottlenecks which are essential to manufacturing (for example, electric-power plants, communications, and, again, petroleum refineries). For the latter, a stockpile of finished components, construction materials, and certain processed items such as wire and pipe are likely to have much greater utility than a stockpile of raw materials, with the exception of petroleum products. To aim higher than these minimum objectives is likely to generate stockpile requirements higher than are politically feasible.

Summary and Conclusions

There are four major themes in the narrative just completed: (1) the gradual and increasing corruption or distortion of a national security program by the pressures of subnational interests; (2) the relative isolation of stockpile policy making from developments in broad defense policy and strategic planning; (3) the multiplication of stockpile programs; and (4) the gradual shift from military to civilian control. The following analysis concentrates on the first two themes, incorporating references to the latter two.

National Security vs. Subnational Interests

We shall not attempt to analyze this theme in terms of any complex theoretical model of decision making. Instead, we shall focus on only two major variables (which surely are the crucial variables in any political activity)—namely *interests* and *power*.[1] In short, stockpiling policies and the outcomes of these policies

[1] Of course, we expect and hope that devotees of more sophisticated decision-making models will have found empirical data in the preceding chapters, which do fit into their particular approach. See, for example, the scheme developed by Richard C. Snyder, H. W. Bruck, and Burton Sapin, *Decision-Making as an Approach to the Study of International Politics*, Monograph No. 3, Foreign Policy Analysis Project Series, Princeton University, 1954.

can be explained largely in terms of the conflicting and common interests of the agencies, congressional committees, and private groups involved, and the relative bargaining power of these groups at various periods of stockpiling history.

It is convenient to divide stockpiling history into four fairly distinct periods: (1) the struggle for control of the stockpile between civilian and military agencies prior to passage of the Stockpiling Act of 1946; (2) the period of predominantly military control from 1946 to mid-1950; (3) the phase characterized by mixed or approximately equal military and civilian influence during the time of the Korean War; and (4) the period of dominant civilian control after 1953.

THE STRUGGLE FOR CONTROL

The negotiations preceding the passage of the Stockpiling Act of 1946 were a case of "bargaining without rules" (or without many), that is, bargaining which was not structured in advance by a set of legally sanctioned roles, procedures, and power allocations. The bargaining, in fact, tended to focus on the issue of the definition of roles and allocation of power for postwar stockpile decision making. The interests of the various agencies, however, were roughly the same as they were later, after Congress had structured the relative power relations. There is one important exception to be noted. While the State Department, in this preliminary round, seemed to be rather strongly interested in making the stockpile do double duty as an instrument for stabilizing the prices of primary commodities, it gave up or failed to press this interest during most of the later history of stockpiling, becoming instead the principal ally of the military in protecting the stockpile program against special domestic interests.

The principal fact which determined the outcome of the bargaining was the community of interest between the Military Affairs Committees and the military departments. The military wanted control over the program; the Committees, especially the House Committee, who had the power to write the legislation, wanted to give it to them. (This ultimate power of the Committee was, of course, a decisive element of structuring; the earlier remark about the unstructured nature of the bargaining applies most accurately to the Executive Branch.) The military departments were forced to accept something more than an advisory role for Interior as a "side-payment" to those committee members with mining constituencies; this concession was better, however, than being *themselves* relegated to an advisory capacity, which would have been their lot under the Administration's bill. After all, Interior would have a real decision-making influence only on the rather abstract matter of establishing stockpile goals, and could be outvoted by the War and Navy Departments anyway.

Perhaps the most interesting aspect of the bargaining was its resemblance to the phenomenon of shifting alliances in international politics during the eighteenth and nineteenth centuries. Alliances were made and broken as interests and the course of events seemed to dictate. The Department of State, which initiated the whole process, was in a weak position from the beginning. Consequently it was the most active architect of coalitions, attempting in the end to save as much as possible of its interests. It lined up first with the war mobilization agencies, then with the military, then with Interior, and finally with the OWMR and the Bureau of the Budget. The military departments, after a brief alignment with State, first attempted to go it alone, and then made unsuccessful overtures to Interior and the OWMR before they finally broke ranks and made common cause with a "peripheral power," the House Committee. After the Executive Branch negotiations, State got its way when the President approved vesting primary decision-making power in the OWMR. The victory turned out to be empty, though, when the military departments decided to oppose the official Administration bill.

The subversive maneuvers of Under Secretary Royall were of course contrary to the usual canons of administrative ethics; in particular, that Executive Branch agencies are supposed to sup-

port the President's program. Apparently, the strong desire of the
military departments to control the postwar program, their enormous prestige and influence in Congress, and the rather low
prestige and influence of President Truman provided sufficient
temptation to disregard ethics. And by prefacing his ambiguous
bid for control at the House Committee's hearing with a statement in support of the Administration bill, and making it appear
that the Committee had decided to drop the Administration bill
on its own responsibility, Royall preserved at least the semblance
of loyalty.

The final important point to be recalled about this early phase
concerns the contrasting attitudes of the agencies involved, particularly those of the military. While the civilian agencies were
willing that stockpiling, consistent with its naturally hybrid nature, should serve a variety of values, the military departments
insisted that it should serve only one, that of national security,
and they defined national security in a much narrower way than
did the civilians. For the military the phrase seemed to be more
or less synonymous with "military security." Hence they were unwilling to move off the strictly military track even so far as to
agree to the stockpiling of materials for minimum civilian needs
in time of war. Moreover, the military were reluctant to allow
even an advisory role for the civilian agencies, fearing that any
influence for them at all would lead to corruption of the program
by values and aims unrelated to the national security. Later,
after a military agency had been granted control of the program,
the military departments retreated from these rather unsophisti-
cated and exclusive attitudes. In fact, by 1952 the military had
shifted to the opposite extreme of wanting to get rid of a program
which they had realized was rather unmilitary in nature, politically controversial, and a competitor for scarce funds with more
important defense programs.

MILITARY CONTROL, 1946-1950

Although the Stockpiling Act did not materially change the interests of the agencies and groups concerned, it did authorita-

tively shape the distribution of power. The Act made clear that a military agency, the Munitions Board, was to have primary responsibility for major decisions. However, this responsibility was qualified in several ways which allocated some influence to other agencies. The Department of the Interior was given a substantial if vague role in that its Secretary was to participate "jointly" with the Secretaries of War and the Navy in the establishment of stockpile objectives. This sharing of power largely followed from the fact that the congressmen on the congressional Military Affairs Committees who took the leading role in writing the Act combined a military interest with an interest in domestic minerals producers. The first derived from their institutional role as members of the Committees, the second from their sectional political constituencies. The Buy-American provision, as well as the statement that one of the purposes of the Act was to "conserve and develop" domestic resources, further reflected the latter of these two congressional interests and conferred a considerable degree of "legitimized" influence upon the Interior Department and mining pressure groups. The interests of the Department of Commerce and materials-consuming interests, and a certain degree of power for these participants, were also given legal sanction by the provision that the stockpile should buy only materials "in excess of industrial demand" and by the specific authority granted to a division of Commerce to make the controlling decisions about the disposition of surplus materials from World War II. Other agencies with different subnational or other-national interests were granted some influence by the proviso that their "cooperation" was to be solicited in the establishment of stockpile goals. A continuing role for Congress itself, especially its Military Affairs Committees, was explicitly written into the law in the disposal provisions. Thus the authority and power of the Munitions Board was circumscribed from the beginning, and the stage was set legally for a continuing struggle between the "pure" national security interest and a variety of other interests.

During the period of its dominant control, the Munitions Board was fairly successful in protecting the national security interest against repeated assaults from the agents of competing interests. However, the Board very carefully observed those provisions in the law which were designed to protect the competing interests despite the existence of escape clauses. A case in point was the provision that the stockpile should avoid competition with industrial consumers only "so far as is practicable." The Board either did not invoke the qualification or was very reluctant to invoke it even after the President had ordered a more active and competitive purchasing policy in 1948. The Board denied any general responsibility for furthering domestic "conservation and development," insisting that this purpose of the Act was meant to be carried out by the research programs of the Interior and Agriculture Departments. Nevertheless, the Board *did* almost always favor domestic producers over foreign whenever the former could meet the world market price or could qualify for the limited price premiums allowable by the Steelman interpretation of the Buy-American Act.

These limited concessions by the Munitions Board can be attributed to several factors. With respect to the competition with industrial buyers, the Board's diffidence in the early years in part simply reflected the prevailing mood of the times, which combined a concern about inflation with a lack of full perception of the threat to security. It also reflected a tendency in the Munitions Board, as a military agency, to lean over backward to avoid giving offense to civilian agencies and groups in administering a program which, by its nature, inextricably combined military and civilian elements and was politically controversial to boot. The Board did not want to expose itself to the accusation of "taking over" or expanding beyond its proper role when questions of choice between military security and nonsecurity values were at issue, and it wanted to avoid involvement in political controversy as much as possible. Hence it simply delegated to the Civilian Production Administration the responsibility for choosing between stockpile acquisition and industrial need. The Board seems to have been extremely careful to avoid contradicting "the will of Congress," hence its failure or reluctance to invoke the escape clause.

Also, many men on the Munitions Board staff, both military and civilian, sincerely believed that domestic development would redound to the national security. Therefore they were glad to prefer domestic sources of supply when domestic purchases did not involve an extra drain on stockpile funds. On the other side of the coin, some also believed that giving industrial consuming industries first call on available materials was only an application of their own view that a sound economy was an essential aspect of national security. To a certain extent, therefore, the attitudes or "myths" held and propagated by the subnational interests were internalized within the Munitions Board's own thinking.

Because of these attitudes, the Muntions Board *did* capitulate to subnational pressures somewhat more than was required by law. Nevertheless, the Board did draw the line at some point— and where it drew the line, it stood steadfastly and fought tenaciously. It firmly resisted strong demands to use stockpile funds as subsidies to domestic producers. It persistently pressed for allocation of stockpile funds according to the criterion of balancing the inventory rather than according to the availability of materials, the latter being in part a cover term for the management of stockpile policy so as to stabilize markets. It insisted that security in raw materials should be no greater than the general level of United States security, against demands from Interior and Congress for "100 per cent security" in raw materials. Against the pressures of the big-stockpile advocates who sought to junk the strategic assumptions of the Joint Chiefs of Staff, the Munitions Board stood fast for the Joint Chiefs. A general hypothesis is suggested here: that a military agency will fight harder in interagency bargaining on issues perceived to be military or strategic in nature than it will on other issues. Thus the Board held fast against a majority of the Strategic Materials Committee on the matter of strategic assumptions but capitulated to the Interior point of view on other matters (such as civilian requirements in wartime) which bore on stockpile objectives. It was only after the Korean War brought a greater sense of urgency into the situation, when Congress became much more generous in granting appropriations, and when the NSRB began asserting itself more aggressively during 1950, that the Munitions Board agreed to adopt the factoring system, which sharply increased stockpile objectives by taking account of political and economic risks which the JCS guidance had either ignored or minimized. (It may be worth noting that it was the JCS decision to stop assessing political and economic factors *at all*, after the alleged need to more fully consider such factors was pointed out, which provided the final impetus for adoption of the factoring system. Thus one might say in partial explanation that the military opted to maintain their "role purity" at the expense of their policy preferences.)

An exception which may in part prove the rule is the fact that the Munitions Board was much more aggressive with agencies responsible for *foreign-policy* programs than in bargaining with domestically oriented agencies. Thus it exerted strong pressure upon the ECA to use its counterpart funds and the bargaining leverage of the foreign-aid program generally to increase foreign production of strategic materials for the stockpile. Conversely, there is no instance on record before the Korean War of the Munitions Board being persuaded to use the stockpile program to serve foreign-policy ends. Part of the reason may be that the State Department did not exercise much persuasion in this direction. Nevertheless, there is reason to suspect two things: (1) that the Munitions Board really did not feel that foreign-policy programs contributed to national security in the same sense that military programs did, and that therefore it was not concerned about the possible conflicts in objective between foreign-policy programs and stockpiling—as was the case with the foreign-aid programs; and (2) that the foreign-policy agencies had weak "constituencies" in Congress and outside the government; therefore any pressure upon, or resistance to, their interests was not likely to backfire in the form of domestic political controversy.

Curiously, the Munitions Board's lack of responsiveness to foreign-policy considerations occurred despite the fact that the Department of State was its most loyal ally on the Strategic Materials Committee (later the Interdepartmental Stockpile Committee). A relevant point is that the Stockpiling Act said nothing about accommodating stockpile policy to foreign policy, whereas it did have a good deal to say about the protection of domestic interests.

In the Introduction it was suggested that one function of the rather rigid, logical formulae which the Munitions Board used to determine both ultimate goals and current procurement programs was to resist domestic political pressures even though the systems may not have been developed primarily or consciously for this purpose. Any agency or group which wanted to increase the objectives or current budgets could be put off by invoking "the formula," which implied that stockpiling policy was, and necessarily had to be, determined in the manner of an objective solution of a problem rather than as a subjective choice between values or interests. Obviously there could be only one "correct" solution to a "problem." Any group which challenged the Board's policies therefore was forced to challenge the formulae which underlay them, which of course tended to reduce the bargaining power of these groups, especially when the formulae emanated from such a prestigious entity as the Joint Chiefs of Staff. The most relevant illustration here is the action of the NSRB in breaking Interior's challenge to the JCS strategic assumptions on the ground that only the JCS had the right and the competence to make such assumptions. But it should also be mentioned that the use of "objective" formulae as a device for policy making and the problem-solving attitude generally were also consistent with the Munitions Board's image of its own role as a "working, factual agency" (to use Admiral Paine's revealing phrase)—that is, an agency which had nothing to do with, and was properly not concerned with, politics and subjective value choices.

On the other hand, it is interesting to note that in defending its

policies before congressional committees, notably the Public
Lands and Interior and Insular Affairs Committees, the spokesmen for the Board did not often invoke the objective formulae
when their policies were criticized. In tête-à-têtes with Congress,
the dominant motive of the Board seemed to be conciliation;
Congress was an organ to be propitiated, not fought with. Thus
the military witnesses would say, typically, something to the
effect that the size of the stockpile objectives was a "matter of
opinion" (thus soothing the congressmen by admitting the possible validity of their own prescriptions), that in fact the Munitions Board would welcome a larger stockpile and was prevented
from planning and buying it only by the failure of the Appropriations Committees to provide enough funds, and so on. To have
defended themselves by referring to objective formulae which
indicated that greater stockpile purchasing would be objectively
"wrong" or "irrational" would have been to take a more comba-
tive stance and might have alienated some congressmen. This
tactic was desirable in dealing with executive agencies of equal
or lesser stature and power than the Munitions Board and the
Department of Defense, but with Congress, appeasement was
the preferred tack.

Somewhat related to the invocation of systematic formulae was
the Munitions Board's tendency to "pass the buck" to other agencies when it came under fire in Congress. "The NSRB makes the
policies, we are only the program agency," "in deciding upon the
source of purchase, we rely upon the Department of the Interior
and the Department of State," or "our quality specifications are
set by our industry advisory committees," etc., etc., were all typi-
cal rejoinders. Thus the formal participation by other agencies
and private interest groups in the policy-making process, however disruptive and productive of conflict it was in the Executive
Branch, nevertheless was politically useful to the Munitions
Board in its transactions with Congress.

It should not be inferred from the preceding analysis that the
attitudes and interests of the civilian agencies (and congressional

committees) were determined entirely by the interests of their private constituency groups. Almost as important, perhaps more important in some instances, was the agency's own perception of its "job," of the role which it played and the aims and objectives it had been given responsibility for serving in the over-all governmental process. Thus Interior's advocacy of a large stockpile and more vigorous buying did not stem simply from a feeling in Interior's Bureau of Mines that it existed primarily to promote the interests of the domestic mining industry. The Bureau, and by extension the whole Department, also believed that it was responsible for strengthening the over-all natural-resource position of the United States in terms of operating productive capacity, discovery of new reserves of minerals, and so on. Relatedly, the personnel in the Department (as is perfectly normal with bureaucrats everywhere) tended to magnify the importance of their own specialty or object of concern, as compared to other governmental programs. Thus Pehrson demanded 100 per cent security in raw materials, even though something less than 100 per cent was being accepted in other defense programs, because raw materials were somehow more "fundamental" than anything else. The Department of Commerce naturally resisted aggressive competition with private users of materials because competition would tend to raise prices and one of its most important responsibilities was to control inflation. The same point can be made in explanation of some of the attitudes and interests of the Munitions Board. Thus the Board did not worry much about the depletion of underground reserves which might be a consequence of its domestic purchasing, or the somewhat questionable security value of just moving materials from below-ground to the surface within the country, because its job was simply to acquire the planned stockpile at minimum cost from whatever source. The Board's direct or predominant responsibility for stockpiling, combined with its equal responsibility for other programs of military procurement, naturally contributed to a small-stockpile orientation, a desire to keep the stockpile in balance, both internally and externally, vis-à-vis other military procurement programs, and related attitudes. The fact that the civilian agencies, and in fact the individual armed services, did not share this responsibility, which of course included the heavy responsibility for developing budget requests, contributed greatly to their differences with the Munitions Board.

Frictions and conflicts *were* rather sharp and characteristic of the stockpile decision-making process from the outset in 1946 until 1953. The primary reason seems to be that no agency's or group's interests were being completely satisfied, and the primary reasons for *that* were the Munitions Board's staunch resistance to nonsecurity interests and pressures and the Board's difficulties in prying funds out of Congress. The process became smoother after 1953, for related reasons, but that is getting ahead of the story.

KOREAN WAR PERIOD, 1950-1953

The partial mobilization program during the Korean War changed the actors in the drama and reshuffled the distribution of power, but did not basically change the nature of the interests concerned. First, the NSRB acquired much greater influence, and the stockpile buyers in the GSA gained their freedom from the most onerous aspects of Munitions Board control. These two changes amounted to a substantial rise in civilian influence in stockpile decision making. Increased power for the NSRB was important in leading to the adoption of the factoring system in September 1950, although a greater sense of urgency and a desire on the part of some participants to tidy up the decision-making processes also contributed. As mentioned earlier, the adoption of this system caused almost a 75 per cent increase in stockpile goals. The Munitions Board was definitely lukewarm about the system and its result, but agreed to go along with its civilian advocates, partly because Congress had become much more generous in granting funds. Also, since the general military budget increased greatly, the norm of equalizing "marginal security utility" across all defense programs permitted a stockpiling increase.

The cast of characters was changed when President Truman created an entirely new industrial-mobilization structure late in 1950. The NSRB dropped out of the picture, and the ODM, the DPA, and a variety of "operating" agencies took over all of industrial-mobilization policy—with the notable exception of stockpiling, which remained with the Munitions Board. The power distribution changed with the enormous grant of legal authority to the new agencies in the Defense Production Act of 1950. These agencies gained the power to allocate materials to all recipients, including the stockpile, as well as the power to plan and carry out a vast program for expanding production, most prominently, of raw materials.

The new power position of the Munitions Board was much weaker and extremely anomalous. While it retained the legal, formal, and publicly recognized responsibility for acquiring a stockpile, the real power to determine the rate of acquisition of which materials had passed to the new civilian agencies. Although restrictions placed by the latter agencies on civilian consumption did make more materials available for stockpiling (at least during certain periods) and the rate of acquisition did increase somewhat, the rate was far short of what the Munitions Board desired. The Board protested vigorously, but to little avail. The impact of the restrictions was felt unevenly across the range of stockpiled materials, resulting in further unbalance. Naturally, the mobilizers permitted large purchases of plentiful materials and sharply restricted the acquisition of those in short supply.

The mobilizers also attempted to persuade the Munitions Board to mold its stockpile procurement programs so as to give support to the mobilizers' program for expanding materials production, primarily domestic. The Board resisted, on the ground that it had no responsibility for the expansion program, which moreover was oriented toward general economic welfare as well as national security. Eventually the Board gave in partially, adjusting its purchases in a limited way to provide a guaranteed market to producers who agreed to expand their output in return for certain incentives. In the process, it reluctantly agreed to var-

ious unorthodox features in its stockpile contracts, notably floor
prices, which required the stockpile to take materials only if their
prices fell below a certain level. In the Munitions Board's view,
this was a form of market stabilization, which it deplored on
principle and also because stockpile intake via such contracts
was highly uncertain. The uncertainty tended to disrupt procurement planning. At length, however, the Bureau of the Budget released the Board from such contracts, as well as from excessively
long-term contracts, by decreeing that materials flowing from
them should go into a new and different kind of stockpile, authorized by the Defense Production Act and administered by the civilian mobilizers. This was the first step toward the proliferation
of stockpiles of subsequent years.

Internationally, United States stockpile purchasing raised some
hackles among Europeans, who mistakenly believed that it was
the primary cause of the inflation of materials prices in latter
1950 and early 1951, adversely affecting the Europeans' "terms of
trade." The row raised by the Europeans was one factor which
led to the International Materials Conference, through which the
European countries as well as some non-European producing
countries exercised influence over United States materials importing. In particular, American stockpile accumulation probably
was somewhat restricted below the rate which might otherwise
have been possible. The Munitions Board was again on the defensive during the IMC negotiations, since the civilian mobilizers
and the Department of State tended to be sympathetic to the
other countries.

During the latter part of the Korean War (1952-1953), supply
conditions improved, largely as the result of the expansion programs carried out by the civilian mobilization agencies. The rate
of stockpile acquisition increased, and the net result of the Korean mobilization experience for the stockpile was substantial
progress toward its ultimate objectives.

To sum up, the deviations of stockpiling policy from the
straight and narrow path of national security, which had been

NATIONAL VS. SUBNATIONAL INTERESTS

evident on a minor scale earlier, continued during the Korean
War mobilization. The differences were that the deviations were
somewhat greater and were the consequence of administrative
decisions by the new mobilization agencies who now held effective power, not of voluntary concessions by the Munitions Board.
To the security-oriented Munitions Board, taking badly needed
materials from the stockpile while allowing consumer durable
goods to be produced at recent peacetime levels appeared as
gross disregard of national security and as kowtowing to domestic pressures. However, to the mobilizers, more broadly responsible for general economic values as well as security, it no doubt
seemed that the economic disruption which would be caused by
fulfilling the Munitions Board's purchase schedules for the very
tight materials would be disproportionate to the security value
received. Also, the mobilizers probably sincerely believed that
using stockpile contracts to support expansion programs was consistent with national security, or at least with a multi-valued conception of the national interest. Nevertheless, there are bits of
factual evidence that the mobilizers *were* influenced by specific
pressures. The decision to permit a very high level of automobile
production, for example, and the withdrawals of copper from the
stockpile were undoubtedly related to the outcries from Senator
Homer Ferguson, other Michigan congressmen, and the auto
manufacturers and workers when mobilization decisions and
scarcity of materials threatened to curtail production. In any particular industry office in the Department of Commerce on any
day of the week during the last weeks of 1950 and early 1951,
small manufacturers could be seen queued up to apply for special extra allotments of materials on grounds of hardship, and
many of these requests were granted. The expansion programs undoubtedly were influenced by pressures from mining-state
congressmen and mining-industry associations. The bloating of
the DPA inventory in subsequent years would seem to provide
prima-facie evidence that some materials producers were effective in getting government incentives and benefits to support a

degree of production expansion which was not justified by either national defense or the economy's capacity to absorb the materials.

The civilian mobilizers distributed materials according to four primary criteria: short-run national security needs, the building of an economic mobilization base for rapid movement to a full-scale war footing if necessary, the long-run national economic welfare, and the short-run minimization and relative equalization of sacrifice by consumers and businessmen. The latter, of course, was a political value. The stockpile program occupied a rather low position on the scale of priorities. To a greater degree than before the Korean War, the stockpile program was used as a selective instrument of economic stabilization both on the high side (relieving shortages) and on the low side (supporting prices and domestic production). In another sense, the civilian mobilization agencies used the stockpile as a convenient, quickly manipulable lubricant or buffer to ease the consequences of frictions, accidents, inconsistencies, and mistakes in other segments of the mobilization program, and generally to relieve the tension between limited supplies and the more imperative and politically potent demands of defense production, expansion programs, and the civilian economy.

CIVILIAN CONTROL, SINCE 1953

The transfer of the stockpile program to civilian control in 1953 was natural because it had become quite evident during the Korean War that the program logically should be integrated with general industrial-mobilization planning and because the ODM and the other mobilization agencies had already asserted *de facto* control over procurement policy. The Department of Defense was in fact quite glad to be rid of the program, having had enough of battling with the civilians, of being legally and publicly responsible (and thus the target of attacks and pressures) while the mobilizers pulled the strings, and of having stockpiling compete with military hardware for funds in the over-all national security budget. The reorganization further shifted the distribution of bargaining power from the military to the civilian mobilizers. Formally the relative power of the other interested agencies remained unchanged; in practice, however, their power increased because of the inherent weakness in the bargaining power of the ODM as compared to that of the Munitions Board. The nature of the *interests* concerned remained relatively unchanged, except that the ODM valued the objective of national security somewhat less intensely perhaps than had the Munitions Board and perhaps defined it somewhat more broadly. It did insist, however, that national security was the sole aim of the stockpiling program.

Nevertheless, during the Eisenhower Administration, deference to subnational interests increased, causing a further distortion of the stockpile from its original criterion of national security. The primary manifestations are the adoption of the long-term stockpile program to prop up domestic prices and domestic producers, ostensibly to nurture the mobilization base, and the increased recourse to withdrawals and diversions from the stockpile to relieve shortages and depress high prices. In short, stockpiling evolved further in the direction of economic stabilization although this function was never openly acknowledged by the administrators.

Two of the reasons for this trend have just been alluded to: one had to do with the *attitudes* prevalent in the ODM, the other with the agency's relatively low status and *power*. The ODM was never as single-mindedly dedicated to national security, to the virtual exclusion of other values, as the Munitions Board had been. Thus the ODM was more vulnerable to outside pressures which sought to manipulate the stockpile program for private gain. More importantly, and further increasing its vulnerability, the ODM lacked the prestige which normally characterizes a military agency, even one so peripheral as the Munitions Board. As a part of the powerful Department of Defense, the Munitions Board had been able to resist extraneous pressures with considerable success. Furthermore it could invoke the logic and requirements of national security with considerably more force and plausibility than could the ODM. Apart from the ODM's own attitudes and power, certain prevalent attitudes in the upper echelon of the Administration also tended to favor subnational interests. Most noteworthy was the Administration's ideological commitment to the notion that a strong economy was just as important for national security as was military strength. Closely related was the belief in the importance of maintaining a strong domestic mobilization base.

The stockpiling policy process during the Eisenhower Administration might be compared to a diffuse taffy pull, with the Commerce Department on one end pulling for the industrial consumers, the Department of the Interior on the other end pulling for the domestic producers, the Department of State pulling (with somewhat more vigor than before) for the interests of producers overseas, and the Department of Defense (now shorn of most of its power) pulling everything toward the middle and trying to minimize the thinning of the middle area, which might be labeled the national security. The ODM acted as referee or compromiser, and in this role its decisions (apart from its more technical, detailed activities) amounted to an attempt to accommodate all the contestants simultaneously. This description is an exaggeration and somewhat unkind to the ODM, but it does point up the general situation.

Several officials in the ODM told this author that there was more "understanding" of the stockpile program in Congress in the mid-1950's than ever before and less conflict among the participating agencies. This was undoubtedly true, and the reasons for it are rather obvious. Every interested agency and group (with the possible exception of the Defense Department, which had lost much of its interest in the program) received a substantial satisfaction of its particular interests. The primary reason for the high degree of conflict which had characterized the Munitions Board's tenure was the Board's stubborn resistance to nonsecurity pressures. Under Eisenhower, domestic producers, particularly of lead and zinc, who wielded the most political power, enjoyed enhanced prosperity, for a time at least, from the long-term price-support operation. Industrial users of raw materials, when confronted with shortages, had only to call upon the Department of Commerce, which provided quick relief, after some persuasion at the ODM. The Department of State occasionally was able to get special consideration for foreign producers, in the form of either stockpile purchases or the postponement of a disposal plan. If fact, the ODM seems to have in effect abdicated a good bit of its formal decision-making authority to these other agencies in the areas of their special concern. This deference to others was most evident with respect to disposals: the ODM usually dropped any proposed disposal if another agency objected.

During this period, the power of the Interior Department particularly increased, partly because of the President's appointment of Douglas McKay, Secretary of the Interior, to head the Cabinet Committee on Minerals Policy. More pertinent was the appointment as Assistant Secretary of the Interior of Felix Wormser, whose force of personality and personal energy seems to have been important. Wormser, a lead-industry executive, worked very hard on behalf of the lead and zinc industry, and apparently it was largely through his personal efforts that the lead-zinc support program was adopted. If Carl Rolle of the Department of Defense deserved the sobriquet of "Mr. Stockpile" before 1953, Felix Wormser deserves it after that date.

Another feature of stockpiling during the Eisenhower Administration was the further proliferation of stockpiles, which was related to the increased influence of subnational interests. The long-term program was really a substockpile; although it was legally justified by the Stockpiling Act, it operated according to quite different assumptions and rules than did the original or minimum stockpile. Both of these together made up the "strategic stockpile." The DPA stockpile continued to thrive and grow. The supplemental stockpile was born in servitude, so to speak, to the Department of Agriculture and was designed to further the interests of that agency and its farm constituency in getting rid of part of its own burdensome "stockpile" of surplus agricultural goods. The Commodity Credit Corporation acquired by barter a certain stock of strategic materials which was not dignified by a name; much of it seemed to be in transit or was expected to be transferred to one or another of the other stockpiles. Only the original minimum program could be justified solely in terms of national security; the others were designed to serve other aims only remotely related to national security.

All of these stockpiles still exist. Current additions are the civil-defense stockpile of the Department of Defense; the stockpile of medical supplies held by the Department of Health, Education, and Welfare; and the stockpile of processed or semiprocessed foods which the Department of Agriculture would like to convert out of its piles of wheat and other farm commodities; a stockpile of post-nuclear-attack survival items which the Office of Emergency Planning has developed on paper; and a planned stockpile of materials and other products to insure industrial recovery after a nuclear war.

It is probably more than a coincidence that the trends toward greater deference to nondefense interests, increasing use of the stockpile and stockpile funds for market stabilization purposes, higher stockpile goals, and the multiplication of stockpiles were accompanied by a trend toward civilian control.

The fear which military spokesmen had expressed before passage of the Stockpiling Act of 1946—that a stockpile in civilian hands would become a political football—has proved to be amply justified. The principal reasons appear to be that the civilian mobilizers were more vulnerable to industry and congressional pressure than was the Munitions Board; they were responsible for a wider range of values than the Board had been; and they defined national security in somewhat broader terms. To a degree, some of the values which the Munitions Board would have considered extraneous were quite legitimate within this broader frame of reference. There is nothing intrinsically sinful about market stabilization. Nevertheless, the introduction of such values, along with the attempt to camouflage them as elements in national security (or the belief that they *were* aspects of national security), tended to blur the ground rules for stockpiling and to open wide the door to dubious manipulation in response to pressures from self-interested groups.

Stockpiling and Strategy

According to logic and common sense, a program of industrial mobilization should be geared to a military strategy. Assumptions about the possible nature of future wars—conventional or nuclear, limited or general, regular or guerrilla—as well as intelligence about enemy capabilities and intent, and most importantly our own plans of response to various possible contingencies have a direct bearing on a program such as stockpiling.

During the early postwar years, stockpile policy and military policy were consistent in a general way. It was assumed in military planning that a future war would be much like World War II. The atomic bomb (which was a United States monopoly until 1949) would help to deter the war and would provide a marginal assist in fighting the war should deterrence fail, but the main burden of combat would rest with conventional forces. Accordingly, it would probably be a long war; military forces, while small at the outbreak, would be greatly expanded during the course of the war by the large-scale mobilization of industry. The various plans for universal military training, to provide a large reserve of readily mobilizable manpower, as well as the stockpile program and the development of industrial-mobilization plans by the Munitions Board and the NSRB testified to the prevalence of this general view.

The Soviet explosion of an atomic weapon in 1949 and the outbreak of the Korean War in 1950 generated simultaneous programs for an increase and diversification of the United States nuclear arsenal, a substantial increase in conventional forces in being, and a buildup of the industrial mobilization base for quick movement to maximum military production after the outbreak of a general war. While there was a somewhat sharper perception of the deterrent and combat potential of nuclear weapons, the basic image of future war remained substantially the same. This image was reflected, for example, in the plan agreed upon at the Lisbon NATO conference of 1952 to create 90 divisions (about half in reserve status) for the defense of Western Europe. The stockpile program was consistent with this image; in fact, it was considered part of the program for creating a broad mobilization base. In general, the Korean War partial mobilization, including the increased stockpile accumulation during the period, followed the mainstream of military thinking. It is true that at least as early as the great "B-36 debate" of 1949, which largely concerned the relative merits of strategic nuclear bombing and conventional military action, a deviant image of a short war in which nuclear power would be decisive had been gaining adherents, especially in the Air Force. Nevertheless, it was still a minority view.

While it is true that stockpiling policy was generally consistent with military strategy before 1953, it cannot be said that it was guided or controlled in a specific and detailed way by an agreed strategic plan. In the first place, the Joint Chiefs were never able to agree on a comprehensive "joint" strategic plan, even though the long war–industrial mobilization image was dominant. The JCS did provide strategic assumptions for use in estimating wartime materials supplies, but these assumptions seem to have been rather routinely prepared, perhaps not out of whole cloth, but nevertheless by a process of crystal-gazing not precisely based on a strategic war plan. A frequent complaint of the civilian stockpiling agencies was that guidance from the JCS was inadequate; this complaint, along with less disinterested pressures (which perhaps were effective *because* of the ambiguity of the strategic guidance), eventually led to adoption of the factoring system, which sharpened up and supplemented the JCS strategic assumptions in the direction of more pessimistic estimates of probable wartime supplies.

Stockpiling policy and military strategy began to diverge much more sharply with the advent of a Republican Administration in 1953. This divergence was the result of logically *opposite* policy changes in both areas. In the realm of military strategy, the Eisenhower Administration reduced conventional forces, attempted to cover a wider variety of military challenges by threats of nuclear retaliation, and sharply downgraded the likelihood of a conventional war of substantial intensity or duration. During the middle and late 1950's, it was generally assumed in the higher Pentagon circles (excluding the Army) that future wars would be nuclear either from the beginning or would become so, or if conventional, would be rather small affairs not requiring any significant industrial mobilization. Nevertheless, the Administration remained committed, during its first term at least, to the continuing importance of intrawar industrial mobilization and actually increased stockpile objectives. The Administration consistently pressed for a greater emphasis on inactive, partially trained manpower reserves as a substitute for active ground troops.

This narrative shows that the Department of Defense was aware of the contradiction between strategy and stockpile policy as early as 1954. The Department made several attempts to convince President Eisenhower of this inconsistency but did not succeed until 1958, after the achievement by the Soviets of a long-range nuclear strike capability had forced a sweeping review of United States defense policy. The result was the adoption of the three-year-war assumption previously favored by the Pentagon and the automatic creation of huge stockpile surpluses, much of which might not have accrued had military strategy and stockpiling policy made connection earlier.

One must doubt, on the available evidence, that the military assumption of a three-year war rested on an agreed military strategic plan. Apparently it did represent an agreed "military mobilization program" before 1957; that is, it was the time assumption for the JCS, Department of Defense, and service prognostications concerning the amount and rate of buildup of military demands on the economy during war. But as such it was a rather arbitrary assumption, made necessary by the administrative need to make "paper plans" for industrial mobilization, and apparently was not intimately connected with *strategic* thinking in either the JCS or the individual services.

Curiously, by the time the three-year-war criterion was adopted for stockpiling in 1958, it was already obsolete in terms of top-level military and mobilization planning assumptions. Approximately a year and a half earlier, the NSC and Pentagon directives had virtually written off any need for industrial mobilization beyond the first six months after the outbreak of war. One reason why the new stockpiling policies did not reflect these directives was political in nature: to have declared all of the stockpile surplus except for a six-months' supply would have set off loud howls of protest from the mining interests.

Another reason relates to the flimsiness of the supposed top-level military "agreement" on war planning assumptions. Anyone familiar with the Pentagon decision-making processes can testify to the remarkable resistance and inertia on the part of the service bureaucracies to the implementation of abstract "policy papers" prepared by the JCS or the NSC. The policy papers generated by the New New Look went far, though not all the way, toward acceptance of the Air Force views. The Air Force apparently continued to plan on the assumption of a very short, highly destructive nuclear war which would leave no scope for industrial mobilization. On the other hand, unreconstructed Army planners continued to assume the possibility of a long conventional war, with substantial intrawar mobilization, and they made *their* strategic plans accordingly. After the Kennedy Administration took office, Secretary of Defense Robert S. McNamara reported as follows:

We found that the three military departments had been establishing their requirements independently of each other. I think the results can fairly be described as chaotic: the Army planning, for example, was based, largely, on a long war of attrition, while the Air Force planning was based largely on a short war of nuclear bombardment. Consequently, the army was stating a requirement for stocking months of fighting supplies against the event of a sizable conventional conflict, while the Air Force stock requirements for such a war had to be measured in days, and not very many days at that.[2]

Thus one reason for the divorce between stockpiling and evolving strategic doctrine was that the three armed services were unable to agree on a strategic doctrine until 1961 or later. That is, there was no generally accepted strategy for stockpiling to be related *to*. So long as there existed a considerable body of opinion in the Army, and perhaps the Navy, that a long, large-scale conventional war was conceivable or more likely than a short nuclear war, the stockpilers could feel at least somewhat justified in their five-year assumption, whatever assumptions to the contrary might be emanating from the office of the Secretary of Defense.

The 1958 assumption of a three-year war, for stockpiling purposes, was essentially a bargained or compromised figure, somewhere between the Air Force and the Army conceptions of the nature of future war. It was not logically deduced from the national policy papers which purported to establish a uniform set of planning assumptions, although it did move stockpiling policy in the general direction of the prevailing trends in strategic planning. It stopped short of full consistency with those trends because of the fundamental disagreement about strategic doctrine within the military establishment, because a large stockpile had already been acquired, because no one was certain that the proponents of the long-war doctrine were wrong, and because a more radical change might have caused unpleasant political repercussions.

It is probably fair to say that the lack of agreement about strategy in the JCS and among the individual services increased the vulnerability of the stockpilers to domestic pressures, contrib-

[2] Quoted in William W. Kaufmann, *The McNamara Strategy* (New York: Harper, 1964), p. 30.

uted to the inflation of stockpile objectives, and resulted in the accumulation of unnecessary surpluses. If the JCS could have firmly agreed on a definite strategic plan including definite assumptions about the length of a future war or mobilization period, they would have been politically capable, as a corporate body, of presenting this plan more vigorously before the Interdepartmental Stockpile Committee, the National Security Council, and the President. Failing this unanimity, stockpiling policy was made in a strategic vacuum, and those who urged a big stockpile for supporting a mobilization base in domestic minerals production enjoyed considerably more influence than they otherwise might have.

The first Eisenhower term was a time of strategic "doublethink" at the highest military and civilian levels. The new implications and potentialities of nuclear airpower conflicted sharply with deeply ingrained traditions and past experience emphasizing protracted intrawar mobilization. A belief in the overwhelming decisiveness of nuclear weapons for both deterrence and the fighting of wars competed with a lingering faith that the most valuable wartime asset of the United States was its great industrial strength. During the heyday of the massive-retaliation policy, the Secretary of Defense could assert that "the Russians are more afraid of Detroit than of the atomic bomb." Such bifurcated thinking was most clearly evident in the mind of President Eisenhower. While repeatedly asserting that the days of the large-scale conventional war were over, he nevertheless approved policies to strengthen the mobilization base, including a large stockpile, which would be relevant only for the contingency which he himself had declared to be anachronistic.

The responsibility for the gross inconsistency between stockpile policy and military strategy must be laid very largely to the President himself. An overwhelming majority of his military and civilian advisers repeatedly urged a retrenchment in stockpiling beginning early in 1954, but he stubbornly refused to be persuaded until four years later. And the modest changes made in 1958 still left stockpiling policy badly out of step with new strategic doctrines approved by the President during the intervening years. It certainly is difficult to reconcile the stockpiling assumption of a war even three years long, implying substantial industrial mobilization, with the Eisenhower Administration's continued commitment to a predominantly nuclear strategy and its assumption at high policy levels that a long conventional war with our major enemy was extremely unlikely.

The present stockpile (exclusive of the surpluses) is more consistent with the military policy of the Kennedy and Johnson Administrations. Under President Kennedy, conventional forces were increased to a point where the United States had the option of a conventional response to a much wider variety of military challenges, and therefore could reduce its dependence on nuclear deterrence or on nuclear strikes in case of war. At the same time, nuclear strength was tremendously increased, underlining the certainty that a *nuclear* attack on the United States or its allies would be suicidal for the aggressor. These actions seemed to add up to a greater likelihood that a major war could be kept conventional. Of course, the two-edged preparation also reduced the chances of any war at all. And if a conventional war should break out between the United States and the Soviet Union, the terrifying shadow cast by the thermonuclear weapons in the background would produce enormous pressures on both sides to end the conflict quickly by negotiation. Even the achievement of full conventional equality between the NATO powers and the Soviet Union would not justify a confident assumption that a long conventional war similar to World War II had become very likely. Nevertheless, it is a possibility which should not be dismissed completely and which could become more plausible as a result of further increases in NATO's conventional arms, or of possible developments in the field of arms control—for example, a tacit or explicit ban on the "first use" of nuclear weapons or an agreement to reduce nuclear arsenals to minimum-deterrent levels. Speculation aside, changes in United States military capability and doctrine since 1960 have removed most of the blatant contradiction between stockpiling and strategy which characterized the previous Administration—when the United States was unprepared to fight, and had no intention of fighting, the only kind of war for which a stockpile of strategic raw materials made any sense at all.

In view of developments in the Far East in early 1965, and the rather belligerent attitude assumed by Communist China in recent years, we should note perhaps that the Soviet Union is not the only great power against which the United States might have to fight a conventional war of substantial dimensions. A war with China over Southeast Asia is distinctly possible (with the Soviets perhaps "lending" China part of their great submarine fleet for the attrition of United States shipping) and could involve wartime mobilization considerably greater than that of the Korean War.

The above remarks should not be construed as a fully developed argument for retaining the present stockpile for conventional war or for not reducing the three-year-war assumption. There are reasons to believe that the present objectives are still too high from the view of probable need and that some items are of rather doubtful essentiality. Nevertheless, it would seem that on strategic grounds extreme suggestions for selling off the entire stockpile are misguided. It simply cannot be shown with sufficient plausibility that the kind of war for which the stockpile would be useful, even crucial, could not occur. And whether or not a future war would take this form may depend considerably on our own choices concerning strategic doctrine and capability. The most imperative need of the age is to reduce as low as possible the probability of nuclear war. A giant step in this direction would be to maintain conventional forces fully capable of defeating the conventional forces of any enemy, thus eliminating the need to initiate nuclear war as the only alternative to defeat. A stockpile of the most critically essential raw materials would be a logical counterpart of such capability and strategy.

The delay in acting upon the problem of stockpiling for post-nuclear-attack recovery is another instance of the isolation of stockpiling from military doctrine and technology. Although the possibility of the United States being subjected to nuclear attack was recognized in higher policy circles as early as 1949, the stockpile planners did not begin to grapple with this contingency in earnest until 1962. Curiously, when nuclear attack was mentioned earlier, it was usually by agencies or persons seeking a rationale for a large stockpile of raw materials. Thus, Interior and the NSRB both used the specter of nuclear war to support their separate drives for higher stockpile objectives in 1949 and 1950, and it was mentioned as partial justification for the Eisenhower long-term program in 1954.

The possibility of nuclear war appeared for the first time in formal stockpile policy statements in 1958, after it had been dramatized by foreseeable developments in Soviet military technology. Even then, however, it was advanced only as guidance for planning a stockpile of raw materials, which would have only limited value for nuclear war recovery, and the formal guidance had little operational effect even in this virtually irrelevant sphere. The only effect, apparently, was to rationalize adoption of the six-months rule, which limited the reduction of the formal stockpile objectives after the Department of Defense had forced a shortening of the assumed war from five years to three. Only after a special Presidential committee had specifically urged action in March 1962 (and after Senator Symington had begun his critical investigation), did serious planning begin for a separate nuclear-war stockpile made up of items more appropriate for this contingency.

OEP personnel explain the delay between 1958 and 1962 in two somewhat contradictory ways. Publicly, they have said that the phrase "general war" in the 1958 policy statement issued by the ODM meant "general conventional war" rather than nuclear war.[3] This clarification does not *explain* the delay but only asserts that it was not inconsistent with the stockpilers' own policy

[3] See testimony by Edward A. McDermott, Director, Office of Emergency Planning, Symington Hearings, Part 9, p. 3109.

declarations. Even so, the attempt at explanation seems spurious because, to almost everyone else familiar with the jargon, general war does mean nuclear war, and because the phrase "nuclear attack (including reconstruction)" actually was used in a 1959 amendment to the policy statement.

Privately, the stockpilers blame the delay on their inability to obtain relevant military guidance. This statement is consistent with the general pattern of military indifference to stockpiling, especially after 1953, and with the persistent complaints from civilian stockpiling agencies about the inadequacy and belatedness of strategic guidance received from the JCS. However, it does not explain why the ODM or its successors could not have developed their own strategic assumptions concerning nuclear war, nor why they waited until the spring of 1962 to get started when they *had* received an "order-of-magnitude" estimate of war damage to the economy from the JCS in January 1961.[4] A balanced judgment would have to allocate the responsibility about equally to military indifference and the stockpilers' inertia. The latter may have been due, in part, to a reluctance by the ODM-OEP to trespass on the sacred domain of military strategy. Apparently the nudge given by President Kennedy and the Executive Stockpile Committee, with Senator Symington looming in the background, was enough to galvanize both sides into action. It is significant, too, that the initiation of planning for a nuclear-war stockpile coincided with the drive by the Kennedy Administration for public and congressional acceptance of a meaningful program of civil defense.

At any rate, stockpiling has finally caught up with the nuclear age. The Office of Emergency Planning is to be commended for the considerable progress made thus far in dealing with this extremely difficult and complex problem. One would expect that, if and when planning matures to the point of appropriations requests and actual procurement, stockpiling for nuclear war will confront the same general kind of political pressures which have

[4] Symington Hearings, Part 9, p. 3121.

bedeviled the accumulation of a conventional-war stockpile, although the pressures are likely to be more diffuse and therefore less potent. Undoubtedly the biggest political hurdle to be surmounted will be that of gaining congressional acceptance of any significant program at all.

In sum, since 1961, stockpiling and military strategy have become more consistent in both the conventional and nuclear dimensions of future war. At the conventional level, changes in military doctrine and capability have increased the relevance and potential value of a stockpile of raw materials. At the nuclear level, changes in stockpiling policy reflect a recognition that recovery from a nuclear war may require a stockpile quite different in its composition from the stockpile maintained for conventional, limited war. These two sets of changes mirror the two principal themes of the military policy of the Kennedy and Johnson Administrations: an attempt to build capabilities which will permit a wide range of conventional responses to conventional aggression, thus minimizing reliance on nuclear retaliation; and at the same time, attempts to alleviate the consequences of nuclear war should it occur despite our best efforts to deter it.

Appendix A

Material	Cost value	Quantity		
		Total	Strategic stockpile objective	Excess over stockpile objective
Aluminum, metal, tons	$893,220,300	1,933,574	450,000	1,483,574
Aluminum oxide, tons	44,482,500	378,359	160,000	218,359
Antimony, tons	34,038,800	52,979	25,500	27,479
Asbestos, tons:				
amosite	12,505,162	51,125	40,000	11,125
chrysolite	10,442,754	16,148	13,700	2,448
crocidolite	10,970,700	41,158	0	41,158
Bauxite, tons:				
metal grade, Jamaica type	125,088,436	8,288,538	5,000,000	3,288,538
metal grade, Surinam type	123,832,900	7,889,966	5,300,000	2,589,966
refractory grade	11,347,800	299,279	173,000	126,279
Beryl, tons	34,244,152	38,050	28,000	10,050
Beryllium metal, tons	18,703,500	153	0	153
Bismuth, pounds	8,263,400	3,871,796	3,600,000	271,796
Cadmium, pounds	27,489,600	15,172,952	5,100,000	10,072,952
Castor oil, pounds	45,809,600	180,187,374	22,000,000	158,187,374

Source: U. S. Congress, Joint Committee on Reduction of Nonessential Federal Expenditures, *Additional Report*, Senate Committee Print No. 59, 88th Congress, second session, October 1964. The figures for each item are the total amounts held in all four of the raw-materials stockpiles: the national or strategic stockpile, the Defense Production Act inventory, the supplemental stockpile, and the barter inventory held by the Commodity Credit Corporation.

Material	Cost value	Quantity		
		Total	Strategic stockpile objective	Excess over stockpile objective
Celesite, *tons*	$ 2,224,993	48,017	10,300	37,717
Chromite, *tons:*				
chemical grade	34,218,200	1,259,096	600,000	659,096
metallurgical grade	527,469,800	6,338,992	2,970,000	3,368,992
refractory grade	30,188,300	1,226,934	1,425,000	0
Cobalt, *pounds*	223,470,000	102,198,706	42,000,000	60,198,706
Coconut oil, *pounds*	2,058,800	13,582,369	0	13,582,369
Colemanite, *tons*	2,636,400	67,636	0	67,636
Columbium, *pounds*	75,815,200	15,698,474	1,176,000	14,522,474
Copper, *tons*	578,188,900	1,102,339	775,000	327,339
Cordage fibers, *pounds:*				
abaca	37,034,400	146,934,136	100,000,000	46,934,136
sisal	41,868,300	309,571,655	300,000,000	9,571,655
Corundum, *tons*	393,100	2,008	2,500	0
Cryolite, *tons*	5,651,300	20,466	0	20,466
Diamond, industrial, *carats:*				
crushing bort	77,402,300	36,659,900	24,700,000	11,959,990
stones	286,850,900	24,745,010	16,500,000	8,245,010
Diamond dies, *pieces*	577,800	18,667	25,000	0
Diamond tools, *pieces*	1,015,400	64,178	0	64,178
Feathers and down, *pounds*	32,838,100	7,925,702	3,000,000	4,925,702
Fluorspar, *tons:*				
acid grade	61,093,000	1,155,981	540,000	615,981
metallurgical grade	18,840,500	412,243	850,000	0
Graphite, natural, *tons:*				
Ceylon, amorphous lump	1,279,100	5,883	5,500	383
Malagasy, crystalline	6,998,000	34,744	18,000	16,744
other, crystalline	1,894,400	5,481	2,800	2,681
Hyoscine, *ounces*	30,600	2,100	0	2,100
Iodine, *pounds*	5,483,300	4,290,276	8,000,000	0
Iridium, *troy ounces*	2,525,800	13,937	17,000	0
Jewel bearings, *pieces*	4,564,600	52,435,065	57,500,000	0
Kyanite-mullite, *tons*	734,300	8,493	4,800	3,693
Lead, *tons*	388,159,800	1,347,006	0	1,347,006
Magnesium, *tons*	125,242,200	172,516	145,000	27,516

Material	Cost value	Quantity		
		Total	Strategic stockpile objective	Excess over stockpile objective
Manganese, *tons:*				
battery grade, natural ore	$ 35,090,100	286,730	80,000	206,730
battery grade, synthetic dioxide	5,620,200	25,051	6,700	18,351
chemical grade, type A	10,055,400	146,914	68,500	78,414
chemical grade, type B	6,802,400	100,838	64,000	36,838
metallurgical grade	681,460,117	12,763,877	7,900,000	4,863,877
Mercury, *flasks*	36,515,800	200,456	200,000	456
Mica, *pounds:*				
muscovite block	74,709,541	19,952,025	6,000,000	13,952,025
muscovite film	10,833,700	1,938,547	2,000,000	0
muscovite splittings	46,824,100	44,866,426	22,200,000	22,666,426
phlogopite block	303,600	223,239	17,000	206,239
phlogopite splittings	5,082,300	5,065,964	1,300,000	3,765,964
Molybdenum, *pounds*	78,293,200	75,173,469	68,000,000	7,173,469
Nickel, *tons*	279,822,800	218,229	50,000	168,229
Opium, *pounds*	13,661,700	196,355	141,280	55,075
Palladium, *troy ounces*	14,249,200	737,935	1,300,000	0
Palm oil, *pounds*	1,988,900	11,050,613	0	11,050,613
Platinum, *troy ounces*	60,904,400	766,342	450,000	316,342
Pyrethrum, *pounds*	415,100	67,065	25,000	42,065
Quartz crystals, *pounds*	70,993,100	5,702,365	650,000	5,052,365
Quinidine, *ounces*	1,846,000	1,600,428	2,000,000	0
Quinine, *ounces*	2,617,000	4,137,733	4,130,000	7,733
Rare earths, *tons*	12,965,800	15,779	3,000	12,779
Rare earths residue, *pounds*	657,200	6,079,983	0	6,079,983
Rhodium, *troy ounces*	78,200	618	0	618
Rubber, *tons*	677,451,900	876,264	130,000	746,264
Ruthenium, *troy ounces*	559,500	15,001	0	15,001
Rutile, *tons*	5,856,500	47,616	51,000	0
Sapphire and ruby, *carats*	190,000	16,187,500	18,000,000	0
Selenium, *pounds*	2,198,919	347,082	475,000	0
Shellac, *pounds*	8,339,800	16,635,181	8,300,000	8,335,181

Material	Cost value	Quantity		
		Total	Strategic stockpile objective	Excess over stockpile objective
Silicon carbide, crude, tons	$ 38,198,100	196,502	30,000	166,502
Silk, pounds:				
noils and waste	1,232,100	979,924	0	979,924
raw	486,600	113,515	0	113,515
Sperm oil, pounds	4,775,400	23,442,158	23,400,000	42,158
Talc, steatite, tons:				
block and lump	494,800	1,269	200	1,069
ground	231,200	3,901	0	3,901
Tantalum, pounds	21,720,200	4,686,532	3,400,000	1,286,532
Thorium, pounds	17,991,700	3,965,428	500,000	3,465,428
Thorium residue, pounds	42,000	848,534	0	848,534
Tin, tons	759,459,800	313,095	200,000	113,095
Titanium sponge, tons	207,982,100	31,263	20,500	10,862
Tungsten, pounds	704,673,200	203,544,890	44,000,000	159,544,800
Vanadium, tons	31,567,900	7,865	1,400	6,465
Vegetable tannin extract, tons:				
chestnut	10,296,900	36,906	15,000	21,906
quebracho	48,855,000	197,456	86,000	111,456
wattle	9,826,900	38,962	15,000	23,962
Zinc, tons	425,721,300	1,517,409	0	1,517,409
Zirconium ore, tons:				
baddeleyite	710,600	16,533	0	16,533
sircon	116,300	1,970	0	1,970
Total:				
National stockpile	$5,594,391,500			
Defense Production Act	1,440,197,800			
Supplemental— barter	1,389,084,274			
Total, strategic and critical materials	$8,423,673,574			

Appendix B

STRATEGIC AND CRITICAL MATERIALS STOCK PILING ACT

(PUBLIC LAW 520—79TH CONGRESS)

To amend the Act of June 7, 1939 (53 Stat. 811), as amended, relating to the acquisition of stocks of strategic and critical materials for national defense purposes.

Be it enacted by the Senate and House of Representatives of the United States of America in Congress assembled, That the Act of June 7, 1939 (53 Stat. 811), as amended, is hereby amended to read as follows:

"That the natural resources of the United States in certain strategic and critical materials being deficient or insufficiently developed to supply the industrial, military, and naval needs of the country for common defense, it is the policy of the Congress and the purpose and intent of this Act to provide for the acquisition and retention of stocks of these materials and to encourage the conservation and development of sources of these materials within the United States, and thereby decrease and prevent wherever possible a dangerous and costly dependence of the United States upon foreign nations for supplies of these materials in times of national emergency.

"SEC. 2. (a) To effectuate the policy set forth in section 1 hereof the Secretary of War, the Secretary of the Navy, and the Secretary of the Interior, acting jointly through the agency of the Army and Navy Munitions Board, are hereby authorized and directed to determine, from time to time, which materials are strategic and critical under the provisions of this Act and to determine, from time to time, the quality and quantities of such materials which shall be stock piled under the provisions of this Act. In determining the materials which are strategic and critical and the quality and quantities of same to be acquired the Secretaries of State, Treasury, Agriculture, and Commerce shall each designate representatives to cooperate with the Secretary of War, the Secretary of the Navy, and the Secretary of the Interior in carrying out the provisions of this Act.

"(b) To the fullest extent practicable the Secretary of War, the Secretary of the Navy, and the Secretary of the Interior, acting jointly, shall appoint industry advisory committees, selected from the industries concerned with the materials to be stock piled. It shall be the general function of the industry advisory committees to advise with the Secretary of War, the Secretary of the Navy, and the Secretary of the Interior and with any agencies through which they may exercise any of their functions under this Act with respect to the purchase, sale, care, and handling of such materials. Members of the industry advisory committees shall receive a per diem allowance of not to exceed $10 for each day spent at conferences held upon the call of the Secretary of War, the Secretary of the Navy, and the Secretary of the Interior, plus necessary traveling and other expenses while so engaged.

"Sec. 3. The Secretary of War and the Secretary of the Navy shall direct the Secretary of the Treasury, through the medium of the Procurement Division of his Department, to—

"(a) make purchases of strategic and critical materials with due regard to the objectives set forth in section 1 of this Act and pursuant to the determinations as provided in section 2 hereof, which purchases (1) shall be made, so far as is practicable, from supplies of materials in excess of the current industrial demand and (2) shall be made in accordance with title III of the Act of March 3, 1933 (47 Stat. 1520), but may be made without regard to section 3709 of the Revised Statutes. A reasonable time (not to exceed one year) shall be allowed for production and delivery from domestic sources and in the case of any such material available in the United States but which has not been developed commercially, the Secretary of War and the Secretary of the Navy may, if they find that the production of such material is economically feasible, direct the purchase of such material without requiring the vendor to give bond;

"(b) provide for the storage, security, and maintenance of strategic and critical materials for stock-piling purposes on military and naval reservations or other locations, approved by the Secretary of War and the Secretary of the Navy;

"(c) provide through normal commercial channels for the refining or processing of any materials acquired or transferred under this Act when the Secretary of War and the Secretary of the Navy deem such action necessary to convert such materials into a form best suitable for stock piling, and such materials may be refined, processed, or otherwise beneficiated either before or after their transfer from the owning agency;

"(d) provide for the rotation of any strategic and critical materials constituting a part of the stock pile where necessary to prevent deterioration by replacement of acquired stocks with equivalent quantities of substantially the same material with the approval of the Secretary of War and the Secretary of the Navy;

"(e) dispose of any materials held pursuant to this Act which are no longer needed because of any revised determination made pursuant to section 2 of this Act, as hereinafter provided. No such disposition shall be made until six months after publication in the Federal Register and transmission of a notice of the proposed disposition to the Congress and to the Military Affairs Committee of each House thereof. Such notice shall state the reasons for such revised determination, the amounts of the materials proposed to be released, the plan of disposition proposed to be followed, and the date upon which the material is to become available for sale or transfer. The plan and date of disposition shall be fixed with due regard to the protection of the United States against avoidable loss on the sale or transfer of the material to be released and the protection of producers, processors, and consumers against avoidable disruption of their usual markets: *Provided,* That no material constituting a part of the stock piles may be disposed of without the express approval of the Congress except where the revised determination is by reason of obsolescence of that material for use in time of war. For the purposes of this paragraph a revised determination is by reason of obsolescence if such determination is on account of (1) deterioration, (2) development or discovery of a new or better material or materials, or (3) no further usefulness for use in time of war.

"SEC. 4. The Secretary of War and the Secretary of the Navy shall submit to the Congress, not later than six months after the approval of this Act, and every six months thereafter a written report detailing the activities with respect to stock piling under this Act, including a statement of foreign and domestic purchases, and such other pertinent information on the administration of the Act as will enable the Congress to evaluate its administration and the need for amendments and related legislation.

"SEC. 5. The stock piles shall consist of all such materials heretofore purchased or transferred to be held pursuant to this Act, or hereafter transferred pursuant to section 6 hereof, or hereafter purchased pursuant to section 3 hereof, and not disposed of pursuant to this Act. Except for the rotation to prevent deterioration and except for the disposal of any material pursuant to section 3 of this Act, materials acquired under this Act shall be released for use, sale, or other disposition only (a) on order of the President at any time when in his judgment such release is required for purposes of the common defense, or (b) in time of war or during a national emergency with respect to common defense proclaimed by the President, on order of such agency as may be designated by the President.

"SEC. 6. (a) Pursuant to regulations issued by the War Assets Administration or its successor, every material determined to be strategic and critical pursuant to section 2 hereof, which is owned or contracted for by the United States or any agency thereof, including any material received from a foreign government under an agreement made pursuant to the Act of March 11, 1941 (55 Stat. 31), as amended, or other authority shall be transferred by the owning agency, when determined by such agency to be surplus to its needs and responsibilities, to the stock piles established pursuant to this Act, so long as the amount of the stock pile for that material does not exceed the quantities determined therefor pursuant to section 2 hereof. There shall be exempt from this requirement such amount of any material as is necessary to make up any deficiency of the supply of such material for the current requirements of industry as determined by the Civilian Production Administration or its successor. There shall also be exempt from this requirement (1) any material which constitutes contractor inventory if the owning agency shall not have taken possession of such inventory, (2) such amount of any material as the Army and Navy Munitions Board determines (i) are held in lots so small as to make the transfer thereof economically impractical; or (ii) do not meet or cannot economically be converted to meet, stock-pile requirements determined in accordance with section 2 of this Act. The total material transferred to the stock piles established by this Act in accordance with this section during any fiscal year beginning more than twelve months after this Act becomes law shall not exceed in value (as determined by the Secretary of the Treasury on the basis of the fair market value at the time of each transfer) an amount to be fixed by the appropriation Act or Acts relating to the acquisition of materials under this Act.

"(b) Any transfer made pursuant to this section shall be made without charge against or reimbursement from the funds available under this Act, except that expenses incident to such transfer may be paid or reimbursed from such funds, and except that, upon any such transfer from the Reconstruction Finance Corporation, or any corporation organized by virtue of the authority contained in the Act of January 22, 1932 (47 Stat. 5), the Secretary of the Treasury shall cancel notes of Reconstruction Finance Corporation, and sums due and unpaid upon or in connection with such notes at the time of such cancellation, in an amount equal to the fair market value as determined by the Secretary of the Treasury of the material so transferred.

"(c) Effective whenever the Secretary of the Treasury shall cancel any notes pursuant to subsection (b) of this section, the amount of notes, debentures, bonds, or other such obligations which the Reconstruction Finance Corporation is authorized and empowered to have outstanding at any one time under the provisions of existing law shall be deemed to be reduced by the amount of the notes so canceled.

"(d) Subsection (b) of section 14 of the Act of October 3, 1944 (58 Stat. 765), is hereby amended to read as follows:

" '(b) Subject only to subsection (c) of this section, any owning agency may dispose of—

" '(1) any property which is damaged or worn beyond economical repair;

" '(2) any waste, salvage, scrap, or other similar items;

" '(3) any product of industrial, research, agricultural, or livestock operations, or of any public works construction or maintenance project, carried on by such agency;

which does not consist of materials which are to be transferred in accordance with the Strategic and Critical Materials Stock Piling Act, to the stock piles established pursuant to that Act.'

"(e) Section 22 of the Act of October 3, 1944 (58 Stat. 765), is hereby repealed: *Provided,* That any owning agency as defined in that Act having control of materials that, when determined to be surplus, are required to be transferred to the stock piles pursuant to subsection (a) hereof, shall make such determination as soon as such materials in fact become surplus to its needs and responsibilities.

"Sec. 7. (a) The Secretary of the Interior, through the Director of the Bureau of Mines and the Director of Geological Survey, is hereby authorized and directed to make scientific, technologic, and economic investigations concerning the extent and mode of occurrence, the development, mining, preparation, treatment, and utilization of ores and other mineral substances found in the United States or its Territories or insular possessions, which are essential to the common defense or the industrial needs of the United States, and the quantities or grades of which are inadequate from known domestic sources, in order to determine and develop domestic sources of supply, to devise new methods for the treatment and utilization of lower grade reserves, and to develop substitutes for such essential ores and mineral products; on public lands and on privately owned lands, with the consent of the owner, to explore and demonstrate the extent and quality of deposits of such minerals, including core drilling, trenching, test-pitting, shaft sinking, drifting, cross-cutting, sampling, and metallurgical investigations and tests as may be necessary to determine the extent and quality of such deposits, the most suitable methods of mining and beneficiating them, and the cost at which the minerals or metals may be produced.

"(b) The Secretary of Agriculture is hereby authorized and directed to make scientific, technologic, and economic investigations of the feasibility of developing domestic sources of supplies of any agricultural material or for using agricultural commodities for the manufacture of any material determined pursuant to section 2 of this Act to be strategic and critical or substitutes therefor.

"Sec. 8. For the procurement, transportation, maintenance, rotation, storage, and refining or processing of the materials to be acquired under this Act, there is hereby authorized to be appropriated, out of any money in the Treasury not otherwise appropriated, such sums as the Congress, from time to time, may deem necessary to carry out the provisions of this Act. The funds so appropriated, including the funds heretofore appropriated, shall remain available to carry out the purposes for which appropriated until expended, and shall be expended under the joint direction of the Secretary of War and the Secretary of the Navy.

"Sec. 9. Any funds heretofore or hereafter received on account of sales or other dispositions of materials under the provisions of this Act, except funds received on account of the rotation of stocks, shall be covered into the Treasury as miscellaneous receipts.

"Sec. 10. This Act may be cited as the 'Strategic and Critical Materials Stock Piling Act'."

Approved July 23, 1946.

Index

tegic assumptions, 223ff
disposal of, 60-62, 246ff
in strategic stockpile, 233-234
Symington, Stuart F., 2, 5, 129, 151, 152, 171, 194, 238ff, 295, 296
Symington subcommittee, 212, 213, 238
    hearings, 239ff
    recommendations, 244-245

Taft, Charles, 21
Talc, 66, 95
Taylor, General Maxwell, 225
Templeton, Richard H., 26
Thomas, Elbert, 25, 97
Thomas-May bill, 25, 30
Tin, 66, 67, 90, 95, 108, 156, 205, 233, 247, 250
Treasury, Department of the, 33, 112, 250
Truman, Harry S., 29, 77, 99, 100, 158
Tungsten, 137, 158, 178, 180, 192, 204-205, 216, 247, 250

Vanadium, 5, 62, 80, 95
Vinson, Fred, 25
Vital Materials Co-ordinating Committee, 156, 159

Walsh, Al, 152
War, Department of, 8, 9ff, 271
War Mobilization and Reconversion, Office of, 8, 12, 13, 14, 24, 25, 269
War Production Board, 17
Wartime supplies, estimate of, 104, 106
Weaver, E. H., 201
Weeks, Sinclair, 193
Wilson, Charles E., 153, 154, 155, 165, 225
Windfall profits, 211-213
Winter, Sidney, 260
Withdrawals and diversions from stockpile, 209ff
Wool, 135, 180
World War II stockpile, disposal of, 60ff
Wormser, Felix, 183, 192-193, 198-199, 207, 208, 209, 217, 227, 285
Worthing, Marion, 59, 63, 114

Zinc, 47, 62, 67, 68, 80, 157, 158, 178, 180, 191ff, 197, 200, 203-207, 208, 231, 233, 240-241, 247, 253, 285
Zirconium, 95